CLARENDON LIBRARY OF LOGIC AND PHILOSOPHY
General Editor: L. Jonathan Cohen

THE DIVERSITY OF MORAL THINKING

THE DIVERSITY OF
MORAL THINKING

———

NEIL COOPER

CLARENDON PRESS · OXFORD
1981

Oxford University Press, Walton Street, Oxford OX2 6DP

OXFORD LONDON GLASGOW
NEW YORK TORONTO MELBOURNE WELLINGTON
KUALA LUMPUR SINGAPORE HONG KONG TOKYO
DELHI BOMBAY CALCUTTA MADRAS KARACHI
NAIROBI DAR ES SALAAM CAPE TOWN

© *Neil Cooper 1981*

Published in the United States
by Oxford University Press,
New York

British Library Cataloguing in Publication Data

Cooper, Neil
   The diversity of moral thinking. —
   (Clarendon library of logic and philosophy).
   1. Ethics
   I. Title
   170   BJ1012   80-41063

   ISBN 0-19-824423-1

*Set in IBM Baskerville by Graphic Services, Oxford
Printed in Great Britain
at the University Press, Oxford
by Eric Buckley,
Printer to the University*

To BERYL

Preface

Attempts by philosophers to answer the question how reason can become practical have been hampered by complacency and despair alike. On the one hand, it has been claimed that the dictates of reason are clear and uniquely authoritative, on the other, that reason is utterly impotent to decide on matters of morals. In this work I shall try to steer a middle course and shall argue that once the diversity of moral thinking is appreciated, scope is afforded for a use of reason which is at once practical and dialectical. It is for this reason that there are no quick ways to the solution or dissolution of the problems of ethical theory; in philosophy Gordian knots need to be not cut but untied. It will not do complacently to accept the promptings of common sense at the very beginning of an enquiry; if philosophy is worth doing at all, it is worth doing the hard way. For it is the journey rather than the destination which is of interest, and it is only one's honest toil which there is joy or even point in submitting to the critical gaze of the reader.

In the writing of this book I have been particularly indebted to Mr L. Jonathan Cohen and Professors R. M. Hare, G. P. Henderson, and Bernard Mayo, who read the original typescript and greatly helped me with comments and criticisms. I owe a very great debt to 'the hard men of Dundee', my colleagues past and present in the Department of Philosophy at Dundee, who have generously given up their time to discuss some of my arguments. I am indebted to Mr Roger Young for comments on Chapters 3 and 6. I have also to thank a number of my pupils from whom I have learnt much in discussion. None of the above are responsible for the thoughts which appear here, although they are responsible for the non-appearance of other, less happy, arguments. I am also grateful to the Department of Philosophy and the University of Dundee for sabbatical leave to complete the book. Above all, I owe an enormous debt to my wife, Beryl, who has scrutinized every sentence and discussed every aspect of the work.

Early versions of some of the material appeared in 'Some Presuppositions of Moral Judgements' (*Mind*, January 1966), 'Morality and Importance' (*Mind*, January 1968), 'Two Concepts of Morality' (*Philosophy*, January 1966), 'Language, Purpose and Morality' (*The Philosophical Quarterly*, July 1973), 'Moral Nihilism' (*Proceedings of the Aristotelian Society*, 1973-4), 'Oughts and Wants' (*The Aristotelian Society Supplementary Volume*, 1968), and 'The Only Possible Morality' (*The Aristotelian Society Supplementary Volume*, 1976). I am happy to acknowledge permission to rework this material. I also have to thank Messrs Macmillan, London and Basingstoke, for permission to use some arguments from my 'Further Thoughts on Oughts and Wants' in *Weakness of Will*, ed. G. W. Mortimore (1971).

I would also like to thank Mrs E. A. Fairweather for typing the book with such accuracy.

N. L. C.

Contents

But if we turn from the matter to the form of morality; if, instead of asking what actions are right or wrong, we ask, what is the essence of right and wrong? how do we know right from wrong? why should we seek the right and eschew the wrong?—we are presented with the most contradictory answers; we find ourselves at once in that region of perpetual antinomies, where controversy is everlasting, and opposite theories seem to be equally self-evident to different minds.

SIR LESLIE STEPHEN
The Science of Ethics, p. 2

Introduction

What is a morality? Moral philosophers have often claimed to discover the essential characteristics of morality. The majority of these rival definitional accounts have been mistaken in so far as they have been held to be true, necessarily true, of all moral judgements, all moral thinking, all moralities. Most of them, however, have in fact been true of some one class of moral judgements or one kind of morality, or have uncovered one genuine aspect or style of moral thinking. The passionate intensity with which these partial and lopsided views have been maintained requires some explanation. It would appear that these views engage the interest and allegiance of their adherents because of their undercover normative character. The contention over rival definitional accounts has concealed both from the antagonists and from their public the real character of their disputes. The real conflicts are not over what moralities are essentially like, but what they ought to be like. One side argues that an aspect or feature which one kind of morality possesses ought to be manifested by any rational morality, while the other maintains the same thesis about an entirely contrary aspect or feature. Both sides in conflicts of this kind appear locked in perpetual antinomies which offer no hope of being resolved. The issues are not ones of definition and so the tools of conceptual analysis are of no avail. Nor is it any good appealing to moral intuitions, since the issues are not of straightforward right and wrong, and the intuitions themselves pull in different directions. The task, then, is to find appropriate procedures for resolving these antinomies in the hope that by learning how to decide these high-level issues of ethical theory we may reach a rational framework which will to some extent circumscribe the content that a rational morality ought to have.

There are three things needful. First, in order to know what a morality is, we have to put aside the shadow-boxing and to treat most of the supposedly rival accounts as one-sided views of the same thing, each perhaps compensating for some inadequacy in one of the others. Second, in order to prepare the way for a new approach to ethical theory one has to learn to see moral thought and language differently by a kind of *gestalt*-shift, so that moral judgements are no longer thought of as aiming at truth and as essentially having the same characteristics as factual statements. Third, to decide what a morality ought to be one has to recognize that the different lopsided accounts of what a morality is can be seen as real competitors, as antithetical conceptions of what a morality ought to be. The three parts of this book correspond to these three considerations.

In Part I the notion of 'direction of fit' is introduced, and it is argued in Parts I and II that the foundations of any morality face in the normative direction of fit and never in the descriptive direction. Part I is largely an extended account of the normative nature of moralities, an account in itself incomplete and requiring the other two parts for its role to be fully understood. Part II works out the consequences of normativism and attempts to show that a morality cannot be 'objective' in the ordinary sense, for its foundations cannot face in the descriptive direction of fit. It is the task of Part II to argue for the demise of objectivity; part of the role that objectivity plays in descriptive discourse has to be demitted to some effective substitute in the field of morals. Objectivity has a cutting edge which enables us to distinguish the acceptable from the unacceptable. Moral thinking and discourse, therefore, need a kind of control or constraint capable of making a more or less sharp divide between what may and may not legitimately be said on matters of morals; otherwise, anything goes. In seeking appropriate constraints, we have to struggle against a natural obsession with the notion of correspondence, the idea that a remark or thought on any topic can only be acceptable if there is something, which is outside the thinker and in the world, to which his remark or thought corresponds. But if, as I argue, the concept of correspondence cannot apply to the foundations of a morality, we have to look for some effective substitute to which our remarks and thoughts have, not to correspond, but at any rate to respond.

The change from an objectivity-dominated approach to a constraints-dominated approach to morals amounts to a quasi-Copernican *gestalt*-shift.

Now if our constraints are to be real constraints, they must not be a mere reflection of our fancies and wishes. An anarchic consequence of this kind can only be avoided if the constraints are genuinely independent of us, just as if they came from outside us. Otherwise, to quote the words of the late Professor Norman Robinson to me, 'morality will only be a complicated way of getting what one wants'. So the constraints have to satisfy two conditions, first, that there is no question of our fundamental moral judgements having to correspond with them, and second, that the constraints are external to us, in the sense of being independent of our individual prejudices and desires. Constraints can satisfy both these conditions if they are concerned with the relation of three elements, the moral agent or group, the morality of the agent or group, and the world in which agents, groups, and moralities interact and have their being. The first kind of constraints concern the structure of moralities and I shall call them 'structural constraints'. We shall find in Part III that structural principles can resolve antinomies concerned with how we ought to think about matters of morals, but that they do not suffice to circumscribe the content of what a morality ought to be. For that task we need to apply empirical or factual constraints also. These are concerned with the relation of human individuals and groups to the world, arising from what is often called 'the human condition'.

The moral antinomies which the diversity of moral thinking yields are unlike those of Logic in that in morals no uniquely effective decision-procedure is in the offing. They do not therefore generate insoluble problems so much as opportunities for reflection and decision. Decision is only made possible by the structural principles and by the facts which constitute the empirical constraints. Since the principles which I shall propose are contestable, none of the offered resolutions to the antinomies can be final or conclusive. The terms on which resolutions to antinomies are obtained may change, for the dialectical process is a continuing one.

PART I

WHAT A MORALITY IS

I

The Logic of Morals

1.1. In Part I of this book I shall try to give a morally neutral account of the concept of a morality, to characterize the concept in such a way as to be compatible with any moral position whatsoever. However, before I start on this account, I need to consider and answer some of the doubts moral philosophers have expressed about the very possibility of such a morally neutral enquiry. This enquiry into or examination of the concept of a morality I shall call 'the logic of morals'. By describing it as 'morally neutral' or 'morally unaligned' I do not mean to imply that the enquiry must be morally unmotivated; there is no objection to moral motives provided that they do not covertly enter into our arguments. All I wish to contend is that we can practise the logic of morals without being thereby committed to any ground-level moral position. I shall try to show further that the logic of morals can be self-neutralizing in that it has the means whereby any backslidings into the moral arena may be reversed or corrected.

One may wonder how the logic of morals could ever have hived off from the live body of moral philosophy, so as even to be thought by some to be the only justifiable residue of Ethics. I shall try, albeit in an over-simplified fashion, to give some kind of historical explanation of this, an explanation the value of which will lie solely in the particular slant it gives. Moral philosophy, I suggest, has arisen as a response to seven main problems concerning moral discourse and beliefs, the problems of unity, consistency, ideality, proof, definition, logical status, and self-interest. These problems arise naturally as soon as serious reflection on morals begins. At first glance our so-called moral intuitions are a farrago. We seem to be faced with a 'heap of unconnected obligations' (H. W. B. Joseph, *Some Problems in Ethics*, p. 107) or, at any rate, with a list of unconnected virtues. There is a pervasive demand, in part aesthetic, that we should seek to impose some kind of unity on our thinking. This is fundamentally the same demand which drives us to reduce Geometry or Propositional Logic to a small number of primitive propositions. This first problem of unity cannot be answered without bringing in the second problem, that of consistency. If our moral code or our moral intuitions are in fact inconsistent, any discovered unity will be entirely spurious or, at best, superficial. We have, then, to decide what we should do about any inconsistencies, actual or potential, in our moral beliefs. If we are convinced that morality is rooted in the nature of things, it will be tempting to impose consistency in the same way that we impose consistency on our scientific thought. A body of truth cannot be inconsistent. If, on the other hand, we eschew such an objectivist approach, we may provide an answer to the problem by pointing out that what makes the moral life so difficult is that equally valid demands and ideals conflict with one another.

The first two problems arise in an attempt to give a coherent description of our moral beliefs and may be solved perhaps only by modifying or even discarding previous moral beliefs. What starts as 'a consecration of men's actual sentiments' (J. S. Mill, *Utilitarianism*, p. 3) may degenerate into or progress towards providing a 'guide'. This development brings about a shift of problem in moral philosophy. If our only data are our moral intuitions and ethical theory has solely a descriptive and explanatory role, we can only systematize, rarely correct, and if we do correct, no rationale for such correction would be available. For our intuitions, if incorrect, could not provide the means by which they themselves might be corrected. Hence arises what I have called, for lack of a better name, the problem of ideality. If our 'actual sentiments' are not adequate as a basis for morality, we have to find some other basis or bases which will be adequate. So we search for some highest good or end or ideal which will, after reflection, appeal both to the heart and to the mind. Plato perhaps was the first philosopher explicitly to search for some highest good outside the corpus of vulgar beliefs. Bentham likewise was a revisionary moralist, as he makes clear in the course of distinguishing in his 'Fragment on Government' between expository and censorial jurisprudence.

The fourth problem is that of finding some kind of proof

or decision-procedure in morals. We can settle questions of arithmetic by calculation, questions of fact by observation, but about questions of morals we disagree and 'cannot come to a satisfactory decision' (Plato, *Euthyphro* 7D). This was the point, as J. S. Mill saw it, of the Principle of Utility; at one and the same time it gave unity to our moral beliefs and provided a decision-procedure either in cases of conflict between existing moral rules or in cases where no established moral rule afforded any guidance.

The problem of definition arises naturally from the first four problems. As Socrates pointed out, we cannot answer questions about the virtues until we know their nature, until we can define them. Nor can we give an adequate answer to the problems of consistency or of proof until we know the meanings of the key concepts we are employing. There is an important distinction between general moral concepts like those of *good* and *right* and specific moral concepts, like those of courage, temperance, justice, and friendship, with whose definition Socrates and Plato were most concerned. The same is true of the work of Aristotle and Theophrastus on the virtues, vices, and character-traits of men. Such work involves moral decisions about what elements one is going to value amongst generally recognized virtues and vices.

Now the problems of proof and of definition have in our century given rise to the sixth problem of logical status. This was largely due to the work of Moore and Prichard. If moral judgements are provable, they have to be proved either from fundamental moral judgements, which only serves to shift the problem back, or from non-moral judgements or from definitions of moral words. But if the basic moral words, namely, 'good', 'ought', and 'right', are indefinable in terms of other words, as Moore and Prichard argued, then no derivation of moral judgements from non-moral judgements via definitions is possible and no derivation of moral judgements from definitions themselves is possible either. This was why Prichard in his 1912 *Mind* article, 'Does Moral Philosophy Rest Upon a Mistake?' (*Moral Obligation*, pp. 1-17) argued that traditional moral philosophy in so far as it demanded the proof of moral principles rested on an error. Since moral judgements were synthetic, they were not self-certifying, nor were they derivable from non-moral statements capable of being known. So either we had immediate knowledge of moral principles or we had no knowledge of them at all. In either case the traditional tasks of the moral philosopher were no longer feasible. The most that moral philosophy could do would be to articulate the principles known by intuition and to investigate the logical structure and status of morality and moral judgements. Wittgenstein had prepared the way for epistemology as the logic of science; so after their fashion had Moore and Prichard prepared the way for ethics as the logic of morals.

The seventh principal problem is that of interest or self-interest. A morality is likely to have points of conflict with the interests of individual agents. The more points of conflict there are, the more pressing is going to be the question, 'Ought I to conform to this morality?', 'Ought I to be moral?', where the point of these questions is to ask either whether it is in my interest or whether it is rational for me to be moral. We shall see that this question, to which Plato's *Republic* may be seen as the first sustained attempt to give an answer, has to be faced, however one defines the term 'moral', whether widely or narrowly. Like the other questions, it leads into an examination of the logic of morals and beyond it. In order to consider the relation between individual rationality and what is sometimes called 'the moral point of view' one has to decide on criteria of rationality, and this is a semi-conceptual investigation (Part III).

1.2. It is often maintained that it is impossible to undertake work in 'meta-ethics' without committing oneself to some particular moral judgements or taking up some attitude. In particular, it is alleged that no definition of the words 'moral' and 'morality' is possible which does not commit the definer to taking sides on moral matters. The ideal of a neutral logic of morals which is no respecter of moralities is, it is argued, a sham and delusion. At the very best, it is an almost unattainable ideal, the approach to which is highly precarious and beset by logical pitfalls. Indeed, many a moral philosopher has begun his researches with high-minded neutralist ideals only in the end to furnish the world with yet another under-cover morality.

I shall begin by adverting to the actual use of the words 'moral' and 'morality'. The sense of the words which I propose to examine is that in which they are not words of praise. I am here concerned with the 'moral'/'non-moral' distinction, not the 'moral'/'immoral' one. The sense of the word I shall be concerned with will be that in which we may talk of moral rules, moral principles, moral arguments, moral problems, moral judgements, and so on. For the moment I do not wish to go further in discussing the concept of a morality. That I leave for the next chapter. In this chapter I wish merely to examine the possibility of a morally neutral or non-aligned logic of morals.

There are many different kinds of statement which we can make about moral judgements and moral concepts. Such statements are often called 'meta-moral' or 'meta-ethical', with the apparent implication that all such statements have some common feature in virtue of which they are 'about' moral judgements. But in fact we can distinguish several kinds of meta-moral statements. First, some meta-moral judgements are themselves moral judgements as well, albeit ones of a higher order, for example, 'It is immoral to believe that evil means can be justified by a good end.' A second class of meta-moral judgements are normative although not moral. An example of such a judgement would be the prudential one, 'It is foolish to condemn a man morally for doing what he cannot avoid doing.' Meta-moral judgements of a third kind serve to describe the morality of a society, for example, 'Among the Navaho it is thought immoral even to look at your mother-in-law' or 'No quarrel between two men about a woman is admissible in the Onge code of behaviour.' A fourth kind of meta-moral judgement is descriptive of the logical relations of our actual moral concepts. The statement, 'It is logically possible for there to be morally good actions which it is not the case that one morally ought to perform' is in this way descriptive of the logical relations of two moral concepts. A fifth kind is concerned with the essential features of the concept of a morality. The statement 'Moral judgements must be universalizable' claims to describe such a logically necessary feature of moral judgements. It is to meta-moral judgements of these fourth and fifth kinds that moral philosophers have commonly intended to refer when they have talked of 'meta-ethics'. To obviate confusion I shall refer to judgements or statements of the fourth and fifth kinds as belonging to the logic of morals. They all purport to describe logical relationships, not empirical or moral ones.

Those who have doubted the possibility of a morally neutral logic of morals have done so for at least three reasons. In the first place, they have maintained that statements of the logic of morals entail, at any rate sometimes, moral judgements, and that the so-called neutrality of the logic of morals is not merely precarious but quite spurious. Second, it has been objected that you cannot explicate a moral concept from the outside; to understand a moral concept you must share it. Third, it has been maintained that since the most general part of the logic of morals is concerned with the concept of morality, it cannot be morally neutral, since to say that something is a moral matter is itself to make a moral judgement. I shall discuss these objections in the next three sections.

1.3. The first group of critics allege that there are some statements of the logic of morals which entail moral judgements. While their allegation is correct, they are not right to infer from this that moral neutrality in the logic of morals is impossible. To see that the allegation is correct, consider the following three judgements:

(1) The concepts of *good* and *ought* are necessarily co-extensive.

(2) There are some actions which are good but which it is not the case that one ought to do.

(3) There are no actions which are good but which it is not the case that one ought to do.

(1) is ostensibly a statement of the logic of morals, while (2) is a substantive judgement of normative ethics. (3) is the contradictory of (2) and must, therefore, share the same logical status and be a judgement of normative ethics. (2), however, would be a counter-instance to (1), and thus (1) must entail (3). There are, then, some statements of the logic of morals which entail moral judgements. However, one cannot infer from this that the logic of morals is not morally neutral. Indeed the very fact that a moral judgement is deducible from

it indicates that this statement of the logic of morals is false. If (1) had been true, no moral conclusion, acceptable or unacceptable, could have been inferred from it. This is a consequence of a more general logical truth, that a synthetic statement cannot follow from an analytic one, although it can follow from a contradictory one. In general, given a term B and a complex of terms C, then if B and C are synonymous, it is analytic that everything which is B is C. By contraposition, if it is not analytic that everything which is B is C, then B and C are not synonymous. If you can infer anything informative, substantial, or synthetic from a statement of synonymy or definition, then the statement of synonymy or definition cannot be correct. Now all statements of the logic of morals appear to state meaning-relationships; they appear to be definitions, quasi-definitions, statements of synonymy, non-synonymy, deducibility, non-deducibility, concept-exclusion, concept-inclusion or necessary concept-coextension. Hence if anything informative, substantial, or synthetic can be inferred from them they cannot be correct or true. In the past it has been a common procedure in moral philosophy to see if a meta-ethical theory has 'counter-intuitive' consequences for morals and, if it has, to reject it. On my view, any statement of the logic of morals which is shown to have moral consequences, whether these be counter-intuitive or intuitive or betwixt and between, is *eo ipso* to be rejected as false. The main argument of the opponents of a morally neutral logic of morals is in this way converted into a rejection-procedure. If you encounter a statement which appears to be a true statement of the logic of morals, ask yourself whether there is any moral conclusion to which you would commit yourself by its acceptance. If there is not, then you may accept the statement, at any rate provisionally; if there is, it should be rejected as certainly false.

The misguided attempt to derive or deduce substantial conclusions from conceptual statements has given rise to some of the most celebrated ethical theories. I shall give two instances of the infringement of this fundamental rule of the logic of morals. First, we have the passage (*A Treatise of Human Nature*, pp. 469–70) in which Hume is commonly interpreted as denying that an 'ought' can be deduced from a neat 'is', a conceptual statement. He goes on to say that 'this small attention wou'd subvert all the vulgar systems of morality . . .' Presumably, if Hume supposes that he has subverted them, he regards himself as entitled to deny any moral judgements contained in these moralities. Whether this is too uncharitable an interpretation of Hume or not, it would be a mistake, analogous to the one he was trying to point out, to suppose that one could derive the rejection of moral views from a purely conceptual premiss. My second example is an argument of J. S. Mill's (*Utilitarianism*, p. 46). He argues that duties of imperfect obligation cannot be assimilated to duties of perfect obligation,[1] because the former cannot be claimed by an individual or mankind generally as a right.

> For if a moralist attempts, as some have done, to make out that mankind generally, though not any given individual, have a right to all the good we can do them, he at once, by that thesis, includes generosity and beneficence within the category of justice . . . whoever does not place the distinction between justice and morality in general, where we have now placed it, will be found to make no distinction between them at all, but to merge all morality in justice.

Mill appears to think that he has provided a conclusive argument, a *reductio ad absurdum* of his opponents' view. Now clearly there is a conceptual distinction between morality in general, in Mill's use of the term, and justice. The two words are not synonymous. But this does not suffice to prove that the two concepts cannot consistently be thought to be coextensive. Thus Godwin was not denying a conceptual distinction when he merged 'all morality in justice'; he was advocating a new morality. From the truth that two moral concepts differ in intension you cannot validly infer that they must differ in extension too. One might just as well argue that the Evening Star could not be the same as the Morning Star since the two expressions plainly do not have the same meaning. Likewise inferences from actual conceptual structure to the truth of moral judgements are always invalid. While this is so, yet the actual conceptual structures of moral language do have a special relation to particular moral viewpoints. If it

---

[1] '. . . duties of perfect obligation are those duties in virtue of which a correlative *right* resides in some person or persons; duties of imperfect obligation are those moral obligations which do not give birth to any right.'

can be shown that two concepts differ in meaning, the view that the concepts are *necessarily* coextensive is ruled out of court, and the way is cleared for the view that the concepts differ in extension also.

1.4. The second kind of objection to the possibility of a morally neutral logic of morals emphasizes the highly complex and rich character of moral language. Time was when a moral philosopher could write one book on the word 'right' and another on the word 'good' as if these were the most typical moral words. The 'logic' of these words can be agreed amongst moralists of different persuasions without great difficulty. Their very generality and blanket character facilitate their use as vehicles for the expression of almost any point of view on matters of morals. They are in fact universals of morality or, more accurately, universals of evaluation. In calling them universals I am not committing myself to saying that certain attitudes or kinds of attitude towards certain kinds of things are universal amongst men. To say that 'ought' represents a universal of evaluation is to say not that everybody recommends that one should perform certain kinds of action or aim at certain ends, but that everybody can engage in that speech act which 'ought' is used to perform, namely, advice or recommendation. I say 'can engage' because I am not warranted in asserting that all human beings must engage in recommendation or advice. I can imagine a people who might not, although they would be rather odd. However, even in their thought there would be a vacant logical space which the word 'ought' or some equivalent to it could occupy.

The logical possibility of formal universals of morality has not, I think, been doubted, although it has never been much discussed, and, indeed, has not the same interest as the actual existence of material universals of morality. A word or expression, like 'ought', which is a distinctive vehicle for the performance of a speech act represents a formal universal. Thus C. von Fürer-Haimendorf in his *Morality and Merit* (pp. 224-5) comments on the South Asian societies whose moralities he considers: 'All of them distinguish between "right" and "wrong" conduct and social approval rewards those who conform to the behaviour considered as "right".' The author does not by these words imply that there is agreement among these peoples. Far from it. What he calls 'the ubiquity of the sense of right and wrong' no more guarantees moral agreement than the ubiquity of the concepts of truth and falsehood guarantees factual agreement. Just as the particular factual beliefs of a society depend on what members of the society regard as true or as false, so the particular moral beliefs of a society depend on what members of the society regard as 'right' or 'wrong', as 'good' or 'bad'.

If general concepts were the only concepts to be employed in morality, moral language would be gravely impoverished. The stuff of moral discourse involves more specific terms and concepts. The logic of such terms is not a common possession of all moralists alike. Merely explaining their meaning appears to be taking a stand for or against certain kinds of behaviour. Those who employ words like 'justice', 'courage', 'loyalty', 'honesty', are taking a stand (sincerely or insincerely). If the use of these latter concepts is universal among men, that is, if they are material universals of morality, this cannot be known *a priori* and will, if true, be an empirical discovery. Specific concepts resemble those theoretical concepts whose meaning can only be explicated within the scientific theory to which they belong. One cannot infer from this that only the supporters of a theory can understand the concepts. Plainly the job of the historian of science is to try and understand a theory, whether he supports it or not; he seeks to understand, say, 'dephlogisticated air' in terms of the science of the time. Likewise the job of the historian of morals is to try and understand the concept of the *megalopsychos*, say, or the concept of 'a gentleman' in terms of the morals of the time.

The second kind of objection to the possibility of a morally neutral logical analysis of moral concepts emphasizes that the typical moral concept is a specific one and that such concepts can only be mastered from the inside. In order to acquire the concept, it is said, you have to learn the correct occasion for its use and in learning this you *eo ipso* acquire certain attitudes. The more sophisticated examination of the nature of the moral concept is parasitic, the argument alleges, on prior everyday knowledge of the meaning of the concept. In this sphere to understand is to believe. It is one thing, it is said, to examine the meanings of words like 'perception', 'meaning', and 'disposition', but moral and other normative words are different. In the case of moral concepts like those of loyalty and courage you can only be said to grasp them if you are able to recognize central and typical instances of them, and this involves coming to share the attitudes inextricably bound up with the use and application of these concepts. I shall try to show that this argument is entirely lacking in cogency.

This can be seen by a consideration of what it is to accept or to reject a concept. Acceptance and rejection apply to those concepts whose use presupposes belief in prior judgements or propositions, and thus especially to theoretical or normative concepts. To accept a concept is to be prepared to apply it in all seriousness to something real or imagined. To reject a concept is not to be prepared so to apply it. If I accept the concept of patriotism, I am prepared to apply the term 'patriotic' as a term of praise to people who put national loyalties first. If I reject the concept of patriotism I am not prepared to use the word as a term of praise. Whether I actually continue to use the *word* is a matter of choice. I may use it merely as a neutral word with no laudatory force; alternatively, I may use it in sneer-quotes or even drop the use of the word altogether, just as the atheist may decline to use the word 'blasphemy' or the anti-racialist to use the word 'miscegenation'. My rejection of a concept may be expressed by my saying such things as 'There is no such thing as patriotism'. Shelley was rejecting the concept of chastity when he wrote in his notes on *Queen Mab*: 'Chastity is a monkish and evangelical superstition, a greater foe to natural temperance even than unintellectual sensuality; it strikes at the root of all domestic happiness, and consigns more than half of the human race to misery that some few may monopolize according to law' (*The Complete Poetical Works of Percy Bysshe Shelley*, p. 808).

Frequently people wonder whether to accept a specific concept or whether to continue to accept it. Many of us have doubts about accepting the concept of patriotism. Were it the case that we could not understand a concept without accepting it, we could never understand the concept which we were wondering whether to accept or not. Further, it is possible to reject a concept which you have previously accepted. There is such a thing as moral apostasy. This happens to many who have abandoned the concept of patriotism. Yet when they come to reject the concept which they have heretofore accepted, they do not abandon their understanding of the concept together with the concept itself. They might indeed say that it is just because they understand the concept so well that they have come to reject it. Again, the proponents of this view assume that learning the meaning of a moral concept is acquiring a disposition to use a certain word in certain circumstances. This is not so. What is necessary is the acquisition of a *capacity* to use the concept in question. A man may reject a moral concept and yet be able to act to perfection the part of somebody who accepts it. Being able to do this would constitute the best possible evidence of understanding a concept. Indeed you cannot be a really successful *agent provocateur* unless you have mastered the value-concepts of your opponents. It was no accident that the Comintern before 1939 used to teach European Communists how to argue in defence of capitalism.

1.5. The third kind of objection to the possibility of a morally neutral logic of morals relates to that most general part of the logic of morals which is concerned with the concept of a morality itself.

   Consider the following situation. I am a member of a local discussion group, which is due to meet in a few days' time. When asked by a friend whether I shall go or not, I answer, 'No, I don't think I will'. When he comments, 'But you ought to', I reply rather tartly, 'That isn't a *moral* "ought".' 'Oh', he says in surprise, 'but it is', and he proceeds to back up his statement with arguments about what would be the fate of this discussion group if everybody behaved as I propose to do. For my part I do not regard this question as a moral question although he does, and yet paradoxically we appear to be engaged in a moral argument. Whether something is a moral question or not appears to be itself a moral question. Consequently it is natural to suppose that, when we call a judgement a moral judgement or a question a moral question, we are not diagnosing the logical status of a judgement or question but rather taking up a moral attitude. Therefore it is concluded that we can never divorce an examination of the concept of a morality or of the use of the word 'moral' from moral commitment. This view is based on a confusion about the use of language. Suppose I said, 'It is a matter of moral principle that I ought to go to the meeting'. In saying this I would be expressing a moral opinion; what I would not be doing is explicitly diagnosing the logical status of my utterance, nor would I be diagnosing the logical status of the utterance, 'I ought to go to the meeting', although I would *show* by the use of the expression 'it is a matter of moral principle' that I was making a moral judgement. This expression indeed acts as a signpost of the logical status of the utterance in a similar way to that in which the words 'I promise' act as a signpost of the logical status of the utterance, 'I promise to help you'. Just as the occurrence of the words 'I promise' makes the utterance a promise under felicitous circumstances, so the words 'it is a matter of moral principle that . . .' make the judgement a moral judgement under normal felicitous circumstances. Hence, in normal circumstances, it would be patently false to deny that a judgement flagged by this expression was a moral judgement. This expression 'it is a matter of moral principle that . . .' functions in a not dissimilar way to the first person present singular of a performative verb. The same goes for the expression, 'It is a moral question whether you . . .', followed by a verb designating an action. Now just as the past and third person present of a performative verb are not used performatively, so we have similar forms of these signpost expressions which are not used to express moral attitudes. Thus I do not make a moral judgement when I say, 'It was a matter of moral principle for me whether I went to the meeting or not', or when I say, 'It is a matter of moral principle for him whether he goes to the meeting or not'. In the last two sentences I am not just saying that I regarded and he regards it as a matter of moral principle; here I am really and truly diagnosing the logical status of the principle involved. The difference between the two kinds of statement may be brought out in this manner. We may observe how a sentence is used on a given occasion by a given person and say, 'That

sentence was used by that person to make a moral judgement.'
Or we may observe how a certain sentence is usually used and
say, for example, about the sentence, 'You ought to keep
promises', that it is usually used to make a moral judgement.
Both of these are examples of our diagnosing the logical status
of an utterance. However, during most of our lives we are
more interested in action than in logical diagnosis. Hence we
may use expressions like 'it is a matter of moral principle that
. . .' to form moral judgements. Thus when I say, 'It is a matter
of moral principle that I should go to the meeting' or 'It is a
moral question whether I go to the meeting or not' or 'It is a
moral principle that one ought to keep promises', I am not
making a logical diagnosis, I am committing myself morally.
We may concede, then, that there are some uses of expressions
involving the word 'moral' which are used for moral commitment, but this does not undermine the perfectly legitimate
use of the word 'moral' in logical diagnosis.

1.6. In this last section I shall undertake a sample investigation and try to show how moral neutrality can be observed
in examining the relationship between two concepts. I shall
then illustrate how disagreement may arise as to the relative
place which these concepts should occupy in one's morality.

It has sometimes been supposed that the concepts of goodness and obligation were necessarily coextensive. Thus Richard
Price (*Review of the Principal Questions of Morals*, p. 120)
maintains that 'to do all the good he can to his fellow-creatures,
everyone is obliged' and (p. 124) speaks of aiming 'at acting
beyond obligation' as 'being the same with aiming at acting
contrary to obligation'. If one was convinced by such statements, one might be led to deny the logical possibility of such
things as works of supererogation, to deny that there logically
can be actions which it is good to do but which it is not the
case that one ought to do. This view of Price's, call it 'logical
anti-supererogationism', would make it a logical mistake to
believe that as a matter of morals there were some good
actions which it was not the case that one morally ought to
perform. Further, it would deprive of any moral substance
the view of people like Godwin who said (*Enquiry Concerning
Political Justice*, II, ii), 'It is . . . impossible for me to confer

upon any man a favour; I can only do him right'. This view, which we may call non-logical anti-supererogationism, can be made into a meaningful moral doctrine if it can be shown that 'good' and 'obligatory' are not synonymous, as Richard Price appears to have thought.

Logical anti-supererogationism appears to be supported by the following argument:

(4) If I call an action 'good', I thereby commend it;

(5) If I commend an action, I must, if consistent, be prepared to recommend it;

(6) If I am prepared to recommend an action, I must, if consistent, be prepared to condemn the failure to perform it.

ergo

(7) If I call an action 'good', I must, if consistent, be prepared to condemn the failure to perform it.

But if (7) is true, then everything which is good is obligatory. This, however, is a moral conclusion. Therefore there must be an error in at least one of the conceptual premisses. The inference is only made possible by an equivocation with the word 'recommend'. There is a difference between recommending an action and recommending somebody to perform an action. (See the *Oxford English Dictionary*.) I may recommend a course of action by saying that it is 'good' or 'worth doing', but I do not thereby recommend or advise anybody to do anything. In talking about the films on at the local cinemas tonight, I may commend or recommend *Jaws, The Deer Hunter*, and *Coma*. Yet they take place simultaneously and on this your only free evening you cannot go to all of them. I recommend *Coma* amongst others, but it is not the case that I recommend you to go to *Coma*; I would not blame you if you went to *The Deer Hunter* instead. We may thus distinguish commendatory recommendation from prescriptive recommendation. The two kinds of recommendation may be distinguished by this feature, that recommending-as may be yoked with 'highly' while recommending-to may not. Thus

(8) I recommend Keith highly for the leadership

is perfectly in order while

(9) I highly recommend you to elect Keith to the leadership

is highly deviant, at any rate according to my linguistic

intuitions. (The word 'strongly', it should be noted, can significantly replace 'highly' in both (8) and (9).) As is commonly
the upshot of a philosophical analysis, we have arrived at a
statement of non-deducibility. We cannot deduce an 'ought'
from a 'good'. This conclusion, however, bars no doors. Rather,
it opens them, for it clears the way to the expression of ordinary
differences of moral opinion about works of supererogation.

Our logical analysis has shown that in the conceptual structure of a morality there is a fissure between goodness and
obligation. Although this conceptual fissure may not be actualized in all moralities, it will be actualized in any morality
which makes a distinction between rules, on the one hand,
and standards and ideals on the other. Our logical analysis
does not show that either rules or ideals or both are logically
necessary ingredients of any possible morality. All it shows is
that we in fact have both in our actual morality. Since, however, we cannot reason from what is to what must be, we cannot infer from knowledge of the actual conceptual structure
of our actual morality to the necessary conceptual structure
of any possible morality. Nor for that matter can one infer
from such knowledge what the conceptual structure of a
morality ought to be.

This example of the fissure between ideals and rules is only
one of many in the conceptual structure of a morality. There
are a number of pairs of aspects of morality between which
there is tension. A logical analysis can reveal these tensions,
but it cannot resolve them; it cannot tell us which aspects are
to be preferred. From this, however, it does not follow that
no rational considerations at all can be brought forward to
decide which aspects are to be preferred. Rather we have to
recognize that here the logic of morals does not suffice and
that we have to find reasons 'capable of determining the in-
tellect either to give or withhold its assent', to engage in what
may be called 'the metaphysic of morals'.

I shall illustrate briefly the kind of conflict which may arise.
Two widely different approaches may be adopted with regard
to the proper relation between ideals and rules. The conservative may say, 'Yes, ideals are very fine. By all means let us
aspire to them, but before that let us do what is required of
us; duty comes first.' On the other hand, the radical may say,

'Damn the rules; it is the ideals which count.' Now both disputants could produce arguments, though less than conclusive ones, in support of their views. Thus the radical could go on to argue that the ideals involve greater goods than the rules do and that it is therefore permissible to break or at any rate neglect the rules in the interests of the 'higher' ideals.[2] The conservative, on the other hand, could object that the radical's argument was not merely inconclusive but also incomplete. 'True', he might say, 'I produce a greater good by attaining my ideals than I produce by conforming to uninspiring rules. But there is the other side of the coin. By failing to act in accordance with the rules I produce a greater evil than I do by failing to attain to the ideals to which I have aspired. Further, if the ideals are properly articulated they will be seen to involve prior conformity to rules'. The arguments on both sides are highly contentious, and the issue is plainly one of moral importance. Although there are no knock-down arguments, the arguments employed by both sides are in a way conceptual. For they are dependent for their articulate presentation on prior understanding of the logical properties of the moral concepts employed. It is the logic of morals which first reveals the conceptual fissures and the rival aspects, styles, and conceptual structures which are the subject of debate. That is why the logic of morals is indispensable to that moral theorizing which I have called the 'metaphysic of morals', and which I go on to consider in Part III.

In this chapter I have argued that objections to the viability of a morally neutral or non-aligned study of the logical properties of moral concepts lack cogency. But the logic of morals neither is nor ought to be the whole of moral philosophy. A less austere conception of moral philosophy is necessary, for there are, in a loose sense of the term, 'conceptual' questions which are concerned with choice between competing aspects of a morality, competing conceptual structures, and competing styles of moral thinking. Once this distinction

---

[2] The fence of rules is for the purblind crowd;
They walk by averaged precepts: sovereign men,
Seeing by God's light, see the general
By seeing all the special—own no rule
But their full vision of the moment's worth.
         George Eliot, *The Spanish Gypsy*, p. 123.

between logic of morals and metaphysic of morals is recognized, there is less temptation to deny the possibility of a morally non-aligned logic of morals. The basis for the denial has been the entirely correct belief that practitioners of the logic of morals have committed themselves to moral theses, while ostensibly trying to produce definitions. The correct inference from this is not that a morally neutral logic of morals is impossible, but that moral philosophers have in the past largely got their logic of morals wrong, that in this area, as in others, to use H. L. A. Hart's words, theory has grown 'on the back of definition' (H. L. A. Hart, *Definition and Theory in Jurisprudence*, p. 7). The aim of Part I of this book is to free definition of its incubus.

The Concept of a Morality

2.1. Since the rest of Part I will be concerned with elucidating the concept of a morality, I need in this chapter to set the stage for that task. It should be noted that I have entitled this chapter 'The concept of *a* morality'. For what I wish to investigate are the distinctive marks of *any* morality and not merely of one particular set of moral judgements or rules, dubbed 'Morality'. I wish, moreover, to spell out what is involved in the concept of a morality in such a way that I do not thereby commit myself to a substantive moral position, since, as I have stressed in Chapter 1, this is a standing danger for any conceptual analyst of the languages of morals.

In the first place, I wish to maintain that the moral philosopher needs to give an account of the distinctive thought and language employed by those who think and talk about matters of morals. The word 'moral', then, must have a classificatory function amongst others. I would distinguish three kinds of words by means of which we classify judgements, statements, and language. First, there are those which contain as part of their meaning the notions of acceptability or unacceptability, words such as 'valid', 'correct', 'rational', 'scientific' (when contrasted with 'unscientific'), 'legal', 'religious', and 'metaphysical' (in the purely pejorative sense). Second, there are words which we use to classify judgements according to the 'topic-neutral' words or logical constants contained in them, words such as 'negative', 'disjunctive', 'universal'. Third, there are words which may be called 'universe-of-discourse words'. It is a necessary feature of these words that they satisfy three formal requirements. If a word 'U' is a universe-of-discourse word, then (1) the contradictory of a U-judgement must be a U-judgement, (2) any non-tautologous disjunction of U-judgements, or any judgement equivalent in meaning to such a disjunction, must be a U-judgement, and (3) any non-contradictory conjunction of U-judgements, or any judgement equivalent in meaning to such a conjunction, must be a U-judgement. The word 'factual' is a word which plainly satisfies these requirements.

These universe-of-discourse words, unlike those of my first and second kinds, are used to classify kinds of disagreement. Unfortunately they are often confused with those of the first and second kinds. Universe-of-discourse words are confused with those of the second kind because both are often indiscriminately labelled 'logical words'. As we have seen, words of the second kind are used to classify statements according to the 'topic-neutral' words contained in them; words of the third kind are used to classify statements according to their topic or subject-matter. Now the topic of a statement is what both it and its contradictory are about; both statements are answers to the same question. Words of the third kind, therefore, are used to classify questions, as well as statements and judgements which are answers to those questions.

Universe-of-discourse words are also confused with those of the first kind, since many words, e.g., 'moral', 'legal', 'scientific', and 'metaphysical', have both kinds of use. Thus the word 'legal' on the one hand means 'in accordance with the law', a sense in which it is opposed to 'illegal', and on the other hand refers to a certain kind of topic or subject-matter. The word 'scientific' is sometimes used as a term of praise, contrasted with 'unscientific', but at other times is used to describe a certain subject-matter, when it is contrasted with 'non-scientific'. It is the same with the word 'moral'. The word 'moral' when it is used as a term of praise is contrasted with 'immoral', or sometimes 'amoral', but is contrasted with 'non-moral' when used as a universe-of-discourse word. The two uses are sometimes confused, as when my grandmother once said of a certain great philosopher that, since he was immoral, he could not have been a moral philosopher.

By proposing that philosophers should use the word 'moral' in its unrestricted sense I do not, of course, wish to deprive anybody of the liberty to make contrasts such as it is customary to make when 'morality' is contrasted with, say, egoism. The distinction between self-interested motivation and non-self-interested ('moral') motivation is as important as ever and the difference between altruism and egoism is no less clear when these words are used (indeed, it may even be clearer) than when egoism is distinguished from 'morality'. Granted, the concept of an altruistic morality is of much greater interest to the moralist than the wider concept of a morality in general. Perhaps some kind of justification for an altruistic morality can be given by examining the narrower concept (see Chapter 15). That is not yet my aim. The priority at this stage is to get clear about the nature of the field in which we express our agreement and disagreement on these matters, that is, we should become clear as to the correct analysis of the wider concept of a morality.

The philosopher in general has a special interest in universe-of-discourse words. It is one of his tasks to investigate similarities and differences between distinct universes of discourse. His respect for the ordinary use of language has therefore to be tempered by an ideal of clarity and logical completeness. Certainly the moral philosopher has to start with the ordinary use of the word 'moral'. But however painstaking our empirical study of usage may be, it will not provide us with an automatic decision on border-line and peripheral instances of moral judgements. For ordinary men a decision on instances of this kind is generally neither important nor interesting; there is seldom need for them to make such decisions. But for the moral philosopher the word 'moral' is one of his tools, and in the absence of clear-cut ordinary usage he has to decide how the word is to be used. It does not follow from this that the moral philosopher thereby moralizes; not all prescription is moral prescription. Just as the judge declares and applies the law where that is clear, but sometimes has to fill in the gaps between statutes, so the philosopher describes the actual use of language where that is clear, but may have to perform an 'interstitial' task as far as universe-of-discourse words are concerned. The end which should guide him is not a moral preconception or prejudice, but an ideal of completeness in conceptual classification. It is this ideal which justifies both the three formal requirements set out above for universe-of-discourse words and my prescription that we should use the word 'moral' in accordance with these requirements.

2.2. Readers of 2.1 may have formed the opinion that I have been advocating a 'formal' definition of what a morality is as opposed to a 'material' definition, a definition which restricts the admissible content of moral judgements. Such an opinion presupposes that the dichotomy between form and content is comprehensive and that we are perfectly clear as to what is meant by 'content'. The word 'content' appears to me to cover two different things, topic and message, and I therefore wish to maintain that there are not just two but three ways in which a definition can restrict what counts as a morality or moral judgement. Three kinds of possible restriction can be distinguished, restrictions on form, restrictions on topic, and restrictions on message. I shall maintain that an acceptable definition of the concept of a morality will restrict form and topic, but not message.

First, restrictions on form need cause us little difficulty, for reasons similar to those mentioned in 1.3. If a statement specifying the essential form that a moral judgement must have is correct, then it will be contradictory to assert that something is a moral judgement and yet lacks the essential form in question. Thus, if universalizability were an essential formal characteristic of moral judgements, it would be contradictory to say of any judgement, 'This is a moral judgement but is not universalizable.' Nothing 'oughty' follows from a statement correctly specifying the essential form of a moral judgement. Thus if all moral judgements are necessarily X-ish, whatever 'X' might be, it does not follow from this that you ought to make X-ish judgements, or that you ought to make your moral judgements X-ish. Indeed, if the statement specifying the essential characteristic is correct, you cannot but make your moral judgements X-ish, and so no 'oughty' question arises about the X-ishness or otherwise of moral judgements.

Second, restrictions on topic are of the greatest importance for determining what a moral judgement is, the topic of any judgement being, as I have already explained (2.1), what both it and its normal contradictory are about. One can certainly think of many topics with which moral judgements are *not* concerned. Moral judgements are plainly not concerned with the behaviour of the stars. It is more difficult to say something positive about the topic of a morality. A contentious topic-restricting statement would be, 'Moral judgements are solely concerned with how people behave to one another'. The question arises whether this statement can be correct. For some of us consider it morally wrong that people should behave in certain ways towards animals, even though we may not count animals as persons. Again, some ecologists talk about an 'ethic of conservation' and this is concerned with how man should behave towards his environment.[1] A less contentious topic-restricting statement, one which appears to me to be correct is, 'Moral judgements are (A morality is) concerned with people, what they do and what is done to them.' Nothing 'oughty' follows from this. It does not follow that one morally ought to make judgements only about people. However, if I make a moral judgement about the behaviour of a stone in rolling downhill, say, 'It was morally wrong of that stone to descend on me so suddenly', then, since it *is* a moral judgement, I shall be implying that the stone is a person. Since stones are not people, my moral judgement is not felicitous and I *ought* not to have made such a judgement. This 'ought', of course, is not a moral one. However, if my utterance about the stone were not serious but facetious, the whole point of saying it would lie in its infelicity. In the example of the stone I so arranged it, by inserting the adverb 'morally', that I made a moral judgement despite the non-moral topic. Had I omitted the word 'morally', it would have been open to somebody to deny that I had thereby made a moral judgement because of the non-moral topic.

Third, usually when philosophers have talked about restrictions on content, they have been thinking primarily of restrictions on the message of moral judgements. Message differs from topic in that the topic is not changed by denial while the message is. We find a manifest restriction on message in Bentham's *An Introduction to the Principles of Morals and Legislation* (Chapter I, § X), where he writes:

Of an action that is conformable to the principle of utility one may always say either that it is one that ought to be done, or at least that it is not one that ought not to be done. One may say also, that it is right it should be done; at least that it is not wrong it should be done: that it is a right action; at least that it is not a wrong action. When thus interpreted, the words *ought*, and *right* and *wrong*, and others of that stamp, have a meaning: when otherwise, they have none.

[1] See John Passmore's *Man's Responsibility for Nature*, pp. 3-4.

The same effect is brought about by Bentham's definition of ethics later in the same work (Chapter XVII, § II): 'Ethics at large may be defined, the art of directing men's actions to the production of the greatest possible quantity of happiness, on the part of those whose interest is in view.'

The thinker who places a restriction on the message of moral judgements I shall, in accordance with current usage, call a 'restrictivist'. The restrictivist, in laying down the necessary conditions for calling a judgement a 'moral judgement', is at one and the same time laying down the necessary conditions for calling a judgement an 'acceptable moral judgement'. Of course, he is not committed thereby to calling all moral judgements acceptable. There is no difficulty about maintaining the existence of some judgements which, although correctly called moral judgements, are unacceptable owing to the utterer having made some factual mistake or being otherwise confused. But the restriction of moral judgements to being judgements with a certain message implies that there are some judgements whose denials are not themselves moral judgements. Worse, it implies that there are some questions to which there are two mutually exclusive but jointly comprehensive answers, only one of which is a moral judgement. We then have to choose between saying that such a question is a moral question, although one of the answers to it is not 'moral', and saying that such a question is not a moral question, even though one of the answers is a moral answer. Either of these alternatives seems to me to be paradoxical and awkward. I am not, of course, denying that there are restrictivist concepts of a morality any more than that there are restrictivist concepts of poetry. While there is a sense in which Cicero and McGonagall were not poets, there is also a sense in which they were poets, albeit fifth-rate ones. Likewise there is an unrestricted sense of the terms 'moral' and 'morality' which enables us to use these words as classificatory terms and in doing so to face the problem of determining the nature of the arena in which people make moral judgements and other people disagree with them. It is this latter problem with which the logic of morals, as I conceive it, is concerned. By defining the term 'moral' narrowly we could not make the problem go away.

It is, indeed, because the problem will not go away so easily

that restrictivist philosophers find themselves confronting unnecessary and self-imposed difficulties. Thus G. J. Warnock
(*The Object of Morality*, pp. 145-6, 152) apparently finds
difficulty in giving a plausible account of the medieval Scottish
chieftain, who acts in accordance 'with the accepted mores of
upper-class Scottish life of the period', and slaughters 'all the
rival clansmen whom he had invited to a banquet'. Warnock says
of him that the chieftain 'has never "got the idea" of morality'.
The chieftain's code thus appears to be relegated to a logical
limbo of non-moral mores. Yet the chieftain must have been
well aware that there was such a thing as Christian morality
and that some of his own peers were not of the same mind as
he; by contrast with them he would have seen himself as a
tough realist and man of the world. Such men have doubtless
had a bad press, but as moral philosophers we have to give an
account of the nature of their disagreement with the morality,
say, of people like St. Thomas à Kempis. Another restrictivist,
Mrs Foot, in her 'Morality and Art' (*Proceedings of the British
Academy*, 1970, p. 16) sees that her own characterization of
morality is so narrow that it is necessary to ask, 'Why, after
all, should we take it for granted that the form of language
already developed is the one we want?' (Mrs Foot's kind of
externalism will be examined in 4.4).

To conclude, the attempt of restrictivists to foist on to the
world of thought a restricted concept of a morality to the
exclusion of all others is to be rejected. However, there will
always be a standing temptation to be restrictivist. For it is
easy to mistake for an essential feature of *any* moral judgement
what is merely a standard feature of the moral judgements
of a particular morality or what is a necessary feature of one
class only of moral judgements. Hence it is important for the
moral philosopher to take, as it were, an antidote to his own
morality and to try and understand some of the more bizarre
and wayward views on morals which have been held by others
at different times and places.

An objector to my position might well argue for an analogy
between science and morals on the lines of S. E. Toulmin's
An Examination of the Place of Reason in Ethics. 'Surely',
he might say, 'when you are considering what science is, you
look at cogent scientific reasoning and true scientific theories.

If you are too slack in the choice of your data, you will include as science everything from Thales' speculations to alchemy, astrology, and phrenology. Likewise when you are doing philosophy of morals you should consider cogent moral reasoning and true or correct moral judgements. Immoralists from Thrasymachus to the Marquis de Sade are more the concern of the psychiatrist than they are of the serious historian or moral philosopher'. My objector, who is not entirely imaginary, is not helped by his analogy with science. Of course you have to explain why, say, the work of Anaximenes would not constitute good science today, and why astrology is ill-founded, but it is quite another thing to exclude such work altogether from science, even from its prehistory. To exclude them because they either were not or are not good science necessarily leads one to deprive the word 'science' of its role of describing a certain kind of activity and to convert it into a word which is favourably evaluative of a much more narrowly defined activity. I agree with the objector that there is an analogy between science and morals; where I disagree with him is in his account of science and the similar account of morality which his analogy leads him to adopt.

Which kind of definition we adopt is, I submit, a matter for classificatory convenience. It is not plausible to suppose that there is something immoral in accepting a wider definition of morality, as if by allowing Nazi morality to be a morality one somehow made it morally respectable. We find D. A. J. Richards (*A Theory of Reasons for Action*, p. 12) speaking of Hare's account of morality compelling him 'too easily to accept what one's deepest moral convictions eschew—the logical possibility of the actual (versus the supposed) morality of the principles of intolerance used by a sincere, universalizing Nazi'. Again, even W. K. Frankena in his 'The Concept of Morality' (*The Definition of Morality*, p. 167) maintains that Hare's 'refusal to define morality by reference to the interests of other people *permits* [my italics] . . . an extension of an aesthetic style of evaluation to take place'. But definitions do not 'permit' or forbid extensions of types of evaluation. It is just as easy for a philosopher who employs a narrow concept of a morality to be an aestheticist as for one who employs a wider concept.

2.3. I argued in 1.3 that any definitional account of what a morality was would be incorrect if it entailed a moral judgement. This is no less true of so-called 'formal' definitions than it is of 'material' definitions. It now behoves me to produce a definitional account of a morality which cannot be faulted in this way. It will not, I hope, be possible to elicit a moral message from my definitional account. This does not, however, prevent me from indicating the topic of moral judgements, since I have already distinguished topic from message. But it does mean that I have so to manage my definitional account of morality that I include all possibilities, even the bizarre ones. At each stage I am bound to cast a reflective eye on my progress and determine whether for some unacknowledged moral reason I have excluded from consideration by definitional fiat attitudes, judgements, or principles which compete with those I regard as 'moral' but which, as it happens, I or my friends cannot share or even imagine sharing. For my characterization of what a morality is is designed not to exclude anything which any reasonable person would want to designate a morality. It has therefore a minimal character and I do not claim that it provides a complete characterization, only one which is sufficient for my purposes.

Before I begin my characterization of what a morality is, I need to make or rather recognize certain distinctions. I need, in particular, to distinguish a social morality, an individual morality, and what I shall call an 'anchored morality'. Moralities, whether social or individual, arise in a social context. They are as much social phenomena as languages, religions, and legal systems. A morality, however, is much more opaque than a legal system. For it is very much more difficult to discover what the moral rules and standards of a society are than what the linguistic or legal rules are. But just as there are objective criteria for determining what the law of a particular country is, so are there likewise objective criteria for determining what the morality of a social group is. Just as there are parts of a legal system whose distinctive use is associated with sanctions, so too there are moral sanctions associated with the application of moral rules and standards. These moral sanctions are, to use Radcliffe-Brown's expression (*Encyclopaedia of the Social Sciences,* Vol. XIII, article on 'Social Sanctions', p. 531),

more 'diffuse' although none the less distinctive. Deviation
from moral rules is met at the very least with that kind of social
pressure which J. S. Mill called 'the reproaches of one's neighbours'. A statement concerning the morality of a group can be
as concrete and objective as, even if less easily verifiable than,
a statement of what the law of a community is. To state that
promise-breaking is regarded as wrong in our society is to state
an objective fact about our social life, not a matter of opinion.
One way of verifying it is by seeing how people behave to
somebody who breaks his promises. He may be shunned,
despised, mocked, or simply ignored. Moreover, a morality is
both less monolithic and less perspicuous than a legal system.
It is less perspicuous because there are no moral statute books
which will enable us to determine what is morally required in
a given society, nor are there universally recognized moral
courts or authorities to give an incontestable interpretation of
either the letter or the spirit of moral precepts. A morality is
less monolithic in that it is possible for only partially identical
moralities to live side by side, although there plainly has to
be some common ground in order that a common legal and
social system should be possible.

In addition to the morality of the group or society there
are also the moralities of individuals. These may be the individuals' versions or representations of the group morality or
their own idiosyncratic moralities. What an individual's
morality is is no less an objective and determinable matter
than what a group morality is. Indeed, the morality of an
individual may be regarded as a limiting case of a group
morality. While the sanction of a group morality is 'the reproaches of one's neighbours', the sanction of an individual's
morality is his own disapprobation and reproaches, the sense
of failing to come up to standards which he has set himself.
Of course, the distinction between individual and social
moralities is of importance where there is a possible or actual
clash between them. For instance, in John Galsworthy's *The
Silver Spoon* (pp. 223-4) the following passages of dialogue
occur between Lady Marjorie Ferrar, on the one hand, and
opposing counsel and the judge on the other:

'. . . Do you believe in current morality yourself?'
'I don't know what you call current morality.'

'I will tell you, Miss Ferrar. I should say, for instance, it was current morality that women should not have *liaisons* before they're married, and should not have them after.'

'What about men?'

'Thank you; I was coming to men. And that men should at least not have them after.'

'I shouldn't say that was *current* morality at all.'

. . . the judge had turned his face towards her. He was speaking.

'Do I understand you imply that in your view it is moral for women to have *liaisons* before marriage, and for men and women to have them after?'

'I think it's current morality, my lord.'

'I'm not asking you about current morality, I'm asking whether in *your* view it is moral?'

'I think many people think it's all right who don't say it, yet.'

The judge here draws a clear distinction between what Lady Marjorie thinks that a society regards as moral and what she *in propria persona* regards as moral.

2.4. The distinction I have drawn between individual and social moralities accounts for some of the uses people make of the term 'morality'. Thus sometimes when somebody says, 'Morality requires me to act so', he means to refer to his own individual morality, while somebody else may be speaking of the positive or social morality of his group or society. There is, however, a further use. People quite commonly speak of 'Morality' with a capital 'M', of 'The Moral Law', of 'natural morality', of the 'Morality of Common Sense', or of 'Common Morality', and in so talking they intend to refer neither to their individual moralities nor to the ordinary social morality of their time, place, and society. What they mean to refer to is an enduring traditional morality of which the contemporary social morality of their society may be only an imperfect reflection. For them traditional morality is not to be thought of as one morality among many, and that is why they may call it 'Morality' without qualification, in much the same way as Christianity is sometimes called simply 'Religion'. The special position of a traditional morality relative to a particular society or to a group of societies enables it to be appealed to when an individual is in conflict with a contemporary social morality. When Sophocles' Antigone[2] appeals to laws superior

_____
[2] Sophocles, *Antigone*, lines 450-70.

to those of the State, she is not appealing to her individual morality, for this would hardly provide her with the leverage she needs; nor is she appealing to the dominant social morality of the Thebans, for that presumably is the morality in terms of which her uncle Creon justifies himself in refusing burial to the corpse of her rebel brother. Her appeal is to the ever-lasting 'laws of the gods' which constitute Greek traditional morality.

A traditional morality is a relatively unchanging social morality which people of successive generations share; it is in the light of such a morality that a conservative individual may judge and seek to change the contemporary social morality which is dominant in his society. When people use the word 'Morality' as the proper name of a particular morality and purport to make a uniquely identifying reference, their intention, when they are not alluding to the contemporary social morality of their society, is normally to refer to their shared, traditional morality. This traditional morality is individuated by its content. The morality which we who originate from a Hebrew-Graeco-Roman culture today regard as traditional has a distinctive content or message. Its principles, rules, precepts, maxims, and ideals are the ones which are commonly called 'moral' and recognized as such. According to it, one ought not to harm others, one ought not to steal, one ought to be truthful, one ought to keep promises, one ought to return services rendered and so on, and it is good to be just, kind, and to promote the happiness of others. This is a basically Natural-Law conception of Morality; indeed, the content of our traditional morality resembles that of Natural Law if we take Justinian's precepts, viz., *honeste vivere, alterum non laedere, suum cuique tribuere* as being not merely *praecepta iuris* but also precepts of Natural Law (*The Institutes of Justinian*, Book I, Tit. I, 3). One may even say that positive social morality is to (traditional) Morality as positive law is to Natural Law.

When a traditional morality is so articulate and stable that people are prepared to give it a proper name or apply to it what is ostensibly a uniquely referring term or expression, calling it 'Morality' or 'The Moral Law', I shall call the morality so referred to an 'anchored' morality. Strictly speaking, of course, it is the referring term or expression which is anchored to the morality in question, but I shall find it convenient to call the morality itself 'anchored', since it is owing to the important and stable role which people ascribe to it within their moral thought and discourse that they designate it so distinctively.

We can only be justified in making an unqualified and uniquely identifying use of the word 'Morality' to refer to a traditional morality if we can be certain that users of the word and of its equivalents in other languages have always intended to refer to one and the same traditional morality. We can have no such certainty. For one thing there are a number of diverse moral traditions. Ours is a tradition in which priority is given to the amiable virtues as opposed to the heroic virtues exemplified, say, by Achilles in Homer's *Iliad*. Moreover, the traditional morality I have specified makes no mention of duties to God or to gods, and would, therefore, appear to be secular. Yet many who purport to make a uniquely identifying use of the word 'Morality' have intended to refer to Christian Morality or to their own suitably glossed version of it, while, as I have remarked, others have used the word to refer to ordinary social moralities. I must, then, to avoid indeterminacy of reference find a device by means of which I can indicate that I am continuing to refer to one and the same traditional morality whenever I use the word 'Morality' in an anchored way. I shall, therefore, from this point onward refer to our secular traditional or anchored morality as 'Morality$_A$', using the first letter of the alphabet to signalize its historical salience. In this way it may be distinguished from other anchored moralities to which different people may from time to time have wished to ascribe a privileged position. It is, I think, of Morality$_A$ that Bishop Butler writes in his 'Dissertation on Virtue' (*Butler's Fifteen Sermons*, p. 148):

For, as much as it has been disputed wherein virtue consists, or whatever ground for doubt there may be about particulars; yet, in general, there is in reality an universally acknowledged standard of it. It is that, which all ages and all countries have made profession of in public: it is that, which every man you meet puts on the show of: it is that, which the primary and fundamental laws of all civil constitutions over the face of the earth make it their business and endeavour to enforce the practice of upon mankind: namely, justice, veracity, and regard to common good.

It is no simple matter to identify a morality as traditional.

We cannot assume that there will be agreement either between different contemporaries or between different generations as to what they decide to regard as traditional. There is, it is true, little problem where moral change is negligible (cf. 8.1); in that case no distinction can profitably be drawn between the traditional morality and the social morality dominant at a given time. Where, however, the rate of moral change is sufficiently rapid, those who wish to identify a morality as traditional have to choose between criteria of identification. One solution would be to identify as traditional the previous generation's morality in its entirety and in consequence of that decision to say that the present social morality was a departure or deviation from traditional morality. Alternatively, one could identify as traditional those elements from the morality of previous generations which survived the moral change. In this event successive generations might revise the standard conception of the content of traditional morality. The nature of the identification will depend in part on the attitude of those seeking to make the identification (the identifiers), whether, say, they welcome the direction of moral change. Hence the attitude of the identifiers in a morally changing community will determine at any rate in part whether the morality dignified as 'traditional' is fairly specific in content or highly schematic. One thing, however, does not depend on attitude and that is the minimum content of the traditional morality. For it is an objective fact that the social moralities of different generations in the same society have some common content, and it is that which constitutes the minimum content of traditional morality. The more rapid the rate of moral change, the more schematic and less specific will be the minimum content of the traditional morality. In the case of our traditional morality, I submit, the rate of moral change is nowadays moderately rapid, which is why Morality$_A$ or the morality of common sense has sometimes seemed to consist only of 'vague generalities', to use Henry Sidgwick's term (*The Methods of Ethics*, p. 342). It is a consequence of the apparently schematic character of Morality$_A$ that those who have sought a solution to the first two principal problems of moral philosophy (1.1), those of unity and consistency, have had to supplement this relatively schematic traditional morality from their own 'moral consciousness'. For they believed that the moral law whose foundations they sought was, in Bishop Butler's words (*The Analogy of Religion*, Part II, Chapter I), 'written upon our hearts; interwoven into our very nature'. It is because of the relatively schematic character of Morality$_A$ that success has eluded so many attempts to unify and systematize it. I submit, however, that a modest measure of unity can be found in the belief in altruism or concern for others or for the common good. I call it a modest measure, since altruism cannot serve as the sole fundamental 'axiom of morality' and is of itself logically insufficient for deducing all the precepts and ideals of Morality$_A$. Moreover, even if Morality$_A$ has altruism or concern for the good of others at its core, yet it contains some other precepts whose connections with altruism are, if they exist at all, extremely tenuous and problematic. To show that altruism is rational, or more rational than egoism, would not, then, suffice to justify these 'peripheral' precepts, which, indeed, may be criticized with the aid of altruistic morality (16.2).

The verbal distinctions I have drawn may appear trivial, but their due observance is of the greatest consequence for our understanding of what we, as moral philosophers, are doing. In addition to the uses I have just mentioned, the word 'morality' is often used without qualification when it is wished to refer to the subject-matter of moral judgements (cf. 2.1), what moral judgements are about. Moral philosophers who have wished to characterize the subject-matter of moral judgements have often asked questions about the definition and nature of 'morality'. Those who have tried to give answers to such questions have supposed themselves to be giving differing answers to a single question. In this they have been mistaken. While some have been trying to find the distinctive and essential characteristics of moral judgements or to understand what it is for something to be a morality, others have concentrated on our traditional morality, Morality$_A$, as if examination of its principal features would illuminate 'the concept of morality'. Thus Warnock in *The Object of Morality* may be interpreted as seeking to determine the purpose or object not of any morality, but of one particular traditional morality, Morality$_A$, by examining its message. If this interpretation is correct, we may guess that it is Morality$_A$ which Warnock's Scottish chieftain (2.2) never 'got the idea of' rather than that he never got the idea of moral thinking or of using moral language; he never made Morality$_A$ the basis of his own morality, although doubtless he would have 'made profession of it in public', when, for example, he wished to conclude a treaty.[3]

'Morality$_A$' denotes a particular morality just as 'Scots Law' denotes a particular legal system. Just as there is no concept of English Law or concept of Scots Law, so there is no concept of Morality$_A$. It does not therefore make sense to ask for a definition of Morality$_A$; we can only ask what constitutes it, where what constitutes it is not a matter for individual decision but of historical fact. If we wish to undertake a conceptual investigation, it is the concept of *a* morality which we have to examine, and this is the topic of Part I of this book.

[3] Some of the different uses of the terms 'moral' or 'morality' are nicely juxtaposed in an account by Virginia Woolf, quoted by Quentin Bell (*Virginia Woolf*, Vol. II, p. 212), of a conversation she had with Beatrice Webb. 'Mrs Webb said she was thankful for her Victorian training in morality; "I said we were moral in fighting that morality. Now there's a morality to make again".' Talk of an individual's morality as opposed to talk of morality *simpliciter* antedates the nineteenth century. Thus Bishop Burnet writes (1680) in his life of Rochester (*Lives of Hale, Bedell and Rochester*, p. 248): 'Upon this he told me, the two maxims of his morality then were, that he should do nothing to the hurt of any other, or that might prejudice his own health; and he thought that all pleasure, when it did not interfere with these, was to be indulged as the gratification of our natural appetites.'

3

Desires and Moralities (1)

3.1. In this and the subsequent chapters I wish to spell out what a morality is. I shall try to show that a morality (1) is in a broad sense 'prescriptive', or, as I prefer to call it, 'normative'; (2) is concerned with the desires and actions of intelligent agents; and (3) is concerned with what its holders regard as 'most important' for action. I shall try in this and the next chapter to give a coherent account of what wanting or desiring is and explain partly in terms of wanting what a morality is. I do not, of course, propose to do anything so crude as to deduce moralities from statements of desire, but it would be just as crude and naïve to suppose that if desires and moralities are not connected deductively they are not connected at all.

Moralities are about human beings and their actions. So too is psychology. As man-watchers we observe people and their actions in order to know what we can truthfully say about them. According to what we observe we judge the utterances of psychologists. The utterances have to fit what we observe. By contrast, the content of a morality provides the standards in terms of which we judge our own actions and those of others. Our deeds have to match or fit our words. Our expressions of desires have a similar relationship to our actions. What we do is judged as satisfying or failing to satisfy our desires. This is why it is important in elucidating the concept of a morality to give an account of desires.

Perhaps the best way of illustrating the direction of fit of moral judgements, this central feature which it shares with expressions of desire and intention, is by adapting Professor Anscombe's example of the shopper and his shopping list (*Intention*, p. 56, § 32). At the beginning of an academic year, I make a list of books which it is necessary for me to buy for the sake of my year's work when I visit the University Book-shop. This is a normative list. I consult it in the bookshop to

remind me of what I should buy; I consult it at home afterwards to see if through haste or forgetfulness I have made an
error or omitted to buy one of the books on my list despite its
availability. I have also another list in my possession, one which
the bookseller has made of the books I bought and which he
has attached to my receipt. This is a recording list. Its direction of fit is opposite to that of my own list. My own book
list was not merely normative but prescriptive; I had listed only
books which I had to buy. At another time when I have more
leisure I may enter the bookshop armed with a list of books it
would be a good thing to have. This list is prescriptive only in
a very broad sense of that term. If I leave some of these books
unbought, I shall not have committed anything that I could
call an 'error'. For my second shopping list is, as I shall say,
only 'mini-prescriptive' or 'commendatory'. But the direction
of fit is the same as in the case of the fully prescriptive list. They
are both lists appropriate for my use in purchasing books, not
for the bookseller's use in recording purchases. I shall say
more about the distinction between degrees of prescriptiveness in 5.2.

For the moment I am only concerned with the common
feature of direction of fit. When I claim that moral language
is 'broadly prescriptive' or 'normative', what I mean is that its
primary direction of fit is the opposite of that of a recording
list, nothing more nor less. I do not mean to imply that every
moral judgement involves one in uttering self-addressed imperatives or prescriptions or anything of that sort. Since the
primary direction of fit of moral language is shared with expressions of desire or wanting, it is important to trace the
connection between desires and moralities. This will be the
concern of the rest of this chapter and of Chapter 4.

3.2. Some desires arise from natural needs although they are
not to be identified with needs. The human infant cannot identify its needs, it merely expresses them. We learn what it is that
we want when we realize that it is food which relieves our discomfort. Conscious wanting in response to a felt need involves
conceptualization, it involves not so much wanting whatever
it is which will assuage the discomfort but wanting *food*, wanting something taken through the mouth and edible. Need-

related desires 'come unbidden' (to employ Benson's useful phrase in 'Wants, Desires and Deliberation', *Moral Weakness*) even if they require conscious direction.

Desires which are arrived at through deliberation are more within our power. The agent's identification of these deliberative or reflective desires is necessarily authoritative. It is because the agent has authoritatively identified them that he can marshal them as reasons in the course of deliberation and coming to a decision. To ignore this leads to absurdity. Consider the following dialogue:

A: I have a strange feeling, of hankering for something. What
   is it that I hanker for?
B: I know what it is. You want to read a novel by Jane Austen.
A: Ah, that's it! Now I know!

What is absurd here is that B should claim to be able to identify somebody else's deliberative desires authoritatively. An identification of somebody else's non-deliberative, need-related desires would not be similarly ludicrous. It sometimes happens even to an adult that he has a sensation of discomfort and is unsure whether he is suffering hunger-pangs or indigestion.

Although need-related desires and deliberative desires differ in the way I have indicated, there is a sense in which a need-related desire can, as it were, become a deliberative desire. Every time I am hungry and then go in search of a restaurant, this is just what happens. In a civilized individual, a need-related desire does not of necessity become a deliberative desire, but its clamant character ensures that its demand to be taken into consideration cannot be totally ignored.

3.3. We acquire the concept of desiring or wanting in the same way as we do other psychological concepts, and this way, as I shall argue, is two-fold. Consider the concept of pain. According to the traditional theory, I know the meaning of the word 'pain' from my own case and I extend the use by analogy and so apply it to others. Concepts of mental phenomena are on this view acquired by some sort of internal perception. The quasi-Lockean theory of meaning, from which this view derives, is untenable, as it would make all communication impossible.

If my words denote my ideas in my mind and your words denote your ideas in your mind, neither of us can determine whether the ideas in each mind can in any sense of 'same' be the same ideas. But since communication is possible, this theory of meaning must be mistaken. The theory, if it has any plausibility, is plausible only for irredeemably private mental concepts which do not appear to have any reference to inter-subjective objects discussable in a common language. However, psychological concepts are part, and can only be taught as part, of a common language. 'An inner process stands in need of outward criteria' (L. Wittgenstein, *Philosophical Investigations* I, § 580). It is through pain-behaviour that we are able to teach the concept of pain. It is through anger-behaviour that we are able to teach the concept of anger and likewise it is through desire-behaviour that we are able to teach the concept of desire.

But are the concepts of pain, anger, love, desire, etc., purely behavioural? All that has been shown is that nobody can know the entire meaning of the words 'pain', 'anger', etc., merely from his own case. It does not follow from this that somebody can acquire the whole concept of pain solely through acquaintance with the pain-behaviour of others. We have rejected the case of the man who has learnt the entire meaning of the word 'pain' solely from his own case as impossible. Consider now the case at the other extreme, the case of the man who has learnt the meaning of the word 'pain' solely from the observed gross behaviour of others. He has seen others groan and grovel and shriek and run away and so on, but he has never experienced pain himself. This is plainly a logically possible case, unlike the one at the other extreme, but it is a queer one, and we should be inclined to say of such a man that he had an incomplete mastery of the concept of pain. Compare being in love. Some of us can remember what it was like when we knew the meaning of 'being in love' only from the bizarre behaviour of others. Until we had had experience of our own, we had an incomplete mastery of the concept. Again some of us, if we are very lucky, never know what fear is in our own case. When after having learnt these concepts in their application to other people, we apply them to ourselves, we may have an 'aha-experience' and feel impelled to say, 'So this is what being afraid is like'. Of course, even after I have acquired part-mastery of the concept from the behaviour of others, I may not be sure that I have correctly applied the concept to my own case. Indeed, it could even be that my initial recognition of my state for what it is depends on my observing my own physical behaviour, actual or incipient. It is because I shake at the thought of the treachery of the man who professed to be my friend that I realize that my principal emotion is anger and not, say, compassion or forgiveness.

To return to the concept of pain. The person who only knows what pain is in the case of others may not recognize what he feels as pain. Such failure to recognize pain in his own case indicates at the very least incomplete mastery of the concept of pain. On the other hand, there may be somebody who initially only knows pain in his own case. To make this intelligible I shall have to spin a tall story. Suppose that a pain-feeler is brought up in a society of 'anaesthetics', people who through some genetic mutation never feel pain. Our pain-feeler never sees anybody in pain but when he falls down and cries, the 'anaesthetics' say to him 'You are not like us, you are like our forefathers, you feel *pain*'. The anaesthetics are able to teach the pain-feeler the internal half of the concept because they have grasped the external half. Were this not possible, we should have an ambiguity in the use of the word, which would have a different meaning in its first-person and third-person uses. However, in point of fact, we are taught the first-person uses of mental concepts by those who have already grasped the third-person uses. Our descriptions of our emotional states and feelings have to be in terms of a public vocabulary in order to be intelligible. Communication is possible between us about our internal states partly, at any rate, because our overt behaviour is broadly similar.

Consider now the case of desire or wanting. We acquire the concept of desire *both* from our own case and that of others. Initially the word 'want' can be taught 'as part of request behaviour. Thus the child learns to say "I want the ball" or "I want some candy" instead of simply "ball" or "candy". At this point he need not think of "I want" as describing a mental state he is in or a mental event he is having, but simply as a prefix used in making requests' (A. Goldman, *A Theory of*

Human Action, p. 121). Later, it will be natural to apply the terms 'wanting' or 'desire' to the tendency or disposition one feels oneself as having when one tends to or is disposed to ask for a ball or candy. Anybody who only learnt the application of the concept of wanting or desire to other people or only learnt its application to his own case would have only learnt part of the meaning of 'want'. If my twofold theory of psychological concepts is true of wanting, then we can account for the two hinges on which the concept appears to turn. It would be a mistake to suppose that we have here two distinct concepts or senses of 'want'. Rather we have two conditions which a concept of wanting or desire must satisfy, first, that 'the inner life' of the agent provides an antecedent means of determining the existence and strength of a desire and second, that the sequel of the desire furnishes an *ex post facto* means of determining the existence and possibly even the strength of a desire. If the second condition were the only one, we should have to regard it as analytic that the strongest desire is that upon which one acts; if the first condition were the only one, we should have to regard it as analytic that the strongest desire is the one which the agent feels as strongest. The two conditions together, although they provide, to use Pears's expression, 'criterial points of attachment to the world' (*Questions in the Philosophy of Mind*, p. 112), do not yield an analytic proposition when taken jointly. If the desire we act on were invariably identical with the introspectively strongest desire, this would be an empirical truth, not a logical one; in fact, I would suggest, it is an empirical falsehood.

We may give a rough definition of a desire as an introspectively accessible tendency to perform an action. A distinction needs to be made between what I shall call *una facie* desiring or wanting, wanting$_{uf}$, and desiring or wanting, all things considered, summary wanting, wanting$_s$. Wanting *una facie* is sometimes spontaneous or need-related, sometimes reflective or deliberative. Summary wanting, on the other hand, is always deliberative wanting. Of course wanting$_{uf}$ and wanting$_s$ may coincide; there may only be one aspect or description under which an action is considered and in that case wanting it under that aspect will lead to wanting it, all things considered. Wanting$_{uf}$ may be thought of as a tendency to do an action if the aspect under which it is wanted is the only aspect under which it is considered.

Now it might be supposed that wanting$_s$ was identical with the strongest or most intense desire. This would be a mistake. The difference is perhaps best brought out by the story of the Catholic priest and the Methodist minister who were passing a pub.[1] The priest made a suggestion: 'Why not go in', he said 'and have a drink?' The minister, somewhat shocked, replied, 'I'd sooner commit adultery', to which the priest retorted, 'Who wouldn't?' One philosophical point of this tale is that often when we say 'I would sooner', or 'I would rather' or 'I prefer', we mean to make an all-things-considered judgement rather than meaning to express a greater liking for or enjoyment of something, although these expressions are commonly used for this latter purpose also.

3.4. In the light of these distinctions we can now look at 'ought'-sentences. Corresponding to the distinction between *una facie* and summary desires, we should distinguish between *una facie* and summary 'ought's. 'Ought's$_{uf}$ are 'ought's which can conflict with one another and yet coexist in the thought of one and the same person, just as desires$_{uf}$ are desires which can coexist in the same agent although conflicting with one another. While we cannot simultaneously try to achieve in full two aims which we know to be incompatible or carry out two decisions which we know to be incompatible, we can have simultaneously two desires whose simultaneous satisfaction we know to be impossible, and recognize that one or both of them will have to go unsatisfied for the present. Since the desires are incompatible, unless a middle way (a compromise of some kind between the opposing desires) is possible, one of them will remain unfulfilled. *Una facie* 'ought'-judgements resemble desires of this kind rather than summary desires or decisions. For there are situations where two or more conflicting 'ought'-judgements apply, and one can only act on one of them, at any rate for the time being. Thus it is sometimes the case that I cannot at one and the same time both tell the truth and refrain from hurting somebody's feelings, and since I believe that I ought$_{uf}$ to tell the truth and that I ought$_{uf}$ not

[1] I owe this story to Dr C. J. F. Williams.

to hurt other people's feelings, I cannot but violate one of my principles in conforming to the other.

However, I wish to claim not merely that there is an analogy between 'ought's and 'want's, but that there is a conceptual relationship. The thesis which I wish to maintain is a version of what has sometimes been called 'internalism'. Anyone who believes that he ought$_{uf}$ to do something *eo ipso* wants$_{uf}$ to do that thing. This connection with wanting$_{uf}$ applies not only to the belief that one ought, but also to the belief that some action is good or, in general, to the belief that some favourably normative expression is applicable to an action. To express the thesis in a nutshell, normative belief necessarily ·involves wanting. Of course if this is to be maintained, it will not do to give an explication of wanting as 'finding attractive', 'being pro', and such like (as Goldman does, p. 49). For this would be a circular procedure. That the thesis is acceptable, at any rate for some uses of 'ought', can be seen by considering how bizarre it would be to say, for example, 'You ought to have a holiday for the sake of your health, but I don't want you to for the sake of your health'. It could be objected that this is not a fair example because the double occurrence of the words 'for the sake of your health', makes the whole sentence appear self-contradictory or, at any rate, almost so. Alternatively, I could have chosen a different sample sentence in which it was unclear whether the 'want' related to the same aspect as the 'ought' did. But in such a case there need be no relation at all between the 'ought' and the 'want'. Any two desires may be compatible if they do not relate to the same aspect of an action.

Of course the desire involved in a normative belief has to be a desire in the very widest sense. When I decide to have my tonsils out, it is not that I want to have my tonsils out *tout court*; I want to get rid of the tonsils because of the consequences of doing nothing about it. In this widest sense of 'want' I want to do everything that I do intentionally.

3.5. The desire which is necessarily involved in a moral belief must be a special sort of desire. It is not *any* sort of desire which is associated with a morality and it is the special character of moral desires ('moral' not being a term of appraisal here) with which I shall be concerned in this section. Moralities do not arise from spontaneous desires, but they cannot but be concerned with them. Desires which come unbidden do not necessarily go away when bidden. Whether, then, we satisfy our spontaneous desires or not, we cannot ignore them in making up our minds how to live. What spontaneous desires a rational organism has may well determine the topic if not the message of those moral judgements he comes to make or accept.

The desires from which moral beliefs spring are reflective desires. By saying this, I do not mean to imply that a moral belief is merely a desire dressed up as a belief. Merely to desire to live in a certain way does not amount to a moral belief. Moreover, the desire associated with a *moral* belief must be a desire of a particular kind, a desire associated with a higher-order desire. If somebody holds a moral belief, it is not enough for him that other people should simply conform to it; when one has a moral belief one desires not merely that others should conform to it but also that they should desire to conform to it. Perhaps this is part of the point of Stevenson's first pattern of analysis of 'good' as 'I approve of this; do so as well' (*Ethics and Language*, p. 26). A moral desire must carry with it the desire that others should both act in accordance with it and desire to act in accordance with it. Non-moral desires do not necessarily carry with them higher-order desires. Spontaneous and unreflective desires are not ramified. My unreflective desire for food does not carry with it a desire that I should desire food, unless indeed I like being a glutton. Sexual desire may even be combined with a desire not to experience it. This is what Catullus felt about Lesbia; he suffered from desire and desired (wanted ?) not to suffer from it.[2] On the other hand, my desire to relieve the needy carries with it not only a desire that others too should relieve the needy but also a desire that others should desire to relieve the needy. One would not call the desire to relieve the needy a moral desire unless one also desired that others should desire to relieve and indeed actually relieve the needy. A man who wanted to be the only person to relieve the needy, who wanted as it were all the moral kudos for himself, would appear not to value the relief of the needy for its own sake and so not really to have a moral desire.

[2] Odi et amo: quare id faciam, fortasse requiris.
Nescio, sed fieri sentio et excrucior. (*Catulli Carmina* LXXXV)

Certainly to approve of relieving the needy involves approving of both oneself and others relieving the needy. If I morally approve of a course of conduct, not only do I desire to act in that way and desire others to act in that way, but I desire others as well as myself to desire to act in that way. For in moral approval and disapproval one's attitude towards the action is necessarily transmitted to the desire to do the action. Indeed a second-order desire to have the desire to relieve the needy is necessary if the desire to relieve the needy is to be a moral desire. If one's *only* second-order desire was to get rid of the desire to do the action one could not be said to approve morally of the action. It does not, however, follow from this that one cannot desire to get rid of one's moral desires and moral principles. I may wish that I did not have the moral principles that I do have, because they are extremely irksome, because, say, they prevent me from doing what I am inclined to do. But if they are to be moral principles, I must at the same time also desire to desire to act in accordance with them. Moral principles to be expressed in language must express the desire to act in a certain way with all its ramifications. If I desire to benefit other people, this is not enough to constitute my morality. My desire must ramify into (i) a desire that I should desire to benefit other people and (ii) a desire that other people should desire to benefit people other than themselves. Moral desires, then, exist at the ground level, where they belong to the moral agent in virtue of his holding the morality in question, and at the higher level of reflective appraisal. This two-level existence is no accident, but is a consequence of the two-level character of moralities in general, of which I shall treat in 6.5 and 6.6.

I have tried in this chapter to elucidate the normative character of moral judgements in terms of the desires which are the necessary concomitants of sincerely held moral judgements, that is, of moral beliefs. Now ordinary factual beliefs have a descriptive direction of fit, the onus is on them to match the world. Desires, on the other hand, have a normative direction of fit, the onus is on the world to fit them. Hence if moral beliefs involve wanting or desiring, they must have a normative direction of fit either in addition to or instead of a descriptive direction of fit. How in the latter case they could still be called 'beliefs' is a question which will have to be left until 9.3 ff.

4

Desires and Moralities (2)

4.1. I shall argue in this chapter that what I have said about directions of fit enables me to replace the fact/value distinction with a fourfold classification.

If the linguistic expression of ordinary beliefs and the linguistic expression of desires have opposite directions of fit, we may distinguish three levels of language, (i) a level at which we express both beliefs and desires, (ii) a level at which we appear to express ordinary non-normative beliefs only, and (iii) a level at which we appear to express desires only. I take the levels in this order intentionally because I shall treat the first level as prior in the order of explanation and shall explain the nature of the other levels in terms of it. The first level I shall call the tied or institutional level or the level of social stability. A fourfold classification, as we shall see, is produced because the tied level is split, some language at this level facing in one direction of fit rather than in the other. When I say, 'John is under an obligation to Mary' or 'James made a promise to Peter', I may merely be expressing a belief about the social relations of John and Mary, James and Peter. In making these statements I neither express my desires nor imply anything about them; I am making a purely external use as opposed to an internal[1] use of these sentences. When, on the other hand, I intend to imply by my use of these sentences that I want John, in some sense of 'want', to carry out what he is under an obligation to do, that I want James to keep his promise to Peter, then I am making an internal use of these sentences.

The distinction between external and internal uses may be best seen in the case of the word 'obligation'. The distinction is reflected in the difference between *asserting* or reporting the existence of an obligation and *recognising* that obligation

---

[1] For this distinction see H. L. A. Hart's *The Concept of Law* (pp. 55 ff.) and L. J. Cohen's *The Principles of World Citizenship* (pp. 38 ff.).

as binding. The former use is common in works of a socio-
logical or social anthropological character. Thus C. von Fürer-
Haimendorf writes of a Dafla's kinsmen (*Morality and Merit*,
p. 57) that they 'are bound to support him in feuds, and he
in turn is under a moral obligation to make every effort to
ransom them if any of them has fallen into enemy hands'. The
author does not intend to commit himself to saying of the
Daflas that they ought to support their kinsmen in feuds and
so on, for he himself does not hold a retaliatory morality. The
second use appears in the following passage: 'We repudiated
entirely customary morals, conventions and traditional wisdom. We were, that is to say, in the strictest sense of the term,
immoralists. The consequences of being found out had, of
course, to be considered for what they were worth. But we
recognized no moral obligation on us, no inner sanction to
conform or to obey. Before heaven we claimed to be our own
judge in our own case.' (J. M. Keynes, *Two Memoirs*, pp. 97-8.)
In this passage Keynes is not falsely denying that there was in
the society of his youth an external obligation to obey; rather
he is saying that he and his Bloomsbury friends did not make
that obligation internal, did not 'recognize' it.

When we use the rules of a social morality and other language of the tied level internally, we intend thereby to provide
reasons for action and reasons for criticism, reasons, say, for
acting in conformity to one of the rules and reasons for criticizing actions which fail to conform to that rule. Making an
internal use of moral judgements involves expressing or applying rules which we ourselves accept. There are, of course,
different modes of acceptance. A man may accept a rule of
social morality out of fear or deference, because of what
'people will say'. Such a man may regard a rule of social
morality as being for him merely a rule of self-interest. An
approach of this kind differs from that of the whole-hearted
adherent of the rules. The latter accepts the rules of a social
morality not because conformity to them promotes one of
his ulterior ends, but because he considers the rules worthy
of obedience or good in themselves. When the rules of a social
morality accord with the moral judgements an individual is
prepared to make independently of the social morality, then
he has no need of making independent moral judgements; for

whenever somebody thinks a rule a good rule, he can make an easy and legitimate transition from external to internal moral judgements.

In some cases the transition from external to internal judgements is facilitated because we have concepts which encapsulate or contain the concept of obligation. This is so, for example, with the word 'promise'; hence the fact that Jones has uttered the form of words conventionally set apart for promising, namely, 'I promise . . .', is taken as a reason, other things being equal, for regarding him as having put himself under an internal obligation. This is why the inference from (1) to (3) goes through in Searle's celebrated argument (*Speech Acts*, p. 177):

(1) Jones uttered the words 'I hereby promise to pay you, Smith, five dollars.'
(2) Jones promised to pay Smith five dollars.
(3) Jones placed himself under (undertook) an obligation to pay Smith five dollars.
(4) Jones is under an obligation to pay Smith five dollars.
(5) Jones ought to pay Smith five dollars.

The key word in Searle's argument is 'obligation', which may be used in two ways, either externally or internally, as providing a reason for action. When used externally, 'Jones is under an obligation to do *a*' means 'Jones is in a position in which he will be breaking a rule (moral or legal or . . .) if he does not do *a*'. Consequently, if the word 'obligation' is used externally in the Searle argument, then, seeing that 'promise' is defined in terms of putting oneself under an obligation, (3) is validly derived from (1) and (2), and from (3) we may infer

(3a) Jones placed himself in a position in which, if he does not pay Smith five dollars, he will be breaking a rule,

and from (3a) we may infer

(4a) Jones is in a position in which, if he does not pay Smith five dollars, he will be breaking a rule.

Here the derivation breaks down. From (4a) we can only obtain

(5) Jones ought to pay Smith five dollars

if we assume some 'ought'-judgement enjoining conformity like

(6) Jones ought not to break a rule.

Such a judgement is plainly not a tautology but a normatively potent premiss.

If, on the other hand, the word 'obligation' and the word 'promised' with it are used internally, we may move smoothly from (2) to (3), from (3) to

> (3b) Jones placed himself in a position in which he will be breaking a rule he ought to keep if he does not pay Smith five dollars,

from (3b) to

> (4b) Jones is in a position in which he will be breaking a rule he ought to keep if he does not pay Smith five dollars,

and from (4b) to

> (5) Jones ought to pay Smith five dollars.

In this case, while the later part of the inference goes through, the breakdown occurs at the very beginning, for if 'promised' is used internally in (2), we cannot without a supplementary premiss derive (2) from (1). A speaker of (2), who used the word 'promised' internally (as somebody does when he says reproachfully, 'But you promised!'), would be endorsing, even if only tacitly, the institution of promise-keeping. The supplementary premiss needed would, then, be to the effect that saying the words 'I promise' constitutes a good *una facie* reason for carrying out the promised action. The asserter of (1) could hardly be committed to this, since in (1) he, unlike Jones, is not using the word 'promise' but only quoting Jones's utterance which contains it. Plainly (1) could be sincerely asserted by somebody who wanted to eschew value-commitments altogether, or even by one who, somewhat eccentrically, saw promise-making as an illicit denial of freedom to his future self. Searle's argument, then, is invalid if he confines himself to only one at a time of the two kinds of uses of institutional words. The argument only derives some plausibility if Searle commits an equivocation and vacillates between external and internal uses of the key words.

In general, arguments from an 'is' to an 'ought' depend on concealed but potent normative premisses. It has been a philosophical commonplace since the seventeenth century that there are certain trivial truths of morals and politics like 'You ought to pay your debts', 'You ought to keep your promises', 'You ought not to steal somebody else's property', and 'You ought not to tell lies'. The crucial words in these sentences are used internally and hence there is an appearance of trivial truth. Despite this there is a sense in which these trivial truths can be denied without self-contradiction. The pseudo-tautology 'You ought to keep your promises' masks and conceals a normative thought which it is cumbersome to express. It might look like this: 'When you consciously and expressly use a form of words intended to put you in a position such that, if you do not perform the action you imply by that form of words you are going to perform, you will be breaking the rules of the society of which you are a member, you ought to perform that action'. To pretend that there is no masking is to commit what may be called 'The Conventionalist Fallacy'. A similar kind of masking takes place in science. It is said to be an analytic truth that one litre of water at 4 °C weighs 1 kg. This is so in virtue of the definition of a kilogram. It is possible to argue from this that we can *deduce* statements of mass or weight from statements of volume or capacity. But surely, we are inclined to object, this is logically impossible. It is surely an empirical truth that such-and-such a volume of water has a certain mass or weight at a given temperature, and this is, of course, true. The 'analytic truth' that one litre of water at 4 °C weighs 1 kg. masks the empirical discovery that a certain volume (roughly 1.76 pints) of water at 4 °C weighs a little more than 2 lb.

The normatively potent premisses which, I have maintained, are concealed are of at least three different kinds. They consist in asserting that uttering a certain form of words, going through a certain partly non-verbal procedure, standing in a certain relationship constitute good *una facie* reasons for certain kinds of behaviour.

The first kind of normatively potent premiss is one which asserts that uttering a certain form of words is a good *una facie* reason for certain kinds of behaviour. I shall take two examples in this area. My first is taken from Baptism in the Church of England. 'They did promise and vow three things in my name', says the candidate for confirmation, who is then asked, 'Dost thou not think that thou art bound to believe, and to do, as they have promised for thee?' One could make use of a Searle-style argument here:

(7) Smith (my godfather) after hearing the words, 'Dost thou, in the name of this child, renounce the devil

and all his works, the vain pomp and glory of the world, with all covetous desires of the same, and the carnal desires of the flesh, so that thou wilt not follow, nor be led by them?' uttered the words 'I renounce them all'.

(8) Smith promised on my behalf that I would renounce the devil, etc.

(9) Smith put me under an obligation ('. . . thou art bound') to renounce the devil, etc.

(10) I am under an obligation to renounce the devil, etc.

(11) I ought to renounce the devil, etc.

Now this argument does not carry with it the certainty of Searle's original example. The reason for this is plain. Promising on one's own behalf is an institution we take for granted and only question when in a very sceptical mood. Promising for others is quite another thing. Thus a commentator on the Prayer Book (C. Wheatly, *A Rational Illustration of the Book of Common Prayer*, pp. 403-4) feels called upon to justify 'the reasonableness of a vicarious stipulation', thus indicating the assumption which lies behind the Anglican catechism, the problematic assumption that promises made for a person by other people can be binding on him.

To take another example, in order to infer 'Smith ought to fight a duel with Jones' from 'Jones uttered the words "I challenge you, Smith, to a duel"', we need to assume that, given circumstances which a nice casuist may specify, having the words 'I challenge you' uttered to you is a good *una facie* reason for fighting a duel. I take this example because duelling is a practice which is dead and which most of us nowadays disapprove of, and hence it needs only a small attention to determine what the concealed assumption is.

The second kind of normatively potent premiss will be found in everyday social transactions, for example, buying and selling. Jones hands a watch to Smith, uttering the words 'That will be £15, sir'. We are entitled to infer that Smith has bought the watch, that he owes Jones £15 for it and that he ought to give Jones £15. To be so entitled requires the assumption that Smith's being behaved to in this complex manner is a good *una facie* reason for requiring him to hand over £15.

The third kind of normatively potent premiss arises out of

natural relationships and social roles. To infer 'Mitya ought to love and honour Pyotr' from 'Pyotr begat Mitya' requires the assumption that a good *una facie* reason for honouring somebody is that he is one's natural or biological father. I shall consider this example at greater length when I have distinguished encapsulated and non-encapsulated obligations.

Searle-type arguments of the kind we have been considering all involve encapsulated obligations. Their apparently smooth running depends on the existence of some word or concept which encapsulates or contains the concept of obligation. Thus promising means putting oneself under an obligation by uttering a form of words, selling means putting oneself under an obligation to hand an article over in return for a certain sum of money. Let us now consider a non-encapsulated obligation, where a superficially similar argument can be constructed without the aid of a conventional form of words containing the concept of obligation. Let us look at the following argument:

(12)   Mr Brown uttered the words to (his son) young Brown, 'I intend to take you to the zoo tomorrow'.

(13)   Mr Brown gave young Brown reason to expect that he would be taken to the zoo on the following day.

(14a) Mr Brown placed himself under an external obligation to take young Brown to the zoo on the following day.

(14b) Mr Brown placed himself under an internal obligation to take young Brown to the zoo on the following day.

(15)   Mr Brown is now ('tomorrow' having arrived) under an internal obligation to take young Brown to the zoo.

(16)   Mr Brown ought to take young Brown to the zoo.

In this argument the transition from (12) to (13) is mediated by the causal knowledge that utterances expressing intention are usually reliable and consequently lead people to expect, give them reason to expect, the fulfilment of intentions so expressed. But the move from (13) to (14a) is unlike the move from

(2)   Jones promised to pay Smith five dollars

to

(3)   Jones placed himself under (undertook) an obligation to pay Smith five dollars

because in the promising-argument the inference is made an

honest one through the meaning of the term 'promised', which can be unpacked in terms of the concept of obligation. The expression 'gave young Brown reason to expect' cannot be unpacked in this way. Rather in the latter argument the move from (13) to (14a) is mediated by the information that in the social morality there is a rule to the effect that people in general and parents in particular ought not to disappoint children unnecessarily. There is, of course, a further move from (14a) to (14b), a move which one is entitled to make if and only if one accepts the rule in question. If one has in good faith given a child reason to expect something he or she wants or hopes for, then, if one accepts the rule, one must accept that one is under an internal obligation to carry out one's expressed intentions if one reasonably can. The inference can only go through if there is a clear recognition and accept-ance of the rule in question. The existence of the obligation, external or internal, is in no way encapsulated or contained in the language used. The word 'disappoint' certainly contains a reference to intentions, but it is not normative on our present use of language. True, a non-encapsulated obligation may become an encapsulated one; it is perfectly possible for a form of words expressing intention to acquire a binding force. But, as things are, it is not a conventional form of words which makes Mr Brown think that he is under an internal obligation to young Brown, but his knowledge that there is a rule of the social morality of his group governing the expres-sion of intentions, his acceptance of that rule as applying to himself and his recognition of the effect his words in fact had on young Brown. The latter is important because if young Brown did not even like the zoo, there would be no question of Mr Brown's being under an obligation.

4.2. I shall now try to explain the nature of the second and third levels in terms of the tied or institutional level. The second level I shall call[2] 'the ostensibly brute-factual' level, and the third the 'free' or 'independently normative' level. It is by reference to the tied level that the nature of the other two levels becomes clear. At the tied level, at which moral or other normative language may be used externally or internally,

---

[2] For 'brute facts' see G. E. M. Anscombe, 'On Brute Facts', *Analysis*, 1957-8.

speakers make indirect reference to rules or standards. These rules or standards may be generally accepted ones, although this need not be so, since any individual who makes a rule or sets a standard of his own can make an internal tied statement in the light of that very standard or rule which he has himself created (see further 9.5). Statements at the tied or institutional level about rules, roles, or institutions or indirectly referring to rules, roles, or institutions, whether or not one commits oneself to support for, commitment to or approval of these rules, roles, or institutions, may be said to state institutional facts. One may depart from institutional fact-stating in either of two directions, either by eschewing all reference to commitment or by committing oneself differently. To make external as opposed to internal institutional statements already constitutes a retreat from commitment, for the external institutional statement refers to other people's commitments and then only indirectly. To describe human action without even alluding to desires, attitudes, and commitments, let alone expressing them, involves a change to the ostensibly brute-factual level, the level of non-institutional facts. I insert the cautionary word 'ostensibly' here for two reasons. First, it is difficult to attain certainty that any particular word or sentence contains no trace of reference to rules, roles, or social relations. We live in a social world of value and it is artificial and requires especial effort to descend to the ostensibly brute-factual level and totally ignore our commitments, roles, and institutions. We may, of course, try to do so as a kind of analytical exercise. One may compare this to the phenomenological attitude in sense-perception. Normally we employ language in an ontologically committed way, we want to describe what it is that we see. It is only when we are standing back from physical objects, taking up an artist's or a psychologist's standpoint or writing a philosophical book about perception, that we are interested in what things look like as opposed to what they are. Similarly, it would be strained and ridiculous to aim in our ordinary discourse to arrive at nuggets of unalloyed brute fact. The ostensibly brute-factual level is only ostensibly so because it is almost impossible to empty tied words of their social meaning, as when one tries to use, say, the word 'father' to mean nothing more than begetter. My second reason for inserting the word 'ostensibly' is because of the normative setting of our descriptions of human actions and situations. Anybody who sets out to describe a situation has necessarily selected from an indefinitely large number of possible statements which he could have made. This is a consequence of 'the inexhaustibility of description' (S. N. Hampshire, *Thought and Action, passim*). The fact that the speaker makes this particular statement rather than some other implies that he considers it relevant to the sequence of thoughts on which he is engaged, and if the sequence of thoughts is a moral one, he must consider the statement in question to be morally relevant, even if considered in itself it is innocently non-normative.

There are two kinds of ostensibly brute-factual statement with which I am concerned here. First, there are those which are only contingently connected with external institutional statements by means of a convention, and second, those which (more or less loosely) are essential components of external institutional statements. An ostensibly brute-factual statement of the first kind would be 'Pyotr uttered the words "I give Mitya this hammer".' It is a contingent matter and a matter of convention that the words beginning 'I give' may be the vehicle by means of which one person gives something to another. An ostensibly brute-factual statement of the second kind would be 'Pyotr begat Mitya'. This, given the current concept of being a father, is an essential precondition of the truth of 'Pyotr is Mitya's father', considered as an external institutional statement. In neither kind of ostensibly brute-factual statement do I, the speaker, imply anything about my desires, Pyotr's desires, Mitya's desires, or the desires of others in the community. Thus, if I say 'Pyotr begat Mitya', I do not imply that I wish Pyotr had not begotten Mitya, or that I would not have liked Pyotr not to beget Mitya, or that I want Pyotr to behave in certain ways in virtue of having begotten Mitya, or that I want Mitya to behave in certain ways in virtue of having been begotten by Pyotr. Nor do I imply the existence of any system of expectations or claims. For all I know begetting could take place on a purely haphazard basis. (The fact that begetting would not take place without desire on somebody's part is irrelevant; in any case, if true, it is an empirical, not a semantic truth.) Further, the sentence 'Pyotr uttered the words "I give Mitya this hammer"' does not imply any-thing about the desires of the speaker (that is, the speaker of the single-quotes sentence). We conduct many of our daily linguistic transactions at the institutional level, at a level fraught with requirements, responsibilities, and roles. We have rules, roles, and institutions because we desire certain ends or certain patterns of behaviour and we cannot describe social roles and institutions without referring, even if indirectly, to the desires and ends of human beings in society. Thus to say that Pyotr is Mitya's father is generally to imply that people in our society believe that Pyotr and Mitya ought to behave in certain ways towards one another. Sometimes, it is true, the word 'father' is used in an ostensibly brute-factual sense, so that the sentence 'Pyotr is Mitya's father' merely means that Pyotr begat Mitya. Until comparatively recently such was the strength of the classical model that it was commonly believed that the word 'father' was almost exclusively used in this ostensibly brute-factual sense. This is plainly a mistaken view. As well as having an ostensibly brute-factual sense the word 'father' is used in both external and internal senses at the institutional level. In which sense it is used depends on whether the speaker commits himself to wanting certain kinds of behaviour.

The third level, the free, autonomous, or independently normative level, can be reached from the institutional level, not by rejecting commitment but by seeking a fresh commit-ment. A way in which this can take place is illustrated by a passage from Dostoevsky's *The Brothers Karamazov* (pp. 789-90) where there is a passage in which Fetyukovitch, the Defence Counsel, discusses what a father is. He takes 'Y is your father' as conventionally implying 'You ought to love and honour Y' and considers the standard criterion of some-body's being X's father, namely his being X's begetter. Accord-ing to the conventional wisdom, 'If Y is your begetter, you ought to love and honour Y.' To say 'Y is your father' says just this in a nutshell. There would, of course, be no harm in this unless it tended to impair our freedom to revise the con-ventional wisdom. The word 'father' is part of our everyday language and its sense and application do not appear to be a matter of controversy. Hence arises conceptual resistance to reform. But, as Fetyukovitch says, 'Let us be bold, gentlemen . . . let us prove that the progress of the last few years has touched even us, and let us say plainly, the father is not merely he who begets the child, but he who begets it and does his duty by it'. So the progressive wisdom will run: 'If Y is your begetter and has done his duty by you, you ought to honour him.' 'He is your father', on this view, is to mean 'he who has begotten and done his duty by you and whom you therefore ought to love and honour'. Now Fetyukovitch in his use of the term 'father' is not using it internally; he is making a free use of the concept of *father* and it will remain free until his progressive wisdom has become the conventional wisdom of a new age. Then what was a free use will become tied and men will make an internal use of it at the institutional level.

4.3. Concepts belonging to the level of social stability I shall call 'intervening' concepts, since they intervene between the ostensibly brute-factual and the independently normative levels. Intervening concepts may be divided into three kinds. First, there are institutional concepts encapsulating the concept of obligation, like those of *promise* and *borrow.* Second, there are concepts of roles, whether natural, like that of *father*, or acquired, like those of *wife* and *teacher.* Third, there are concepts connected with the virtues and vices or with conduct displaying them, for example, those of generosity, cowardice, and murder.

The meaning of intervening concepts is determined by two sets of conditions. The first set consists of pre-conditions of application and may be called the antecedents or antecedent determinants of the concept. The antecedents are in some cases specifiable in ostensibly brute-factual language only, but in other cases mention needs to be made of intentions, roles, and rules in an ineliminable fashion. For example, in 4.1 the best I could do in unpacking the meaning of 'You ought to keep your promises' was 'When you consciously and expressly use a form of words intended to put you in a position such that, if you do not perform the action you imply by that form of words you are going to perform, you will be breaking the rules of the society of which you are a member, you ought to perform that action'. Here the expressions 'consciously and expressly', 'form of words', 'intended', 'breaking the rules of the society' unavoidably and irreducibly belong to the external institutional level. The final 'ought' belongs to the free level, and thus my 'unpacking' sentence connects the external institutional level with the free level. A similar connection is made by Fetyukovitch in his progressive wisdom when he says that 'the father is not merely he who begets the child, but he who begets it and does his duty by it', where 'duty', I take it, belongs to the external institutional level, while a free use is being made of the concept of *father*.

The second set of conditions which determine the meaning of intervening concepts refers to the normative consequences, the consequences so far as what-is-to-be-done is concerned, and may be called the sequents or sequent determinants of the concept. Once we have intervening concepts, we have no need of connecting judgements which connect the ostensibly brute-factual or the institutional factual, on the one hand, with the free/independent level on the other, that is, which connect antecedents with sequents. The conceptual advantage of intervening concepts is that we operate with them within a relatively stable framework. The reason for this stability is that intervening concepts can survive a certain amount of change; they can be narrowed, extended, deepened, and refined. This is why they are at the heart of a society's language of morals and argument can go on within this language in terms of these concepts. So long as argument is carried on in this way, reference to connective judgements linking 'facts' with 'values' is superfluous and confusing. Only the professional analyst, interested in what is going on when intervening concepts are extended or refined, needs to reflect on what changes in connective judgements are correlated with extension or refinement of these concepts.

The connection between the antecedent and the intervening concept is complex. As far as the ordinary, non-forensic use of intervening concepts of the third kind is concerned, it is not possible *in general* to specify necessary and sufficient conditions for their application. When, however, such terms as 'murder', 'theft', 'cruelty' are used within a legal system, it is needful to provide necessary and sufficient conditions as verification-conditions, indispensable where legal proof is required. But even in their non-forensic use moral intervening concepts admit of specifiable necessary or sufficient conditions in respect of central and typical cases. All cases of murder are cases of killing, and so killing is a necessary condition of murder. Deliberately killing somebody solely for the sake of financial gain is a sufficient condition of murder within our language of morals. Somebody who accepted the concept of murder and denied the previous sentence would be involved in a contradiction, but a contradiction dependent on prior acceptance of the concept. More will be said about this in 7.2.

The first two kinds of intervening concepts are more tractable. As in the Searle promising-argument you can move inferentially from the antecedents to the external use of an intervening concept by the mediation of a constitutive convention. Such a constitutive convention may stipulate that uttering a certain form of words, together perhaps with appropriate actions, constitutes issuing a challenge or taking an oath, or that standing in a certain biological relationship within a specific kind of family structure constitutes being a father, or that performing certain actions or transactions constitutes being a purchaser. While a constitutive convention of these types is sufficient to bridge the logical gap between the ostensibly brute-factual level and the external institutional level, it is insufficient to justify inference from the external use to the internal use of an institutional intervening concept. Only prior acceptance of the concept justifies such inference.

The level which I call 'free' or 'independent' is not conceptually visible, so to speak, in the socially stable state of language, where somebody says all that he needs to say at the tied level. The views of the orthodox do not need expression independently of the use of language and thought at this level. When, however, we have heterodox or rebel moralists, who reject the intervening concepts and wish to expound a morality of their own, their position cannot be expressed at this level, and therefore they must have recourse to the free level, and combine ostensibly brute-factual and independently normative language until such time as they create intervening concepts of their own at the tied level. At any given time the views of the orthodox may be expressed in independently normative language whenever it is necessary for them to do so, for example, when they do battle with their heterodox opponents. To employ independently normative language does not imply that you hold heterodox moral views. The independent level is the level at which questions are not begged; the existence of such a level makes it possible for a heterodox morality to be expressed and for both orthodox and heterodox moralists to express mutual disagreement.

We can now see how past views of the fact/value distinction have erred through a partial and incomplete understanding of a complex situation. The proponents of the classical view have primarily emphasized the ostensibly brute-factual and the free levels. Hence they failed to give a convincing account of intervening concepts and confined their investigations to general or blanket words of commendation, condemnation, and re-commendation. The anti-classicists or fusionists, on the other hand, have been so obsessed with the tied level that they have been tempted to deny the existence of ostensibly brute-factual and free levels. It is as if we were so impressed by the fact that we could not unscramble scrambled eggs that we denied that any legitimate distinction could be made between the ingredients.

4.4. In the last chapter (3.4) I put forward a version of internalism. At that point I had not sufficiently developed my account of the relationship between moralities and human desires to comment on the general problems of choosing between internalism and externalism. But now that I have given an account of the different levels of language, I am in a better position to adjudicate on this issue.

The issue between externalist and internalist[3] may be expounded as follows. The externalist maintains that if a person ought (has an obligation) to do something or believes that he ought (has an obligation) to do something, then there is reason for him (or he has reason) to do it, but he may or may not have any desire or motivation to do it. The internalist, on the other hand, maintains that the only way something can be a reason for action is if it is internalized, if it is desired by the

---

[3] For an extended examination of the issue see W. K. Frankena's 'Obligation and Motivation in Recent Moral Philosophy'.

agent in question, and hence the 'fact' that somebody ought (has an obligation) to do something can only be a reason for his doing it if the agent believes that he ought (has an obligation) to do it.

According to the account I wish to give, both sides are making important points, although the internalist has a better understanding of the nature of moral thought and language. There are indeed uses of moral words of which each theory is true. The 'external'/'internal' distinction (4.1) proves useful here. Thus

(17) I ought (have an obligation) to, but I don't want to in the least

is perfectly in order if and only if either the 'ought' is an external one or 'obligation' is used in its external sense. Likewise,

(18) You ought (have an obligation) to, but I don't want you to in the least

is in order if and only if the word 'ought' or the word 'obligation', as the case may be, is external. On the other hand, if the words 'ought' or 'obligation' are used internally or if the word 'ought' is used independently, both (17) and (18) are self-nullifying in a similar way to

(19) It is raining but I don't believe it.

'Ought' is, I maintain, primarily an internalist word. This is supported by the naturalness of saying

(20) I ought to *but* I don't want to,

the 'but' here indicating that the two limbs of the sentence pull, logically speaking, in different directions.

My argument is not that a morality necessarily provides reasons for action, but that it necessarily provides reasons for action *to anybody who accepts it*; moreover, and this is sometimes overlooked, a morality provides reasons for criticism to anybody who accepts it, reasons for criticizing his own conduct and that of others. This modest internalist thesis, however, does not warrant anybody's believing as a conceptual thesis that (Traditional) Morality necessarily provides reasons for action; to say of Morality$_A$, for example, that it provides reasons (that is, justifying reasons[4]) for action for anybody

---

[4] For the distinction between 'justifying' and 'exciting' reasons see Francis Hutcheson's 'Illustrations on the Moral Sense' (1728), section 1, in *British Moralists*, Vol. I, pp. 403 ff.

whatever is to indicate adherence to Morality$_A$ on the part of the speaker. Presumably the speaker would not think that just *any* system of rules provided justifying reasons for action. The thesis which I am maintaining is not a moral but a conceptual one; it relates not to justifying reasons but to exciting reasons, that is, to desires and motivation. In this sense of 'reason' it is the acceptance, not the existence, of a morality which provides reasons for action. This moderate internalist thesis may be accepted even by externalists. Thus Mrs Foot, a sceptical externalist, writes ('Morality and Art', p. 14), 'In one sense it is true that moral judgements necessarily give reasons for acting, but in that sense it is also true that, for example, codes of etiquette must do so'. However, somebody who maintains that Morality$_A$ necessarily gives reasons to anybody, *whether he accepts it or not*, is not merely trying to make the judgements of Morality$_A$ genuinely categorical, he is also trying to make them self-authenticating, that is, he is trying to make them provide reasons for their own acceptance. Such a tactic cannot work; the only self-authenticating utterances are those which are self-verifying, such as 'I am writing', written here and now by me at the time of writing these words. What is happening is that those who want to argue for an objective morality often adopt an externalist view, trying to make 'morality' at one and the same time both capable of proof and necessarily motivating. They start from the commonsense view that there are moral truths which can be proved, such as that Hitler was 'a moral monster', that one ought not to inflict gratuitous pain, and so on. Mrs Foot sees quite clearly that morality conceived from the externalist point of view admits of proof to some extent but cannot at the same time be necessarily motivating. To claim that it can be would be to make morality if not magical at least mysterious; it is, at any rate, to indulge in a kind of pretence which Mrs Foot sees as dishonest. It is for this reason that she has expressed her unhappiness about 'morality' conceived of as consisting of categorical imperatives.[5] Her position sounds strange and strained. Nevertheless what she says can be shown and said with less strangeness if a purely externalist way of

[5] See her 'Morality as a System of Hypothetical Imperatives' in *Virtues and Vices*.

talking and thinking is abandoned. In so far as a morality is necessarily motivating, it is not susceptible of proof (this is the position of the internalist); in so far as (a) morality is susceptible of proof, it is not necessarily motivating (this is Mrs Foot's position). Both positions are perfectly compatible, indeed they are complementary. This provides us with an argument against the objectivity of morals. For if an externalist theory is accepted, morality is susceptible of proof and can be called 'objective', but at a heavy price. For if it has this sort of objectivity, it is not necessarily motivating, and thus the kind of objectivity we have attained is quite worthless. As Aristotle put it, the Form of the Good, even if it exists, is not *to prakton agathon*, the good which can be acted on (*Nicomachean Ethics*, i, 1097a23).

Perhaps an analogy with the code of honour might be useful here to reinforce my point. The code of honour could be treated from an externalist standpoint and it could be maintained that it is an objective truth that it is dishonourable to decline a duel with a gentleman (let us suppose that it is objectively determinable whether somebody is a gentleman[6]). Clearly, then, we can produce any number of objective truths involving defunct or obsolete codes. But they are of little more than academic interest unless we can show some good reason for following them.

To conclude, while I have maintained that normative beliefs necessarily motivate, I have not thereby implied that normative beliefs in general or any body of normative beliefs in particular imply or presuppose any prior or antecedently existing motivation or desires. However categorical a normative or moral utterance may be, it only necessitates conforming desire or motivation if it is assented to. It may after all fall on deaf ears, on the ears of those who have no natural desire for the good of others or who think of justice disparagingly as 'other men's good'. Alternatively somebody may acquire a moral belief solely through parental or other indoctrination and so may give a bare intellectual assent. Here, as in J. S. Mill's case

---

[6] 'The word *gentleman* originally meant something recognisable; one who had a coat of arms and some landed property. When you called someone "a gentleman" you were not paying him a compliment, but merely stating a fact. If you said he was not "a gentleman" you were not insulting him, but giving information'. (C. S. Lewis, *Mere Christianity*, p. 10.)

(see *Autobiography*, Chapter V, pp. 112-13) the end may 'lose its charm'. In such an event a desire whose sole causation lies in dry intellectual assent suffers the price of such independence, a certain precariousness. If the desire so created should lose standing, as it were, should no longer pull effectively, the intellectual assent from which it derived would be placed in peril. The position would be very different with assent grounded in an antecedent desire. Where there are antecedent desires, there is a ready answer to the question 'Why should I?', for one may say something like, 'Well, you want the good of others, don't you?'.

It would, however, be naïve to think of human motivational responses solely in terms of simple desires. Yet astonishingly, apart from the valuable treatment of morality and the emotions by such philosophers as B. A. O. Williams and R. S. Peters, much recent moral philosophy has ignored the emotions. There have been several reasons for this neglect. First, the rejection of Stevensonian and other forms of emotivism as inadequate led to an over-reaction in the logical analysis of moral concepts. The common features of moral and non-moral normative discourse were highlighted and there seemed to be as little reason for including talk about emotions in the analysis of what it was to be a good man as for including it in the analysis of what it was to be a good carpenter. Second, and this point is related to the first, the logical analysis of general concepts like those of *right* and *good* needs to mention nothing at all about emotions. The use of these general concepts appeared to be associated with certain speech acts, like commending and prescribing, and the names for these acts had little to do with the expression of the emotions. Third, the classical problem of how thought can bring about action, of how reason can become practical, appeared to require for a solution the existence of desires solely. There was no need to regard men as anything more than practical-reason machines which, given an input of factual information and desires, could churn out the appropriate decisions. From the point of view of practical reason, love and hatred, gratitude and resentment, and all the other emotions were gratuitous appendages, having no place in the moral life. Of the classical triad, the cognitive, the conative, and the affective, the third could apparently be dispensed with.

I wish to maintain not merely that moral beliefs necessarily involve desires but that they necessarily involve emotions also. I have three principal reasons for this view. First, although it is true that the logical analysis of our most general moral words does not require mention of emotions, there is a large portion of our moral discourse whose logical analysis must bring them in. Some of these words we could not sincerely apply to anybody without feeling the appropriate emotion, for example, 'contemptible', 'admirable', 'pitiful', 'loathesome', 'lovable'. In addition, there are epithets which are suitable vehicles for expressing emotions partly, at any rate, because they are not intended to be taken literally, like 'swine' or 'bastard'. Second, human beings do not merely have desires and knowledge, they react to them, and it is these reactions which constitute the emotions. If I know that I have not reached the standard I have set myself, the standard which I think I ought to have reached, I experience emotions like disappointment, regret, and remorse. If I know that I am about to suffer something bad, I feel fear. A practical-reason machine who believed that his wife had been unfaithful to him might kill her because he regarded himself as having been injured by her and wanted to return all injuries. But this account is strange and almost incredible; we cannot understand Othello's conduct unless we know what the emotions of love and jealousy are like. It is because human beings react to and reflect on their desires that they have the rich inner life which is the concern of dramatists, poets, and novelists. It is our emotions which make us more than practical-reason machines. Third, the desires which moral beliefs necessarily involve cannot be made sense of without their associated emotions. A moral belief that one ought to help the needy necessarily involves wanting to help the needy. An utterance to that effect is unlikely to exercise any leverage on somebody unless he understands what it feels like to be needy. It is this understanding from which the emotions of sympathy and compassion flow.

I have argued, then, that not only is a modest version of internalism essential for the correct understanding of moral thinking and the language in which it is expressed, but also that an enriched internalism is needed for an adequate understanding of what it is fully to accept a morality.

5

Evaluation, Prescription, and Two Logical Gaps

5.1. We saw in Chapters 3 and 4 that moral language faces primarily in the normative direction of fit. In this chapter I want, first, to distinguish within normative language between the evaluative and the prescriptive (5.1-5.3), second, to indicate the existence of a logical gap between the mini-prescriptive and the maxi-prescriptive (5.2), and third, to argue for a second logical gap between prescription and action (5.5-5.6).

I have used the term 'normative' to apply to all language in which the direction of fit is from the world to language, where the 'onus of match' is on the world to fit the language. I am using the word 'normative' with much the same meaning as other writers give to the word 'evaluative', or even to the word 'prescriptive'. I need some word which will apply to all language facing in the same direction of fit and I choose 'normative' not because it is the ideal word for the job, but because it is the least objectionable word I can find. The word 'evaluative' is unfitted for the task of indicating a direction of fit. When a judgement is ordinarily called 'evaluative', or when somebody is said to 'make an evaluation', there is, it appears to me, invariably an implied reference to a prior standard or ideal in the light of which the evaluative judgement or evaluation is made. If this is the current use of the words 'evaluative', 'evaluate', and 'evaluation', we have to accommodate the following consequence. Although any judgement in which a rule is laid down or a standard or ideal is set up lies in the normative direction of fit, this does not apply to evaluative judgements, according to the meaning I have given the word, which, I maintain, is the ordinary meaning of the word. For evaluative judgements, if they are to be acceptable, have to correspond to or conform to some prior standard, and hence their primary direction of fit is not

normative but descriptive. Of course, to say this is not to deny
that they have a normative use also, for evaluative utterances
face in both directions of fit. If this is so, it is evident that the
term 'evaluative' is entirely unsuitable as a generic label for
the genus comprising all terms whose direction of fit is from
the world to words.

5.2. My next task is to try and determine what relation evaluative language can have to other kinds of normative language
and to prescriptive language in particular. Amongst other
things I want to examine whether and how it is possible to
make some kind of logical move from an evaluation to a prescription.

Plain prescription is only one of the many speech acts which
we perform in using normative language. There are also commendation and condemnation, and, as I pointed out in 1.6,
two kinds of recommendation. Even permitting is a normative
speech act. One fits the deeds to the words. If you are in
authority over me and say to me, 'You may go now', and I go,
I act on your permission. If, as I leave the room, you suddenly
ask, 'Why are you leaving the room?', my natural answer
would be 'Because you gave me permission.' It is clear, then,
that one can act on or, at any rate, avail oneself of a permission.

The strongest word of prescription in English is 'must',
which in common with 'may', has no normative use in the
past tense. This tenselessness is not shared by 'should' and
'ought', which can be used in the past tense to censure, blame
or indicate an undesirable omission, clearly normative functions. There are, as some philosophers (John Ladd, *The Structure of a Moral Code*, Chapter V) have recognized, degrees of
prescriptiveness. That prescriptiveness has degrees is suggested
by people saying, as a character in Richardson's *Sir Charles
Grandison* does at one point, 'You should, you ought, nay
you must . . .' The word 'must' here plainly has maximum
prescriptiveness or, as I shall say, is 'maxi-prescriptive'. There
is a simple test of maxi-prescriptiveness. An operator or auxiliary verb 'O' is maxi-prescriptive if and only if the conjunction
of 'Op' and 'O not-p' is logically inconsistent. Thus both 'must'
and 'ought' are plainly maxi-prescriptive operators. I shall say
that an operator 'O' is mini-prescriptive if and only if the

conjunction of 'Op' and 'O not-p' is self-consistent. Thus the word 'nice' is mini-prescriptive; that is why we can consistently say, 'It is nice to get up in the morning but it is nicer to stay in bed'.

The word 'good' is likewise mini-prescriptive. By telling somebody that it would be a good thing if he took a holiday, I do not thereby prescribe that he should take a holiday, although one might be said to have 'suggested' that he should. But suggestion is weaker than prescription, and that is why a proper prescription cannot be deduced from an ordinary 'good'-judgement. True, people sometimes say things like 'It is good to lie in the sun; so I am going to lie in the sun'. The 'so' here suggests the presence of an inference, but this is the 'so' of decision, not of deductive derivation. (If the 'so' is replaced by 'therefore', is the result semantically deviant or just pompous?) Likewise, there is no deductive derivation in the famous words of Odysseus in *Iliad* II, line 204: 'The rule of many is not a good thing; let there be one ruler' ('ouk agathon polukoiraniē, heis koiranos estō'). Here the Greek word *agathon* is not used attributively, as in 'good ruler' or 'good king', but as a mini-prescriptive modal operator. There was no logical necessity in Odysseus' going on to say 'let one be the ruler'. He might have said, perhaps more in the style of some latter-day Nestor: 'The rule of many is not a good thing, but since our greatest hero sulks in his tent and Agamemnon seems fully occupied with Briseis just at the moment, unless we all want to perish here unwept and unsung by any sacred bard, we must be realistic and submit to a form of collective leadership. After all, what is good for the gods on Olympus could not be all that bad for us. However, collective leadership is one thing and mob rule is quite another. For there is nothing worse than when a man does not know who are his betters.'

I have maintained, then, that the expressions '. . . is a good thing' or 'it is a good thing to . . .' represent a mini-prescriptive modal operator and that you cannot validly derive a maxi-prescriptive conclusion from a mini-prescriptive premiss.

5.3. It is tempting to speculate whether the mini-prescriptive and the evaluative could perhaps coincide, for if this were so, we could demonstrate a corresponding logical gap between the evaluative and the maxi-prescriptive. Those who have a relish for logical gaps might find this one particularly attractive, although, as I shall show, it is illusory. 'But surely', somebody might say, 'words like "good" and "nice" are evaluative. "Good" is the typical evaluative word, if ever there was one.' This is certainly true. What is more, even such maxi-prescriptive words as 'ought' and 'must' are sometimes used with reference to antecedent standards or rules, and it would follow from this that it is not just mini-prescriptive words which have evaluative uses.

What, then, is the difference between those contexts in which these words are used evaluatively and those contexts, on the other hand, in which they are used mini-prescriptively or maxi-prescriptively? We have already had a look at the word 'good' in its mini-prescriptive role. The uses we were looking at were predicative and not attributive. We were not looking at uses of the word 'good' in such sentences as 'That is a good car' or 'He is a good king'. We used the word 'good' mini-prescriptively when it was used as a modal operator in contexts of the form 'It is a good thing that . . .' or 'It is a good thing to . . .' or '. . . is a good thing'. Any sentence in which the word 'good' is used in this way quite clearly faces in the normative direction of fit and in that direction alone. On the other hand, when we talk of a car being 'a good car' or, for that matter, a man being 'a good man', what we are saying appears to face in the descriptive direction of fit also, for it implicitly refers to prior standards of goodness for cars and men respectively.

Let us now see whether we can find the same sort of distinction among uses of 'should' and 'ought'. Of course, 'should' and 'ought' cannot, grammatically speaking, be used as adjectives. (My own neologism 'oughty' obviously does not count, as it belongs to the meta-language.) We can, however, compensate for our linguistic ill-fortune by what I shall call 'talification'. Any verbal phrase, even one containing a modal auxiliary like 'ought', can be given the logical role of an adjective by separating it from the noun phrase by the expression '. . . is such that . . .' (The neologism 'talification' is derived from the Latin 'talis' meaning 'such'.) While we can use the words 'should' and 'ought' in a summary way to express a decision or a resolve, or to prescribe a particular course of action on a particular occasion, we can also say of an action that it is such that one ought to do it or of a person that he is such that he ought to behave or to be behaved to in a certain way. Often we do not need the talificatory circumlocution; we just covertly use talified 'should's and 'ought's without putting up a talifying signpost. Thus all *una facie* 'ought's[1] are talified, but not all talified 'ought's are *una facie*. A talified 'ought' also differs from the decisive, summary 'ought' in this respect: two contrary decisive 'ought's cannot apply to the same action at the same time, while two contrary talified *una facie* 'ought's can, provided, of course, that the two relate to different respects (*facies*).

There is a second way in which vehicles for performing speech acts like prescribing and permitting may be formed in English with a logically adjectival role. By adding postfixes like '–ible' and '–able' to English speech-act verbs associated with the modal auxiliary, an evaluative adjective may often be formed. Such words, unlike strictly performatory expressions like, say, 'I advise', are amenable to tense-modification. Thus, 'permissible' is the evaluative counterpart of the modal 'may' and of the performatory 'I hereby give you permission', while 'advisable' is the evaluative counterpart of the performatory 'I advise' and, perhaps, of the modal auxiliary 'should'. There are other English words of the same family which are not formed so simply, for example, 'imperative' or 'mandatory'.

The distinction between the two 'ought's also helps one to make sense of Hare's imaginary conversation between an Existentialist and a Kantian ('Universalizability', in *Proceedings of the Aristotelian Society*, 1954-5, reprinted in Hare's *Essays on the Moral Concepts*, p. 21):

E: You oughtn't to do that.
K: So you think that one oughtn't to do that sort of thing?
E: I think nothing of the kind; I only say that you oughtn't to do that.
K: Don't you even imply that a person like me in circumstances of this kind oughtn't to do that kind of thing when the other people involved are the sort of people they are?
E: No; I only say that you oughtn't to do that.
K: Are you making a moral judgement?

[1] I am indebted to Basil O'Neill for discussion of this topic.

E: Yes.

K: In that case I fail to understand your use of the term 'moral'.

The Existentialist here is using 'ought' purely prescriptively, the Kantian evaluatively. Whether one denies that the Existentialist's 'ought' is a moral 'ought' is quite another matter. That is going to depend on how we define the word 'moral' and I have yet to argue in 8.2 that universalizability is not a defining feature of moral judgements.

The effect of talification is to convert maxi-prescriptive and mini-prescriptive expressions into evaluative expressions. This conversion ensures that these expressions face in both directions of fit. A talified 'ought'-sentence faces in the descriptive direction of fit in so far as it contains an implicit reference to some rule or standard to which it has, in some sense, to correspond. The same sentence faces in the normative direction in so far as there is an onus of match on the prescribed conduct to fit the 'ought'-sentence.

It is because we use covertly talified 'ought'-sentences so frequently that philosophers have falsely supposed all 'ought'-sentences to have the same logic. This error has had unfortunate consequences. Thus, it has been thought that nobody could make an 'ought'-judgement or, indeed, any moral judgement at all, without having reasons for making it (Marcus Singer, *Generalization in Ethics*, p. 56). This is true of all talified 'ought'- judgements, but is not true of all untalified 'ought'-judgements. In the case of a talified 'ought'-judgement the subject is always *such* that one ought to act in an appropriate way, and hence there must be some characteristic or attribute of the subject in virtue of which it is *such*, but this does not apply to an untalified 'ought'-judgement, which a moral agent could make without having any reasons at all.

5.4. As we have seen, the effect of talification is not to reverse the direction of fit, but to add the descriptive to the normative direction of fit. There is, however, one method by which we can decisively reverse the direction of fit of a clearly normative judgement, even if it contains a normative modal auxiliary. I shall call this the method of 'simple embedding'.

I shall first expound the method dogmatically and then put forward an argument in support of my view. Consider any normative sentence formed by means of a genuine modal operator, like 'ought', 'should', 'may', or 'it is good that . . .' Then, if the modal operator is iterated, the result is either nonsense or the reversal of the direction of fit of the embedded operator. If this sounds like gibberish, let us look at an example. If you embed the 'ought' in 'Children ought to honour their parents' by iterating the 'ought', you obtain the problematic sentence

(1) It ought to be the case that children ought to honour their parents.

My contention is that either this sentence is nonsense or the second and embedded 'ought' in (1) faces in the descriptive direction of fit. Let us consider possible interpretations of (1). First, somebody might just conceivably think of it as a bizarre way of emphasizing the honour which children owed their parents. This is very unlikely, since in deontic logic 'Op' does not entail 'p', and so one would expect 'OOp', if it made any sense, not to entail 'Op'. So the 'ought's are unlikely to reinforce one another. Second, it might be of some help to think of 'ought' as more analogous in its logical properties to 'probable' than to 'necessary'. Thus, in the iterated logic of probability 'It is probable that p is probable' does not entail 'p is probable', although, of course, it is compatible with it. Indeed, where it is only probable that p, it is possible that not-p. Hence, if it is only probable that p is probable, it is possible that p is not probable. On the other hand, anybody who went so far as to agree that it was probable that p was probable would not be exactly surprised if p were probable or, indeed, actually true. One might think of our probability-judge in this case as much more taking p's side, as it were, than taking not-p's side.

Let us now, bearing in mind the logical behaviour of the word 'probable', look at 'ought'-judgements. In making an 'ought'-judgement, we normally imply that what we are making an 'ought'-judgement about has not yet come to pass. Thus if I say, 'There ought to be a law against smoking in cinemas', I imply that there does not yet exist such a law. Anybody who retorted, 'But there *is* a law against smoking in cinemas', would have rebutted my 'ought'-judgement. 'And so there ought to be', I might say somewhat peevishly, this time prefixing the words 'And so', and thereby cancelling the conventional implication of my previous utterance. What emerges from this example fairly clearly is that it is pointless for me to make an ordinary 'ought'-judgement if what is recommended has already been brought about. In brief, 'ought' conventionally implies 'is not' (see Hans Reichenbach, *Elements of Symbolic Logic*, p. 339).

Let us apply this to our problematic sentence
  (1) It ought to be the case that children ought to honour their parents.
If 'ought' always (except when preceded by a cancelling 'And so') conventionally implies 'is not', this applies to the outer 'ought' in (1) also. If this is so, (1) conventionally implies
  (2) It is not the case that children ought to honour their parents.
But if somebody genuinely believes (2), that is, rejects the moral belief that children ought to honour their parents, it is difficult to understand what sane reason he could have for asserting (1). For in so far as my linguistic intuitions function at all here, they suggest that, just as the man who asserted that it was probable that *p* was probable was, in a sense, on *p*'s side, albeit only very mildly and very guardedly, so in the case of (1) any sane man who sincerely asserted it must regard at any rate with mild favour the idea of children's honouring their parents. But the truth that (1) conventionally implies (2) conflicts with the likelihood of the asserter of (1) being favourably disposed towards children's honouring their parents. This interpretation of (1) leads, then, to inevitable incoherence, and it is therefore clear that, if we are going to give some sense to (1), it will have to be by abandoning some common assumption upon which the above arguments were based. The common assumption on which I would pin the responsibility for the incoherence is the assumption that the second, embedded, 'ought' in (1) is an honest-to-goodness 'ought', which unshakeably faces in the normative direction of fit, notwithstanding the almost traumatic experience of being embedded.

Let us, then, abandon this disastrous assumption and make (1) into an honest, intelligible judgement. If we think of the embedded 'ought' in (1) as an external 'ought', an interpretation is not merely possible but easy. We can now interpret (1) as meaning the same as

    (3) It ought to be the case that there is a rule to the effect
        that children ought to honour their parents.

This interpretation supports the intuition that anybody who asserted (1) would be favourably disposed towards the idea of children's honouring their parents. Certainly one would expect anybody who asserted (3) to be favourably disposed in this way and to be prepared, whensoever the rule in question comes into being, to internalize it and apply it in the normative direction of fit. It does not follow from this that the embedded 'ought' is really used internally; indeed, if an 'ought' is used internally, then either a rule is thereby created or it implies the existence of a prior rule in accordance with which it is used. Either possibility, however, is precluded since (3) conventionally implies that no such rule exists. We are entitled, then, to conclude that the embedded 'ought' of (1) cannot be interpreted as independently normative without making nonsense of (1), and that, when (1) is interpreted as meaning much the same as (3), the embedded 'ought' cannot be internal either. The embedded 'ought' in (1) must, therefore, be a purely external 'ought' and face in only one direction of fit, the descriptive. In this way, then, the embedding of 'ought' in (1) has reversed its direction of fit. Likewise, the embedding of other normative modal operators like 'It is a good thing that . . .' reverses their direction of fit in the same kind of way. Moreover, I suggest, a similar kind of reversal takes place when the embedding and embedded modalities are quite distinct.

    In case my argument may have convinced some of my readers, it is as well to look at some apparent counter-examples. First, the following has been suggested to me as a counter-example by J. R. Cameron:

    (4) It is a pity that everything I want to do is either illegal
        or immoral or fattening.

It is out of the question to criticize 'It is a pity that . . .' as not being a typical modal operator, just because owing to a comparatively sheltered life its logical behaviour has escaped the attention of logicians. Second, it is quite easy to construct other counter-examples on the model of (4) which do not merely embed a clearly normative expression but also iterate it. Thus we have, for example,

(5) It ought to be the case that everything which I don't
want to do I ought to do,

and

(6) It ought to be the case that everything which I ought
to do I want to do.

Sentence (5) might plausibly be uttered by a singularly perverse masochist who had read Kant's ethical writings in a
hurry, while (6) might just conceivably be uttered by a child
nurtured on Kantian principles and aspiring to a career as a
Holy Will when he grew up.

All three of the above examples, both Cameron's and my
own two, have a common feature. In all three the embedded
normative expression is not directly acted on by the outer
operator. Thus in (5) and (6), although the embedded operator
'ought' is the same as the outer operator, the outer operator
is acting on a concealed implication. This becomes clear if
the whole of the embedded clause is paraphrased in an 'if . . .
then' form. If we do that (5) becomes

(5a) It ought to be the case that for all x, if I don't want
to do x, then I ought to do x,

and (6) becomes

(6a) It ought to be the case that, for all x, if I ought to do
x, then I want to do x.

Here the outer operator 'it ought to be the case that . . .'
operates directly on the 'if . . . then' and we do not have a
case of a genuine iterated modality any more than we do in
the case of ordinary modal logic in such formulae as '$L(Lp \supset Mp)$'. Sentences (4), (5), and (6) furnish examples of complex
embeddings; my rule about embeddings applies only to simple
embeddings. I conclude, then, that a simple embedding of a
normative modal operator in an atomic normative sentence
suffices to reverse the direction of fit.

There is one more result which I need in order to determine
the relationship of evaluation and prescription. It is tempting
to think of evaluations as somehow weaker than prescriptions,
and to conclude that you can never deduce a prescriptive
conclusion from an evaluative premiss. This is false. True, if
you have a talified *una facie* premiss which relates to one
aspect only, then you cannot, of course, deduce a completely

untalified conclusion. However, if your premiss is

(7) *a* is in all respects (*omnibus faciebus*) such that you ought to do it,

then

(8) You ought to do *a*

quite clearly follows. Sentence (7) is evaluative in the sense I have given to the word, and (8) is prescriptive and may express a decision and resolve. We have no reason for refusing to allow that the 'ought' in (8) is maxi-prescriptive. Hence, here we have an example of an evaluative premiss which entails a maxi-prescriptive conclusion. Likewise we can have evaluations which entail mini-prescriptive conclusions.

It is clear, then, that we have only so far discovered one logical gap, and that is the gap between the mini-prescriptive and the maxi-prescriptive. However, before I proceed to consider the second logical gap, I need to indicate the possibility of a moral position which the logical gap between the mini-prescriptive and the maxi-prescriptive cannot be used to demolish. The logical gap I have indicated is part of the actual logic of our moral language. However, the actual logic of our moral language cannot furnish any good reason to preclude its own revision. Indeed, there are some, I think, who are temperamentally disposed towards this. A surfeit of moral seriousness persuades them that, if anything is good and within their power, they ought to do it. A fanatical act-utilitarian may be convinced that he morally must maximize happiness for everybody at every moment of his life. For him counsels of perfection will be no different from obligations, for was it not written (Matthew 5:48) 'Be ye therefore perfect, even as your Father which is in heaven is perfect'? For such people the most mini-prescriptive words of our language acquire maxi-prescriptive force and the actual logic of our language with its convenient logical gap appears to be the work of latitudinarians and backsliders, who have rigged our language to suit their weakness and their flippancy. This moral position, whether you call it 'moral athleticism' or 'moral protestantism', cannot be ruled out of court by any appeal to the actual logic of our moral language. One can indeed be a moral athleticist without wanting to revise it, for that actual logic has sufficient 'give' in it[2] to allow the moral athleticist's position to be stated in the form of a substantive moral judgement like 'One ought to do all the good in one's power'. On the other hand, to revise the actual logic of our language in such a way that the possibility of any mini-prescription was ruled out as 'illogical' or 'contradictory' would be a logically retrograde step. The logic of morals should, I think, have the same logical tolerance for diversity as Carnap forty years ago thought the logic of science should have. The logic of morals *ought* not, in my view, to prejudge questions of moral substance, and this is why I have been chary in this book of saying that all moral language is 'prescriptive'. For the unqualified use of this term suggests, I think, maxi-prescriptiveness, although I doubt whether this was in Hare's mind when the term was first used by him in *The Language of Morals*. An argument about mere words would interest none of us. My own choice of technical terms for talking about the languages of morals has been designed solely to enable us as moral philosophers to describe all the diversity there is, and that is why I have adopted the position which I call 'normativism'.

5.5. I have distinguished the evaluative from the prescriptive and I have argued that there is a logical gap between the mini-prescriptive and the maxi-prescriptive. I wish now to consider whether there is also a gap between prescription and action and, if so, what kind of gap this is. The relation between moral belief and action has perplexed moral philosophers since Socrates. The rival theories about the nature of moral judgements face difficulties of opposite kinds. The descriptivist who holds that moral judgements describe moral facts, that they are static, theoretical, and contemplative, has to explain in an *ad hoc* way how it is ever possible for people to act on their moral beliefs, how it comes about that moral judgements can be reasons for action. The descriptivist finds it difficult even to start the ball rolling. The prescriptivist, on the other hand, can get the ball rolling, but cannot explain how it can ever stop; he cannot explain except in an *ad hoc* way how anybody can ever fail to perform a physically possible action which his moral beliefs require. Whichever of the two theories

[2] Cf. Hare's remarks on 'give' in *Freedom and Reason*, p. 73.

one holds, there is a problem about what I shall call 'moral failure', the failure to do what one believes to be morally required. There is, however, less of a problem for the prescriptivist. You can, after all, construct an ethical theory which explains away acting contrary to one's beliefs, but it would be no kind of an ethical theory at all which explained away acting on one's beliefs. Some middle way appears to be dictated by common sense, but it has to be a middle way which inclines towards the prescriptivist account.

If a man believes that he ought to perform a certain action a, wants to do what he believes he ought to do, and correctly believes that he can perform a, then he will perform a in what I shall call the 'simple case'. If he does not, we shall seek for an explanation and it will no longer be the 'simple case'. The following complications can occur. First, the man may be insincere or, at any rate, may not fully or genuinely believe that he ought to perform a. Second, he may be, in some sense, 'in two minds' or a divided self. Third, the 'ought' may be of a subordinate kind; while he believes that he ought to perform a from one point of view, from another point of view, which he considers more stringent, important, or overriding, he thinks that he ought not. Fourth, even though he believes that he ought, he may not want, in some sense of 'want', to do what he believes that he ought to do, and as a consequence he either cannot or believes that he cannot perform the required action. Most attempts to explain moral failure have attempted to subsume it under one or more of these four complications.

I shall try to argue for a logical gap between prescription and action by first of all attempting a description of the kind of moral failure which occasions the difficulties. Let us take an example. Let us suppose that a man is questioned by the police for an alleged driving offence. He believes that he ought to tell the truth (or, to put it negatively, that he ought not to tell lies), he knows that he can tell the truth, but he tells a lie, because he thinks that he will be charged if he tells the truth. In this case he is quite sincere in thinking that he ought to tell the truth and this is shown by the fact that he is conscious of condemning himself while he is telling the lie as well as afterwards. He is further conscious while he is telling the lie that he could have spoken the truth. He has no feeling while he is speaking that the lie is being forced from him by factors beyond his control; this would be to experience psychological necessity. It is because he is conscious that he could have done otherwise that he blames himself for lying, even though he gets off scot-free as a result. Such a man would be said by us to 'succumb to temptation'. Of course, if a man always succumbed to any temptation, however small, we should rightly doubt the sincerity of his professed principles. The delinquent I have described is a moral lapser; while he often or even usually lives up to his moral principles, he is mindful of them at the time of his lapses and conscious on the particular occasion of his failure that he could, in some sense of 'could', live up to his principles.

It would be a mistake to try and subsume my moral lapser under the first kind of complication, the case of the man who is insincere. It is of course true that many people pay lip-service to moral principles which they do not in fact hold. In such cases their insincerity is revealed in their behaviour. True, some people may show what they really believe only when the external sanctions which they fear are removed, but one's real beliefs are shown not only by one's actions but also by one's feelings and emotions. A man who is insincere not only makes no genuine attempt to live up to the moral principles he pretends to hold, but does not experience guilt or remorse at his failure to do so. It is not to be denied that such people exist, but they are not examples of genuine moral failure, since they do not depart from their real moral principles, only from their pretended ones.

It would likewise be mistaken to identify moral failure with the second kind of complication. The moral lapser is not necessarily to be seen as a divided self. Such a model is sometimes helpful when we are concerned to understand systematic and pathological weakness. It is conceptually attractive to see the tempted man as like Shakespeare's Launcelot Gobbo in *The Merchant of Venice* with a dramatized devil inside him. But after all we do not think of scientists or philosophers as divided selves when they face conflict between the theories they favour and the theories towards which 'the facts' seem to drive them. Nor should we be seduced into overdramatizing the ordinary moral failure of the moral lapser.

The third kind of complication cannot cater for moral failure either. For, as I shall argue in Chapter 6, an individual's moral beliefs are ones which he believes should override, and hence failure to act on beliefs which the individual considers ought to be overridden cannot be moral failure.

The attempt to assimilate moral failure to the fourth kind of complication presents the most serious difficulty. That moral weakness is typically a kind of psychological impossibility has been forcefully argued by Hare in *Freedom and Reason* (Chapter 5). He argues that in weakness, as the meaning of the word indicates, a man is overpowered by desire and that thus we have here a case of psychological impossibility which by an application of the 'ought'-implies-'can' principle downgrades or reduces the moral 'ought' or makes it 'off-colour'. In so far as this view explicates what is involved in calling somebody 'morally weak', in the strictest sense of the word 'weak', it is unobjectionable. However, one can only infer from it that the moral lapser, as described by me, is logically impossible if it can be shown that the latter's condition, in common with other instances of moral failure, is also an instance of weakness in the strict sense. My purpose in focusing attention on the moral lapser is to highlight a case which is not an instance of this kind. The moral lapser does not succumb to temptation invariably but only from time to time. Moreover, he has good reason to suppose that he can resist temptation since he often does succeed in resisting it. Of course, it is easy to be sceptical of any claim by somebody to have been able to do something which he did not in fact do. But it is our practice outside philosophy to support the contention that on a given occasion we could have performed an action which we did not perform by pointing to similar occasions when we did in fact perform a like action. (We reason *ab esse* on other occasions *ad posse* on this one.) Now the way in which we use words depends not on the way things are but on the way we think they are.[3] Any ordinary 'ought'-user, unless he is a self-righteous saint according to his own morality, recognizes that he is capable of becoming a moral

[3] For the way in which our everyday use of language is compatible with the falsity of determinism, see my 'The Concept of Probability', *British Journal for the Philosophy of Science*, 1965.

lapser. While it is possible that all moral failure is psychologically determined in some deep sense, we talk as if this were
not so. It is surely a fact that the moral failures of people like
my moral lapser are generally believed to be avoidable. Consequently, the word 'ought' is used both by and to people who
believe that it is possible for them either to do or not to do
what they believe they ought to do. There is no contradiction,
then, in our acknowledging that we ought to perform a possible action which we do not in fact perform. This is all that is
needed to show a logical gap between prescription and action.

We may appeal also to the phenomenology of temptation.
While it is certainly true that some people at some times are
conscious of its being psychologically impossible for them to
act in accordance with their moral beliefs, this is not true of
all cases of moral failure. There are indeed some people who
are unable to control themselves on some occasions, and these
are the most dramatic cases of moral failure. But they are not
the most typical cases. There is a difference between the
soldier who runs away in a moment of blind panic and the
soldier who after deliberation yields to the temptation to
desert. To suggest that all failure is basically psychological
impossibility is to confuse losing control of oneself with
ordinary succumbing to temptation. We need to be reminded
that we may 'succumb to temptation with calm and even with
finesse' (Austin: 'A Plea for Excuses', p. 24). When we are
faced with temptation, we are not conscious, when we yield,
of finding it psychologically impossible to do what we believe
we ought to do, nor are we conscious, when we successfully
resist temptation, of merely acting in accordance with psychological necessity. Rather we are conscious of finding difficulty
in doing what we believe that we ought to do; sometimes we
do what we ought to do despite the difficulty, while at other
times we fail to do what we ought to do because of the difficulty. We praise those who overcome the difficulties and
blame those who allow themselves to be overcome or deterred
by them. Whether we ought to allot praise and blame in this
way may indeed be questioned, but it is a fact that most of
us do so. We think, whether rightly or wrongly, that we are
responsible for the way we respond to temptation, and since
our use of language is determined by the way we think rather

than by the way things are, we employ a clearly on-colour 'ought' in addressing and talking about those who succumb to temptation and those who resist it, and this we shall no doubt continue doing until the dawn of 'Walden Two'.[4]

Three other kinds of moral failure need to be mentioned. First, the prescriptive moral belief which a moral agent consciously deviates from may be a belief derived from the positive or social morality of his society. He may think other values to be of greater importance. He may consider that, while the positive morality of his society provides reasons for action, these are not conclusive or overriding reasons. Hence, if we are making positive-moral judgements from the internal point of view, it is no self-contradiction to say 'I know that I ought to do a, but I am not going to'. There is no conceptual difficulty in accommodating moral failure within an account of social morality. We often do feel guilt of a kind when we deliberately violate the rules and conventions of the society in which we live, even when these rules and conventions do not embody the standards and values which we ourselves think to be most important and overriding. But these are not central cases of moral failure. The central cases occur, not when we succumb to a temptation and so fail to live up to a social or positive morality in some respect, but when we fail to live up to our own individual morality, when we fail to live up to the standards which we have set ourselves. The same considerations arise with reference to Morality$_A$ or any anchored morality. A man may recognize that Morality$_A$, say, provides him with reasons for action and yet decide that other considerations are of greater moment and should prevail. The condition of this man is common, but it is not a central case of moral failure.

Nor does any difficulty present itself with regard to the conscious failure to conform to beliefs which are not fully prescriptive. Since the move from a mini-prescriptive utterance to a full prescription is not logically necessary (5.2), this ensures that there is a gap between the mini-prescriptive and action. This kind of failure may be called 'mini-prescriptive'. One can take the following example of mini-prescriptive failure. Suppose I believe that certain actions are supererogatory,

---

[4] See B. F. Skinner's novel *Walden Two*.

that they are good but not obligatory; then, while I think it is better to do the supererogatory than not to, I do not think it blameworthy not to. Failing to do what I regard as supererogatory, I see the better course and approve of it, although I pursue the worse course. The better course is within my power, but I may think it would be unreasonable to require me to pursue it. Thus a widow might accept what a former Pope once said, namely, that it is better for widows not to remarry although they commit no sin if they do, and yet she might remarry. This would be 'mini-prescriptive failure' and presents no logical difficulty.

In what follows I shall be concerned with moral judgements which are both independent and maxi-prescriptive. Moreover, they will also have to contain summary 'ought's. For it is plain that there is no difficulty in the idea of somebody's failing to live up to a *una facie* 'ought'. As we saw in 3.4, somebody who believes that he $ought_{uf}$ to perform an action, $wants_{uf}$ to perform the action. But $wanting_{uf}$ may be only one competing desire among others and hence in such a case no special explanation is needed for a man's failing to do what he merely $wants_{uf}$ to do. Consequently no special explanation is required to explain a man's failing to do what he morally $ought_{uf}$ to do.

We are now in a position to discuss what I consider to be a central case of moral failure. This is the case of a person who, correctly believing in his ability to perform an action and fully believing that he ought morally to perform the action all things considered, yet fails to do it. Consider the extreme pacifist who holds that one ought never under any circumstances on any account to take human life and therefore does not allow that any other moral 'ought'-principle ought to override his all-things-considered principle. Such a man might genuinely believe that he ought never on any account to take a human life and yet might in fact kill somebody in defence, say, of his wife or children.

Let us consider two objections which could be raised to the logical possibility or coherence of my description of what I have called 'a central case'. The first difficulty is this. If the agent really thinks that he ought *on no account* to take life, surely he could not have a reason for killing someone. If he did kill somebody, it might be objected, it would be through some surge of hatred or anger or some other factor beyond his control. Consequently this would not be a central case of moral failure, for it would be a case of *propeteia,* as Aristotle called it (*Nicomachean Ethics*, vii, 1150b19), when the agent's passions or impulses leave him no time for deliberation. The objection is powerful, but not insurmountable. It has not been shown that it is logically impossible for a man to believe that he ought on no account to kill and yet to have a reason for killing. This could only be shown, if at all, if it was first demonstrated that inconsistency was impossible, and although some philosophers have believed this, it is plainly false.[5] Since inconsistency can occur, it is perfectly possible to believe that one ought on no account to kill anybody and at the same time to have a (conscious) reason for killing a particular person. To be aware of any reflective desire to do something is to be aware of a reason for action. Let us suppose that our pacifist has an enemy, a tyrant (call him 'A.H.') who is about to inflict grievous injury on the man's wife and children and that there is no legal or other power capable of restraining the tyrant while he lives. It is for this reason that the pacifist desires to remove the danger in the only possible way, by killing his enemy if he has an opportunity. This cannot be interpreted as being merely a natural inclination or need-related desire to defend his family; it is a belief-dependent and reflective desire. For it originates, let us say, from the belief that his enemy intends to do his family a grievous injury unless he prevents it. Since, however, the pacifist holds that he morally ought on no account to kill anybody, he does not acknowledge this desire to kill his enemy as morally good. Nevertheless it is his desire, not somebody else's, and if he acts on this desire and kills A.H., it would be gross sophistry and hypocrisy on the pacifist's part if, when asked his reason for killing A.H., he replied, 'No reason at all, since I believe that I ought never on any account or for any reason to kill anybody.' Of course, in so far as the pacifist does not approve of his desire, does not acknowledge his desire as good, he cannot say that he has a *good* reason for killing A.H. There is a difference between reasons and good reasons. The example of the pacifist suggests, then, a possible description of the predicament of one kind

[5] See my 'Inconsistency', *The Philosophical Quarterly*, January 1966.

of moral lapser. The moral lapser in question believes that he morally ought not, all things considered, to perform a certain action which is open to him and which he has a reflective, belief-dependent desire to perform. Although he acknowledges that desire as morally bad, he is not logically precluded from regarding the desire in question as providing him with a reason for action, albeit not one which he regards as a good reason, morally speaking. From the fact that he has a fully prescriptive, summary moral belief it follows that he desires to desire to refrain from the proscribed action (3.5) and hence to that extent desires not to have the recalcitrant desire. The genuineness of that belief is evidenced by his earnest efforts either to rid himself of the desire or, failing that, to ensure that it does not determine his conduct when the occasion or opportunity for action presents itself. However, since these efforts take time, the occasion for action may arrive in the meantime and our potential lapser may 'succumb to temptation'. If he does so, some may seek to represent him as temporarily under the control of his recalcitrant desire. This move is confusing as well as tendentious, since it misguidedly tries to assimilate what is a reflective, belief-dependent desire to compulsions and addictions. The desire in question should not be misrepresented as if it were an external force against which the agent is temporarily powerless to struggle. Even if he morally disapproves of it, the desire is *his* desire, the reason is *his* reason, where the words 'he' and 'his' refer to the whole person. We are not justified in making an arbitrary Platonic division of the self and in attributing to one part of it privileged 'moral' beliefs and desires to the exclusion of other beliefs and desires capable of conflicting with them. While it is clear that the recalcitrant, reflective desire conflicts with the moral lapser's moral belief, this cannot be used to justify a factitious division of the lapser's self unless the possibility of inconsistency is mistakenly denied. My answer, then, to the first objection has consisted in arguing for the logical possibility of one kind of moral failure in which the agent acts for a reason.

5.6. The second difficulty arises from reflection on the relation between strength or intensity of desire and action. The usual picture of moral failure is of a man who has very strong

or intense desires, under the influence of which he acts. Surely,
the objection goes, if a moral 'ought' is in some sense an overriding 'ought' and if accepting an 'ought'-judgement necessarily
involves having a desire, then accepting an overriding 'ought'-
judgement must involve having a desire stronger or more intense than any of its possible competitors. But if action is
determined by the strongest or most intense desire, anybody
who genuinely holds a moral belief cannot fail to act on it,
and moral failure, on this argument also, turns out to be logically impossible.

The argument which leads to the denial of moral failure
may be reconstructed as follows (where '→' means 'strictly
implies'):

(1) X believes that he morally ought to do a → X believes that
    he ought to do a in preference to anything else which he
    thinks that he non-morally ought to do. (To be argued
    for in Chapter 6.)

(2) X believes that he morally ought, all things considered,
    to do a → X believes that he ought, all things considered,
    to do a in preference to anything else. (A legitimate trans-
    formation of (1); the implicans implies that all conflicting
    moral 'ought's have been considered and overridden.)

(3) X believes that he ought to do a → X wants to do a. (Argued
    for in 3.4.)

(4) X believes that he ought, all things considered, to do a in
    preference to anything else → X wants to do a, all things
    considered, in preference to anything else. (A legitimate
    transformation of (3).)

(5) X wants to do a, all things considered, in preference to
    anything else → X wants to do a more strongly (or intensely)
    than he wants to do anything else.

(6) X wants to do a more strongly (or intensely) than he
    wants to do anything else → X tries as hard as he can to
    do a.

(7) X tries as hard as he can to do a → X does a if he can.
    (Necessary truth linking trying, possibility, and action.)

(8) X believes that he morally ought, all things considered, to
    do a → X does a if he can. (From (2), (4), (5), (6), and (7)
    by repeated application of Hypothetical Syllogism.)

(9) X believes that he morally ought, all things considered, to

do *a, and* X can do *a* → X does *a*. (By Principle of Impor-
tation from (8).)

Proposition (1) will be argued for in Chapter 6. The transformation of (1) into (2) is, I contend, legitimate. Sentence
(1) has to be qualified by the words 'which he thinks that he
non-morally ought to do', because the implicans is not a
summary (all-things-considered) judgement and non-sum-
mary moral 'ought's may override one another. This qualification is no longer necessary in the implicatum of (2), because
the words 'all things considered' appear both in the implicans
and in the implicatum. If X says that he morally ought, all
things considered, to do *a*, he implies that he has considered
all other 'ought's, moral ones as well as non-moral ones. X's
belief, then, described in the implicans of (2), is a belief held
at the end of deliberation, not at its beginning. The transformation of (1) into (2) is thus justified.

The transformation of (3) into (4) is easier to see. Sentence
(3) was argued for in 3.4, and the transformation of (3) into
(4) requires us to accept that if an 'ought'-belief necessarily
involves a desire, the content of that desire is dependent upon
the content of the 'ought'-belief. Thus, if I think that I ought
to love the Lord my God with all my heart, with all my soul,
and with all my might, then it follows that I want to love the
Lord my God with all my heart, etc. If I think that I ought to
do *a* rather than *b*, then it follows that I want to do *a* rather
than *b*. Likewise, if I think that I ought, all things considered,
to do *a* in preference to anything else, then it follows that I
want, all things considered, to do *a* in preference to anything
else. Thus the derivation of (4) from (3) is acceptable.

The two problematic premises in the argument are (5) and
(6). Indeed I shall argue that at least one of them is false. To
show that at least one of the premises is false does not, of
course, suffice to invalidate the argument's conclusion, but
I suggest that it is an argument of this structure and content
which tempts thinkers to deny the existence of moral failure.
I shall deal with (6) first. Sentence (6) claims an analytic connection between intensity of desire and action (trying). If our
sole criterion of what is a man's strongest desire is the action
which is its sequel, then, of course, it is necessary that we all
act in the line of least resistance. In fact, I am prepared to

maintain that what a man does is only a part-criterion of what
is his strongest desire. Our criteria for what somebody most
or most strongly or most intensely wants are in part also his
introspective reports prior to action and, where appropriate,
the behavioural criteria of these intense desires. We know that
a man wants very strongly to run away before he actually
runs away not merely because he may say 'I am terribly
frightened', but also because he turns very white, trembles
uncontrollably and stumbles in his speech. Psychologists have
suggested more refined tests of drive-strength involving such
things as free association. Once such tests are accepted we
can significantly ask such questions as 'Under what conditions
can we refrain from acting in accordance with our most intense
desires?' It is customary to talk of the strength of desires as if
there was only one dimension of strength with respect to
desires. As soon as we begin to distinguish, say, the kind of
strength which we associate with stability and resilience from
the kind of strength commonly called 'intensity', then the
answers to questions like the above are by no means clear. In
Aesop's tale the bramble proved stronger than the oak; its
strength was of a different kind. Analogies of this sort suggest
that desires are not the only determinants of human action
and that their introspectively felt intensity is not the only
relevant determining factor. In any case, I do not require for
the purposes of my argument to refute (6) in the sense of
showing that it is naïve or uninstructive to take the sequel of
a desire as the criterion of its relative strength. Let (6) be
interpreted in such a way as to make it necessarily true. Then,
seeing that I have accepted all the premises of the argument
except (5), if I accept (5) too I must accept the conclusion.
However, (5) is false. To say that I have a desire to do a in
preference to anything else or desire to do a in preference to
anything else is to say nothing about the intensity of that
desire. (See the story of the Methodist minister and the
Catholic priest at the end of 3.3.)

The second difficulty, then, can be overcome. For we have
to recognize that there is no necessary one–one correlation
between the order of priority of a man's moral principles on
the one hand and the order of strength of his desires on the
other. My most intense desire may even be *not* to do what it

is my summary desire to do. Our emotions and passions, as is well known, are not at the immediate beck and call of our moral principles and beliefs, although we may seek to educate our emotions so as to bring them into closer alignment with our moral beliefs. Emotions and passions can come and go, but relatively stable moral beliefs are not necessarily affected by their passage. To venture into the moral arena very briefly, I maintain that in the well-tempered moral agent moral principles and beliefs are able to weather almost any emotional storms. The exceptions are what I call 'crucial experiences' which can affect the whole tenor of a man's life. The nature and possible appraisal of these experiences as 'rational' or 'irrational' I shall not examine until we reach the intricacies of 14.4.

I have argued, then, for a second gap between thought and action, a gap between prescriptive language and action, which makes moral failure logically possible. From this account there emerges a picture of moral beliefs and of the reflective desires which go with them as having a relative stability and immunity to sudden impairment by fluctuating desires, emotions, and passions. But a man's moral beliefs are immune to impairment not only from the passions but also from other normative beliefs. In the next chapter I shall argue for this by relating the concept of a morality to that of importance.

6

The Practical Hierarchy

6.1. Moral judgements have so far been characterized only as normative. But what distinguishes moral judgements from other kinds of normative judgement? In the first place, they are relevant to the making of decisions and to action, they are practical. In this they differ from pure aesthetic judgements. I may judge a sunset to be beautiful or the Niagara Falls to be sublime, but nothing appears to follow from these judgements about what one should do, e.g., that I and others should try to see similar sunsets as often as possible or that I should visit Niagara. Moral judgements, on the other hand, are characteristically used not only by moral critics but also by moral agents in coming to decisions. A non-practical contemplator of human actions who issued judgements *sub specie aeternitatis* would not be a human moral agent.

Relevance to action may be regarded as a normative counterpart of being empirical. A statement is empirical if some observation or experience is relevant to deciding whether it is true or false. A judgement is practical if it is relevant to deciding whether to do something or not. Both characteristics are matters of degree. A statement may be only remotely empirical, for example, the statement that every event has a cause. A judgement may be only remotely practical, for example, a moral judgement about an unrealizable ideal or about some unique historical character. For example, if somebody says that King Charles the Second was morally at fault in digging up and hanging Cromwell's corpse, what he says is only remotely connected with questions about what we ought to do here and now or in the future. Nevertheless, it does have some practical relevance; the speaker may believe that respect for the dead is of paramount importance and that no amount of moral turpitude on the part of a man can justify another's treating his corpse with contumely. Every moral judgement is to some degree practical.

The second feature distinctive of moral judgements is that not only are they normative and practical, but they are also high up in the hierarchy of practical normative considerations. It seems to follow almost from the very meaning of the word 'moral' that moral considerations are not trivial ones. It would be an extremely bizarre character who claimed that he had a morality but thought that it ought not to play a large part in his life or anyone else's. Those who distinguish moral from non-moral considerations have intended to draw a distinction between those reasons for action which are comparatively important and those which are less so. Unless, indeed, the term 'moral' singled out comparatively important practical normative considerations, it would be necessary to invent a term which did. So whatever variations there may be in the actual use of the term, I shall use it in this magisterial sense.

Now it is tempting to say without qualification such things as 'Morality is important' or 'Moral considerations are important considerations', as if 'Morality' were a specific and determinate object and there were an authoritative and definitive catalogue of moral considerations. There may indeed be considerations, principles, and rules which the dominant part of a society regard as most important and these may be regarded as embodying 'Morality'. In that event there is no necessity for everybody to regard these considerations, etc., as most important. Succeeding generations in the same society may have a different mind on the matter. Be this as it may, once the term 'morality' is anchored to specifiable considerations, principles, or rules, it is possible for different people to take different attitudes towards the morality it names, some holding that it is more important than other things, others that it is less important. If the term 'morality' (with or without a big 'M') is used as a proper name for a body of rules or considerations, if Morality is a re-identifiable object, it is possible for the same person to take up different attitudes towards it at different times and for different people to take up different attitudes towards it at the same time. This applies to Morality$_A$ or any other anchored morality as well as to the dominant social morality of one's society. Any of these could be referred to when people purport to make a uniquely identifying use of the term 'Morality'.

On the other hand, sometimes when people talk of 'what is required by morality' they are using the term 'morality' in its non-anchored sense to refer to whatever happens to be their morality; if they change their minds about moral matters, they will use the term 'morality' to refer to their new position. A man's morality, then, will consist of what he thinks that 'morality requires'. Thus 'to will the good' is to will many things. If we are discussing moralities in this sense, we have to decide what place a morality must have in a person's practical thinking in order to be called 'his' morality. My thesis in this chapter is that there is an intimate connection between moral considerations and considerations which somebody thinks most important for the conduct of his life. Consequently, we shall find that considerations which are regarded as 'moral' by one man will not necessarily be so regarded by another. (That is why, as we saw in 1.5, the expression 'It is a matter of moral principle for me that . . .' is used to make a moral commitment, while the expression 'It is a matter of moral principle for him that . . .' is used to make a logical diagnosis.) It further follows that one man may think some considerations more important than considerations thought to be moral con- siderations by some other individual or by his society, as well as more important than considerations derived from Morality$_A$ or some other traditional morality. It is a consequence of these differences of locution that there are alternative ways of describing and of thinking about the same normative posi- tion. These will be discussed in the next section.

6.2. Among maxi-prescriptive moralities two views may be taken about the number of ends or activities to which other ends and activities should be subordinated. Those who main- tain that there is only one end or activity, to which all other activities, etc., should be subordinated, I shall call 'monolithic' thinkers. Those, on the other hand, who maintain that there is more than one end or activity to which all other ends and activities should be subordinated I shall call 'polylithic' thinkers. I shall deal with polylithic thinkers first.

Most social moralities are, like Morality$_A$, polylithic; there

are in such moralities a number of first principles, independent of one another, representing different and sometimes
conflicting moral values. Faced with a morality of this kind
some moral philosophers have responded by trying to reduce
the number of values, either making the morality monolithic
or, if they are less Procrustean, determining an order of priority amongst a small number of fundamental values, so that
they are not saddled with 'a heap of unconnected obligations'.
Nevertheless many moralities seem to be just such heaps. Their
fundamental principles appear to set up disparate ends or lay
down diverse values capable of conflicting with one another,
although collectively they present themselves as entitled to
override all other considerations.

In typical polylithic moralities there are principles which
set up ends and also principles which enjoin the performance
of actions for their own sake. Many of these embody side-
constraints and may be termed 'means-restricting'. Some
philosophers in the Kantian tradition do indeed regard a
morality as containing principles of this kind to the exclusion
of all others. But a typical morality contains principles setting
up ends as well as means-restricting principles. In such a
morality it is thought that means-restricting principles like
'Ends must be pursued in such a way that individual liberties
are not infringed' ought to override and are more important
than end-stating principles. If my thesis is correct that there
is an intimate connection between a man's morality and his
most important principles of action, it is not surprising that
the totality of means-restricting principles are sometimes
thought of (e.g., by deontologists) as constituting the whole
of a man's morality, while the end-stating principles are
thought of as merely auxiliary. Nevertheless, some end-stating
principles should be counted as belonging to a person's morality. Plainly there is a big difference between those special
ends which somebody decides to pursue when, for instance,
he chooses a career, and those all-pervasive ends which relate
to the totality of human endeavour. Their very all-pervasive-
ness makes one want to classify them with means-restricting
principles rather than with choices of specific ends, like choosing to become a doctor, which cannot be regarded as principles.

Let us now consider monolithic thinkers. Aestheticists think that one human activity, Art, is more important than any other. As William Gaunt (*The Aesthetic Adventure*, p. 14) says of the Bohemians, they 'had one law, one morality, one devotion and that was—Art'. Presumably Gauguin and Somerset Maugham's Strickland in *The Moon and Sixpence* held this point of view, in so far as their attitudes were capable of being articulated. Again, the Machiavellian thinks that the State is paramount and that its interests have priority over all others. Perhaps another example of a monolithic attitude is that of capitalist moralists in whose morality financial success is of overriding importance. The pattern of a 'monolithic' belief is 'Let anything conducive to — be brought about, whatever the consequences', where the blank may be replaced by 'art', 'the will of God', 'the State', 'the ego', 'freedom', 'truth', 'justice', and so on. Some of those who hold monolithic views we should term 'fanatics', although we tend to reserve that term for those monolithic thinkers whose claims we totally reject. Some of these monolithic theorics I shall consider in Part III (13.2) when discussing 'open-cheque moralities' and I shall there give reasons for regarding them as rationally-defective. Here, however, I am only interested in characterizing these theories in order to have a better understanding of the connection between the concepts of a morality and of importance.

One way of talking, however, does militate against my thesis. Monolithic theorists often describe themselves or are described by others as 'subordinating morality' to, say, art or the State or success and so on. In this way of talking, it is no contradiction to describe morality and moral values as subordinated to other activities and values. For the morality which is meant is generally Morality$_A$ and this may be quite correctly described as being subordinated to other values. Nevertheless, there is much to be said in favour of a different way of talking and the different way of thinking which goes with it. While, for example, Machiavelli in *The Prince* (especially Chapter 18) may be described as 'subordinating morality to prudence or expediency', it is enlightening to think of him as rather specifying circumstances in which one may be excused from conformity to moral laws. He is not saying, 'You ought to put the State and political advantage first and ignore

Morality$_A$.' On the contrary, he is saying something like this: 'Ideally if all men were good you should obey the laws of morality, but in point of fact most men are bad and therefore you are permitted, morally permitted, not to conform to moral laws when you are dealing with affairs of State.' This interpretation is confirmed by Bacon's description of maxims like those of Machiavelli as 'these dispensations from the laws of charity and integrity' ('The Advancement of Learning', Book II, in *Bacon's Advancement of Learning and The New Atlantis*, p. 215). Likewise Gauguin, although he can be described as subordinating Morality$_A$ to art, may be more enlighteningly pigeon-holed if we think of him as subordinating ordinary moral values such as family loyalty to the exigencies of art. Even Kierkegaard's 'knight of faith' (*Fear and Trembling*, pp. 79–101) may be thought of not so much as subordinating Morality$_A$ to the commands of God, but as advocating a 'Put God first' morality. If I understand rightly what Kierkegaard means when he speaks of Abraham's intended sacrifice of Isaac as involving a 'teleological suspension of the ethical', he is not committing himself to the position that Abraham's action, while ethically wrong, was made right overall because of his faith. Rather he appears to hold that Abraham's faith is relevant in a moral assessment of his action and that in the light of it he was 'not guilty of sin' in being ready to sacrifice Isaac.

My aim in these examples has not been to denigrate those who describe what is done as subordinating morality to something else. But since my task is to explain the concept of *a* morality, I have stressed the rationale of alternative locutions. Clarity on this topic enables us to make sense of such controversies as that between the aestheticist and the ethicist. The aestheticist who thinks that art should be pursued 'for art's sake' will hold that if he has something artistic in mind it ought to be created and that no other consideration ought to override this one. His holding such a view has consequences for his family and himself and society at large, and produces what some may describe as a conflict between art and morality. There is a conflict here between those moral rules, i.e., Morality$_A$ or perhaps the social morality of his society, which require the artist to put his family first, and his own morality,

according to which his overriding duty is to his art. The ethicist, on the other hand, maintains that art must serve morality
not merely in that it should conform to the requirements of
Morality$_A$ but in that it should actively express moral ideas
and precepts. As Tolstoy puts it (*What Then Must We Do?*,
p. 293), 'Since man existed, true art which was highly esteemed
has had no other purpose than to express man's vocation and
welfare.' Tolstoy's ethic here leads him to give a persuasive
redefinition of art.

The conflict between aestheticism and ethicism is not an
aesthetic one, it is not a conflict about what is beautiful or
what merits being called 'a work of art', but is over the question how to live and what place the practice of art ought to
have in the economy of life. The aestheticist's answer is that
art should be dominant, while the ethicist holds that art, like
other forms of human activity, should be subordinate to what
are ordinarily regarded as moral values, human welfare, altruism, and so on. Those who have talked of a conflict 'between
art and morality' have been either referring to Morality$_A$ or
contrasting things which are not on a par. Art is not an alternative pursuit to morality, it is one amongst many aspects of life
the relative importance of which a man has to decide upon.
Aesthetic values like beauty, sublimity, greatness, compete
not with an individual's morality, but with truth, freedom,
happiness, and other things we value. It is only in the minds
of fanatics that there are hard and fast rules about the proper
order of priority. To form a balanced attitude to life—and
here I stick my moral neck out—all our values have to be considered and each person's style of life differs from those of
others according to the different weights each gives to the
things he values. The conflict between aestheticism and ethicism is, I maintain, itself a moral conflict, as is any conflict
concerned with the ordering of the differing things which
people value, for an agent's morality, as I shall argue, is concerned with his whole economy of life.

6.3. I have maintained that the alternative locutions I have
indicated are the effect of shifting between anchored and
non-anchored uses of the term 'morality'. Those who only
recognize the anchored use have difficulties in accounting for

the apparently inexplicable tendency to identify with morality (i.e., Morality$_A$) those considerations which are thought to be most important. Thus Mrs Foot (*Virtues and Vices*, pp. 186-7) notices how we 'accommodate the exceptions *within* morality', as when one is taught that it is morally permissible to tell social lies; she attributes this to the 'flexible' way in which we happen to 'teach morality'. She notices that 'etiquette, unlike morality, is taught as a rigid set of rules that are on occasion to be broken' (p. 186). However, with what she calls 'morality' the exceptions are 'incorporated' into the rules. But it is surely insufficient to record this merely as a stubborn fact. There must be some explanation of this practice. On the account given here such an explanation is forthcoming. When we teach a morality, in particular when we teach Morality$_A$, we are doing both of two things, we are teaching a particular body of rules, etc., that is, teaching that certain modes of conduct are required or forbidden, and we are also teaching people moral thinking.

Now the point of moral thinking, I contend, is to arrive at decisions and this it can only do if it determines what considerations should come foremost in a given situation. It would doubtless be easy to teach a definitive list of rules or principles which specify that actions under such-and-such descriptions are to be done or avoided, as the case may be. But such rules or principles would not of themselves indicate how they were to be applied. To apply them mechanically would be possible, but by so doing one would be assuming that one knew in advance all the possible heads of description under which an action might fall and that this knowledge was fully taken account of by the rules of the taught morality. Moreover, one would also have to assume that no action was so complex that its description fell under two conflicting rules or principles, whose relative stringency was not indicated by the morality in question. Such a manner of teaching moral thinking would ignore the inexhaustibility of description so illuminatingly emphasized by Hampshire in his *Thought and Action*. Since any description of an action in a situation is inadequate, no finite set of rules, dependent on such descriptions, can provide a definitive answer in each and every situation to the question, 'What should I do?'. A circumscribed set of rules plus deduc-

tive logic does not suffice. To ignore immutable facts is irrational and the inexhaustibility of description is an immutable
fact. But a method of teaching moral thinking which presents
it as mechanical deduction from a determinate set of rules
ignores the inexhaustibility of description. If, then, the teaching of moral thinking is to be rational, it must take account
of the indefinite revisability of our descriptions of human
action. A complete description of any human action is unattainable. Hence, a requirement of *total* evidence in morals is
unfulfillable. One might say that only an omniscient God
would be able to make a moral judgement which was not relative to its grounds. From these reflections arise (i) a principle
of realism or total available grounds, that a moral agent/judge,
to be rational, must take into account every relevant ground
of judgement available to him, and (ii) a principle of unattainable ideal rationality, that it is irrational to think that one
actually knows the complete description of an object in all its
particularity, to think that one knows all relevant grounds of
judgement (see 11.5 for further treatment of these principles).

Now if moral thinking is to be rational, it must be taught
as part of practical thinking satisfying the two principles I
have mentioned and in conjunction with whichever morality
is being taught. Since rational practical thinking takes into
account the inexhaustibility of description, a particular code's
relationship with practical thinking in general will depend on
whether that code also takes the same factor into account.
If it does, it will be taught 'flexibly', to use Mrs Foot's term;
but if it does not and comprises a rigid set of rules, like
etiquette, then it will be sundered from other practical thinking and be applicable exclusively to one portion of one's
practical life. This is certainly true of etiquette, the point of
which is to facilitate social intercourse by obviating the necessity of reflection. The price, then, of not teaching a morality
flexibly is that its scope, like that of etiquette, would be
restricted and that the practical thinking which would ac-
company it would be purely routine or mechanical. If, then,
we wish our morality to be capable of responding to changed
circumstances and to be closely connected with the rest of
practical thinking, we should teach it flexibly. My style of
argument here anticipates that of Part III, but this has been

necessary to provide a rationale for the flexible teaching of moralities. The advantage of my account as compared with Mrs Foot's is that it removes the suspicion that the flexible way in which 'morality' is taught is merely a cunning attempt by its adherents to ensure that it is never 'on the losing side' (*Virtues and Vices*, p. 187).

6.4. It is through its connection with importance that we can distinguish a morality from both manners and prudence, for all three are normative and practical. Manners are plainly thought of as having less importance than morals and that is the reason why they are sometimes called *les petites morales* or 'the lesser morals'. Most judgements of manners are concerned with conventional obligations. We judge that it is bad manners to do *a* because we live in Y-land and people in Y-land consider it bad manners to do *a*. It is arguable that fundamental judgements of manners are concerned with such matters as showing respect and refraining from giving offence; they state that one ought to show people the appropriate marks of respect depending on the fashion, the place, and the time. It is not open to people to pick and choose their manners. I cannot decide that thumbing my nose shall be *for me* a mark of deep respect or that raising my hat between the thumb and forefinger of my right hand shall be *for me* an obscene insult. When in Rome it is good manners to do as the Romans do and consequently a private-enterprise theory of manners is not even a starter.

Now, on the account I am giving of what it is for something to be a morality, a code of manners or etiquette could function as a morality. This would be a non-standard morality, for the standard view is that manners and etiquette embody less important rules than morality or prudence. Nevertheless fanatical sticklers for etiquette are sometimes encountered. Perhaps one such appears in a story of Thorstein Veblen's ('The Theory of the Leisure Class' in *The Portable Veblen*, p. 90) about 'a certain king of France, who is said to have lost his life through an excess of moral stamina in the observance of good form. In the absence of the functionary whose office it was to shift his master's seat, the king sat uncomplaining before the fire and suffered his royal person to be toasted beyond recovery. But in so doing he saved His Most Christian Majesty from menial contamination.'

Prudence likewise in at any rate one of its senses may become coextensive with 'morality'. First, we should distinguish technical prudence, which is solely a matter of means–end rationality, from private prudence (see A. P. Griffiths and R. S. Peters, 'The Autonomy of Prudence', *Mind*, April 1962). Private prudence involves a proper regard for one's own interests. It is about what one should do 'in so far as one is considering one's own interests rather than the interests of others' (p. 163). I would contend that for some people (e.g., John Ladd's Navaho in *The Structure of a Moral Code*, pp. 212-13) prudential and moral considerations are coextensive. Those for whom this is so would 'merge all morality' in prudence and would be precluded from contrasting 'moral' and 'prudential' considerations. However, the concepts of prudence and of a morality are distinct and thus those for whom all 'morality' is not merged in prudence will be able to contrast the one with the other.

6.5. I have so far been using the expressions 'important' and 'more important than' as if it were already sufficiently clear how they were to be understood. In this and the following two sections I shall try to fix the sense of these expressions by linking them with notions of overriding, justification, and the functional *a priori*.

I will begin by explaining what I shall mean by 'override'. The word is used ambiguously. In the first sense a consideration is said to 'override' or to be 'overriding' if those for whom it is a consideration in fact allow it to prevail over all others in their conduct; in the second sense a consideration is said to 'override' or to be 'overriding' if those for whom it is a consideration think that it should or ought to prevail over others in their actual conduct. From this point onwards I shall use the term in its first sense, so that users of the word in its second sense will mean the same as I do by 'ought to override'.

Let there be a possible course of action *a* for an agent, John, and let *W* and *R* be the only features of *a* judged by John to be relevant to his decision whether to perform it or not. Let *W* be a wrong-making feature and *R* a required-making feature of a. Then John thinks that the consideration that Wa (i.e., a has the feature W) ought to override the consideration that Ra if and only if he thinks that he ought to perform a, all things considered. Furthermore, if John is free from what I have called 'moral failure', bad faith, etc., the first consideration will override the second. The case of John's thinking that the second consideration ought to override the first may be explained *mutatis mutandis*. We can now explain 'being more important (maxi-prescriptively) than' in the following way. A person thinks that one consideration is more important (maxi-prescriptively) than another if and only if, when there is a conflict between the two considerations, he thinks that the first ought to override the second.

The interpretation of 'important' that I have given for maxi-prescriptive judgements is not appropriate for mini-prescriptive moral judgements. A judgement of supererogatory merit would be one of these. In a normal morality a man who chooses not to do something which it would be heroic or saintly to do may be described as allowing some non-moral normative judgement to override a supererogatory moral judgement. Despite not conforming to it, he is committed to holding that it would be *good* for his supererogatory moral judgement to override. This, therefore, gives us an interpretation of 'more important than' for mini-prescriptive moral judgements. A person is committed to thinking his mini-prescriptive moral judgements to be more important (mini-prescriptively) than his non-moral normative judgements, if and only if he thinks that it would be good that the former should override the latter. Or, to put my point in a formally analogous way, I may say this: a person thinks that one consideration is more important (mini-prescriptively) than another, if and only if, when there is a conflict between the two considerations, he thinks that it would be a good thing for the first consideration to override the second. Let a be the possible action of an agent John and let G and U be the only features of a judged by John to be relevant to his decision, where G is a morally-good-making feature and U is an unwelcome-making feature. Then John thinks that, although it is not the case that the consideration that Ga ought to override the consideration that Ua, it would be a good thing if it did, if and only if John thinks that, although it is not the case that he ought to perform *a*, it would be a good thing, all things considered, for him to perform it. Further, if John is saintly or heroic or otherwise to be commended in that dimension, the consideration that *Ga* will override the consideration that *Ua*, and John will in fact perform *a*.

I can now restate the thesis of this chapter. A man's moral principles are practical principles which he thinks ought to override or which he thinks it would be a good thing to override non-moral normative principles. We have so far, however, no reason to support the converse of this thesis. We have not found any argument so far to support the view that any practical principle which one thinks ought to override other practical principles must *eo ipso* be a moral principle.

Consider a monolithic morality where supposedly the only moral considerations are concerned with some all-embracing end or activity, T. Let us assume that there are some situations in which as far as T is concerned it is indifferent what you do, that is, in these situations it is morally indifferent what you do. But in some of these situations one may consider that one's deliberations ought to be guided by some maxi-prescriptive principle and this principle *ex hypothesi* must be non-moral. Thus one may think that in such 'morally indifferent' situations everybody should put self-interest before other considerations. While the maxi-prescriptive principle of self-interest will be non-moral, the further hierarchy-ordering principle should, I contend, be called a 'moral principle'. For this to be tenable we shall have to say that when we talk about a monolithic morality we are talking about the ground level only. On the higher level there will be hierarchy-ordering or order-of-priority judgements to the effect that considerations pertaining to T ought to take precedence over all others, as well as judgements to the effect that amongst non-T considerations those pertaining to S, say, ought to take precedence. The topic of these higher-order judgements is what ought to or what it is good should be overridden by what. Belonging to a higher order is one way for practical judgements, etc., to be important.

In concluding this section one caveat is needed. I have repeatedly talked of 'moral principles' as if every morality logically required them. In fact there are moralities constructed in a no-principle style. For instance, particularist moralities in which moral judgements are not universalized cannot be said to deal in principles, although such a morality may be misrepresented and reconstructed in a principle-style. Again, a morality without prescriptions or proscriptions, a permissive morality, will not need what we should recognize as principles, for it is hardly necessary to have distinct principles to specify what is permissible where everything is permitted. I do not, then, wish to be taken as implying that all moralities are necessarily capable of being expounded in the principle-style. Where I have mentioned principles for the sake of convenience, the word 'beliefs' may be read as easily. What I mean to imply by the use of the word is generality, stability, and shareability, which are not necessarily connoted by either of the terms 'belief' and 'judgement' on their own.

6.6. In the last section I explicated the concept of importance in terms of overriding. In this section I shall illustrate the operation of the concept in terms of justification.

Moral philosophers have often remarked that moral judgements are about ends, not means. It is indeed true, as Aristotle implied (*Nicomachean Ethics*, i, 1094a15–16), that within any morality which distinguishes ends and means, ends are more important. For given an end which is not itself pursued as a means to any further end and given means which are pursued solely for the sake of this end, the means cannot be as important as the end; if they were, they would be pursued for their own sake too. Thus, in general, an end is more important than the means to it. Now when we wish to justify a course of action, we may try to justify it as being a means to an end. We justify what is less important by reference to what is more important. What is thought of as justifying, is *eo ipso* thought of as more important than what is justified. Indeed, those principles which are most important are those to which we ultimately appeal when justifying our decisions and choices. An individual's moral principles are principles he considers most important and appeals to in justification of his practical decisions and choices.

Now ultimate moral principles are either maxi-prescriptive or mini-prescriptive. If a person accepts as ultimate a maxi-prescriptive moral principle and acts on it, he will be likely to appeal to it if required to justify his action. If he fails to act on the principle, no 'justification' of his action will be possible. On the other hand, let us consider the person who accepts as ultimate a mini-prescriptive or commendatory moral judgement, one perhaps which commends to us the saintly or the heroic or at any rate an action which goes beyond what duty requires. Let us suppose that a widow (5.5) accepts the mini-prescriptive moral principle/judgement, 'It is good, morally speaking, for widows not to remarry.' If she abides by her moral belief, she will be able to appeal to it if she is required to justify her conduct. So far the analogy between mini-prescriptive and maxi-prescriptive principles holds. But suppose that the woman values the companionship which a second marriage would bring her and hence decides to remarry despite her belief that it would be better, morally speaking, for her not to do so. If she is required to justify her decision, she may say that it is only through the companionship which marriage brings that a woman can fulfil herself and that a woman ought, so far as is consistent with morality, to fulfil herself. Her ultimate maxi-prescriptive principle, then, in justification of her action is:

(1) Every woman ought to fulfil herself, but only so far as is consistent with morality.

Such a principle as this seems to be non-moral since it explicitly restricts itself to the domain of what is morally permissible and selects from that domain. The 'ought' in (1) would seem, then, to be a non-moral 'ought'. On the other hand, (1) strictly implies a moral judgement, viz., (2)

(2) No woman ought to fulfil herself if her so doing is inconsistent with morality.

Anybody who asserted (1) but denied (2) would appear to be contradicting himself. Hence if we wish to add to the formal requirements of 2.1 that any judgement which strictly implies a moral judgement is itself a moral judgement, we shall be committed to saying that (1) is a moral judgement also. Whether or not we accept this additional formal requirement, (1) certainly functions as a moral judgement when it is used as an ultimately-justifying judgement. We may conclude, then, that ultimately-justifying principles function as moral principles, whether we choose to call them 'moral' or not.

However, not all moral principles are ultimately-justifying ones. Where there are conflicting moral considerations or principles, some of them have to take a subordinate place even if they are capable of being ultimately-justifying in the absence of superior moral considerations or principles. Where there are conflicts in a morality, adjudicating principles are needed to settle an order of priority. Such adjudicating principles are of a higher order and are logically stronger than the first-order principles between which they decide. However, the language of 'overriding' would sound odd here. For the holders of an adjudicating principle to say that it ought to override both the overriding and the overridden lower-order moral judgements would mistakenly suggest that all three were on a par. This implication can be avoided if people make use of the language of justification and say that the adjudication principle is ultimate in the order of justification and hence more important than both the lower-order moral principles between which it decides.

A morality, then, exists at two levels. On the lower level are the values, principles, considerations which the adherents of the morality think to be more important, maxi-prescriptively or mini-prescriptively, than non-moral values, principles, considerations. On the higher level, on the other hand, a morality is concerned with the order of priority of lower-order moral values, principles, considerations, and so on.

The distinction between first-order and second-order moral principles and judgements can be drawn with respect both to social and individual moralities. An individual in making up his mind what considerations he should regard as most important, what should be his 'master-concerns' (Matthew Arnold's expression in *Culture and Anarchy*, Chapter V), can take into account not merely his own attitudes and preferences but also the social morality of his own society, as well as Morality$_A$, where it is distinct from that social morality, and the individual moralities of other members of his society. Of course the individual may have the same order of priorities as the social morality of his society; in that case he will not need an order-of-priority principle giving first position to the social morality. But if this is not the case it will be necessary for him to accept an order-of-priority principle determining which of his values are prior under what circumstances to the social morality of his society. His own morality is the compound of his first-order moral values and his second-order order-of-priority principles, and clearly that compound cannot be one among the many things which he himself weighs in the balance, for all of the latter are competing first-order considerations. His own morality can be put into an order of priority only in the context of somebody else's morality or of the morality of his society, and there would only be occasion for the social morality to place his morality in an order of priority where his morality diverged from it sufficiently.

I conclude that if the position maintained in this chapter is correct, a morality has a peculiar complexity, involving as it does first-order values and second-order principles of priority. It is in this sense that the language of morals is, to adapt Aneurin Bevan's phrase, 'the language of priorities'.

6.7. It might be thought that one way of explaining the connection of the concepts of a morality and of importance would be through the notion of what has been called the 'functional *a priori*'. It is tempting to try and draw an analogy between moral principles on the one hand and high-level principles in the physical sciences on the other. On the Quine-Duhem view high-level principles like the Laws of Thermodynamics are not straightforwardly verifiable or falsifiable but function almost as *a priori* statements. We do not actually refuse to count anything whatever as evidence against them, but we regard them as true *almost* come what may. We would only want to modify them in the last resort when genuinely alternative means for coping with recalcitrant experience had not been found. The same might be said of our moral principles, if they are 'functionally *a priori*' practical principles. Suppose that a moral principle which is used to provide an ultimate justification justifies an action which appears 'intuitively' wrong or unjustifiable. If it is genuinely 'functionally *a priori*' and the analogy with holistic physical science holds, then the agent whose moral principle it is will try all legitimate alternatives before abandoning or modifying his moral principle. For a moral principle, on this view, is a principle you abandon only in the last resort, if, that is, it really is your moral principle. The 'justified' wrong action may after all have certain features which were not taken account of in the original 'justification'. Perhaps haste or bias caused the agent to ignore features which, when given their due weight, lead him to deploy others of his acknowledged moral principles and thus come to a different view of the action in question. However, if his 'intuitive' judgements of wrongness are constantly at variance with justifications furnished by his ultimately-justifying principles, he will be warranted in questioning those principles.

It is tempting, in the light of these considerations and a moderately attractive analogy, to assert that moral principles cannot be abandoned except in the last resort and to suppose that in saying this we have indicated something about the meaning of the expression 'moral principle'. But if the 'cannot' is a logical 'cannot' the assertion is unwarranted. It is perfectly possible for people to abandon or modify their moral principles before the stage of 'last resort'. One is inclined to qualify the assertion and say that such people would not have properly and thoroughly thought out their moral principles in the first place. People who have thoroughly thought out their moral principles will have already considered some of the difficult situations which, if they occurred, might lead them to abandon or modify their moral views. To say this, however, is not to provide another semantic characterization of the concept of a morality; my use of the normative words 'properly' and 'thoroughly' indicates that we are making a normative, not a semantic, claim connecting the concepts of a morality and of importance, a normative claim which belongs rather to the metaphysic than to the logic of morals.

6.8. I have argued that a morality is concerned with what a man or group think most important for the guidance of their lives, with their master-concerns. It sounds vacuous to say that human beings care most about what they think to be most important, that they are most concerned about their master-concerns. Yet to say just this makes it clearer how inadequate would be a view which explained how moral beliefs issued in action solely by invoking those desires which were necessarily implied by the mere holding of moral beliefs. This is why we need to take into consideration that enriched internalism of which I talked in 4.4. Whichever account we may arrive at in the end, the fact that we get 'steamed up' about the things we consider most important must not be made to look surprising.

When an established morality is functioning in a routine way, when its principles, rules, standards, and ideals are explicit, and when the method of their application is clear, there is no need for the adherents of the morality to express strong emotions. It would serve no useful purpose. It is a very different thing when the principles of an established morality are challenged. If anybody asks me for my opinion about academic freedom, I shall doubtless say that I think it very important. An immediate display of intense emotion would not merely be inappropriate, it would be ludicrous. But let my belief in academic freedom be challenged or let my practice of it be threatened, and then the emotional force behind my beliefs will become only too apparent. The role of emotions in morality may be compared to our everyday attitude towards causes. When, say, my car is *not* involved in an accident, nobody asks for the causes, although, of course, there are causes (e.g. my careful driving). On the other hand, when my car *is* involved in an accident, we do look for a cause. After all, 'accidents don't happen, they are caused'. Perhaps, in a similar way, my passionate attachment to academic freedom is only manifested if it is challenged or seriously threatened. But to be so elicited the passionate attachment must in some sense have been there all along, and my original calm and low-key statement that academic freedom was 'very important' could not have been sincerely voiced without the prior existence of that passion. What is essential to a moral belief is a disposition to express appropriate emotions in the appropriate circumstances. What emotions are appropriate and when depends on such circumstances as whether one's ends are realized or not, or whether one's moral beliefs are facilitated by co-operative people and amenable facts or frustrated by perverse people and recalcitrant facts. Depending on these circumstances it will be appropriate and justifiable to feel satisfaction or disappointment, relief or regret, joy or sorrow, gratitude

or resentment, hope or fear. These emotions[1] are conceptually connected with one another, and the several dispositions to feel and express them form a complex which is necessarily associated with every sincerely held moral belief. It is
such complexes which may take the form of a passionate moral
faith or a deep and lasting moral commitment.

An analogy from the theoretical sphere may be helpful. Let
us suppose with Collingwood that all of us have absolute presuppositions. Because they are absolute presuppositions, we
do not go around discussing them, unless we are either lunatics
or philosophers; we take them for granted, and a careless observer might suppose that we did not attach much importance
to these beliefs of which we so rarely spoke. He might even
think that we would not make much ado about abandoning
them, if we were sufficiently pushed. In this he would be
seriously mistaken, for as Collingwood used to say, 'people are
apt to be ticklish in their absolute presuppositions' (R. G.
Collingwood, *An Essay on Metaphysics*, p. 31). Likewise, the
fact that, when coolly stating my commitment to fundamental
moral principles, I do not evince great emotion does not in any
sense imply that these emotions are not there, at any rate dispositionally.

This is even clearer when we consider the utterances and
thoughts of a moral reformer. In the case of these, deep and
powerful emotions do not merely exist dispositionally, are not
merely in the offing behind the actual verbal expression, but
are actually being expressed. For it is typical of the moral reformer or rebel that he wishes to change the world, to persuade
people to aspire to a new ideal or to express indignation at or
disgust with the established order; he seeks to appeal to the
dormant sensitivity of his audience, something he can do most
successfully if he evinces strong emotions himself. In due
course the moralist's converts no doubt settle down to routine
moral thinking once again, when it is no longer necessary to

---

[1] 'Consider the following series, for example: sadness—yearning for the absent
good—hope that it will be ours—the desire to bring it about—the courage to make
the attempt—the decision to act. The one extreme is a feeling, the other an act of
will; and they may seem to be quite remote from one another. But if we attend to
the intermediate members and compare only the adjacent ones, we find the closest
connections and almost imperceptible transitions throughout' (F. Brentano,
Psychology from an Empirical Standpoint, pp. 236-7).

parade the driving passions behind what have now become settled and stable moral beliefs. All this is just what one would expect if, as I have argued, the role of moral principles in our practical thinking bears some resemblance to the role of functionally *a priori* propositions in scientific thought, since the latter are often identical with Collingwood's absolute presuppositions. The expression of strong emotion is appropriate in moral exhortation or in defence of moral principles or in an attack on the well-established moral principles of others, even if their expression in routine moral thinking is nothing more than an irrelevant histrionic display.

It is not just any emotions which are associated with our moral principles and beliefs. In any morality there are specific emotions which have an especially close relationship with the fundamental moral principles or beliefs of that morality. There is after all some resemblance between a man's desire to revenge a particular wrong and a desire for justice. But Titus Andronicus' manner of revenging himself is unlikely to be regarded as justice by anybody but Titus himself, though Bacon says at the beginning of his Essay on Revenge, 'Revenge is a kind of wild justice'. The point which I wish to make about the relation between moral beliefs and concepts, on the one hand, and emotions, on the other, might be made by turning Bacon's dictum round and saying,[2] 'Justice is a kind of tamed revenge'. Many a specific moral concept has an especially intimate relationship with a certain passion or emotion, in that it expresses a socialized version of that passion, which it tames, civilizes, regulates, and directs in a way likely to be acceptable to members of a society, whether they experience the passion in question or not.

Those of our moral principles which we consider to be more important than others are intimately related to those emotions which we judge most important to regulate. Such, for example, are lust and revenge. But the sanctions of a social morality are too diffuse and uncertain to be relied on in the case of emotions which it is thought so important to regulate effectively. Social institutions are necessary in order that the regulation and

[2] Cf. J. S. Mill, *Utilitarianism*, p. 60, where he talks of 'the natural feeling of resentment, moralised by being made coextensive with the demands of social good . . .'

canalization of these emotions should be effective. As was so crisply said by Sir James Fitzjames Stephen:[3] 'The criminal law stands to the passion of revenge in much the same relation as marriage to the sexual appetite'. It is clear, then, that some of the emotions from which moral principles derive their power have an importance commensurate with the principles which regulate them, an importance evidenced by the authority we confer on the appropriate institutions.

The emotions furnish not only the motive force behind moral beliefs, but also the topic with which moralities are concerned. Any morality must have some answer to the question 'What are we to do about the emotions?' The nature of the answer will vary from morality to morality. A morality may after all proscribe emotions altogether, urging the moral novice to pursue freedom from craving. An ascetic may recognize that emotions play an important part in the lives of the rest of us and deplore the fact that this is so. Paradoxically for this very reason his belief that one ought to cultivate freedom from emotion or freedom from at any rate the lower emotions is his most important practical belief. Thus his morality too has emotions as one of its principal topics. Nobody, then, can ignore the actual importance of emotions in our lives. This is common ground between the saint and the voluptuary. Were things different, it would be less tempting to be a voluptuary and much easier to be a saint.

Whether we live up to our moral beliefs or whether we depart from them, some emotion will figure in the explanation of our behaviour. Since one of the principal topics of a morality is the emotions, we may regard a morality as furnishing an answer to a very general question about emotions, namely, 'Which emotions, if any, are to be cultivated and to what extent?' There is logical space here for many diverse answers, ranging from 'None of them to any extent' to 'All of them as much as possible'.

I conclude, then, that if the main argument of this chapter is sound, if a morality is a body of settled normative beliefs which a person or group considers to be most important for

---

[3] Quoted by Oliver Wendell Holmes, *The Common Law*, p. 41, from Stephen's *General View of the Criminal Law of England*, p. 99.

guiding their lives, then the passions and emotions not only furnish the motive power behind moral convictions but are themselves one of the principal topics with which moralities are concerned.

PART II
THE DEMISE OF OBJECTIVITY

Introduction

'At bottom', wrote a contemporary philosopher[1] some years ago, 'we all feel that ethical judgements are rooted in the nature of things'. If this feeling is justified, it is good sense to look for an agreed inter-subjective decision-procedure in morals, a decision-procedure which would be invulnerable to scepticism. The feeling, however, is in my view due to an illicit extension of the concept of objectivity into our thinking about moral thinking. That concept provides an ideal towards which we aspire in our epistemic undertakings, in all our various attempts to acquire knowledge. The concept is at home whenever a cutting edge is needed to distinguish reality from appearance. But if the account I have given in Part I is correct, it is difficult to see how the concept of objectivity could be applied to moral thinking. It would, however, be mistaken to go to the other extreme and suppose with F. P. Ramsey (*The Foundations of Mathematics*, pp. 288-9) that 'the objectivity of good was a thing we had settled and dismissed with the existence of God'.

I shall argue in this Part II that the 'objective'/'subjective' distinction is unilluminating when applied to moral thinking and that the concept of objectivity has suffered a 'demise' in the sense that some of the tasks normally undertaken by the concept have to be handed on to other substitute concepts. It will be the aim of Part III to try to provide one such substitute by extending the concept of rationality.

[1] Professor H. D. Lewis in a letter to *The Times Literary Supplement*, 21 August 1970.

7

Logical Freedom of Dissent

7.1. I shall try to show in this chapter that there are no moral values which either institutional or non-institutional facts compel us to accept on pain of inconsistency. I shall be arguing for what I call a 'logical freedom of dissent'. Perhaps it is misleading to use the word 'freedom' here at all. It is merely the logical possibility of dissent which I am arguing for and I do not wish to imply that such a logical possibility is a good thing, whatever that would mean. The freedom which matters to people is, after all, an empirical freedom and that is circumscribed by psychological, environmental, and other empirical factors beyond our control.

Normative concepts range from the very general to the very specific. In the extreme case of perfectly general normative concepts, it is the user's decision which determines the application of the concepts. That is why they exist at the independent level. There need be no initial resemblance between the objects comprising the extension of one of these concepts other than that certain language-using moral agents have in the light of their purposes and interests decided to apply that concept to these particular things. If they do so uniformly, then it is likely that there is some external cause for their reacting in the same way to these particular things. Any physical resemblance in the extension of such a concept may, then, be discovered afterwards, and it might be a consequence of this that general normative concepts ceased to be completely free-ranging. General normative words are words like 'good', 'nice', 'right', and 'ought', the kind of word which Moore, Ross, and Hare chose as paradigms of moral language. If there are psychological constraints which prevent us from being for or against certain classes of things or actions, then one can understand how it is that normative concepts appear perfectly general when considered abstractly, while yet appearing not to be general when considered in concrete examples. Such perhaps are 'morally good' and 'evil'.

At the other extreme are specific concepts. These plainly do not exist at the independent level, for they are externally controlled, that is, it is the external world which determines to what we apply specific concepts. Thus a fair game is a game in which the probabilities of any particular participant's winning, skill apart, are equal or roughly equal. Thus football, cricket, and chess are, in this sense, fair games. If some advantage is given by, say, batting first or playing White, this minimal advantage can be fairly allocated by using a randomizing procedure such as tossing a coin. Cases of complete external control are rare. Most specific normative concepts are such that, while the central cases are externally controlled, the peripheral cases are to a great extent dependent on the decision of the agent/thinker/speaker. The agent/thinker/speaker has to judge whether the cases he has in mind are *sufficiently* similar to the central cases. These specific concepts are intervening concepts of the third kind (4.3). That specific concepts are at the same level as institutional and role concepts is shown by the way in which explanation of the meaning of role-concepts or institutional concepts might be facilitated by use of specific concepts referring to the virtues and vices. Thus an explanation of what a soldier is might make mention of courage. Again, an explanation of what a loan is might mention honesty.

Some normative concepts share features of both general and specific concepts. Thus the words 'good' and 'bad', although they appear to be general in some contexts, behave like specific concepts in certain contexts. When they so function I shall say that they function as 'semi-specific' or 'mixed' concepts. The differences are illustrated in the following three contrasting dialogues:

Dialogue 1.
   A: Look at this cricket-bat. It is split right down the middle and will no doubt shatter completely if hit by a cricket-ball.
   B: Yes, that is what I call 'a good cricket-bat'.
   A: Oh, don't be absurd. It might be a good cricket-bat for throwing at the umpire, but it is not a good bat for playing cricket with, which is what we normally mean by 'a good cricket-bat'.

Dialogue 2.

A: Look at this man. He always resorts to force and in using it inflicts as much pain as possible, enjoying the spectacle.

B: Yes, that is what I call 'a kind man'.

A: Oh, don't be absurd. If you are serious, you obviously don't know the meaning of the word.

Dialogue 3.

A: Look at this man; he will stop at nothing to satisfy his desires and realize himself; he enjoys making people suffer and kills as effortlessly as he drinks.[1]

B: Yes, that is what I call 'a good man', a morally good man.

A: If you think that, you must be Satan himself.

B: Yes, I am.

It is clear from the second dialogue that we cannot say without self-contradiction, absurdity or a change in the meanings of the key words, 'Honest, be thou my dishonest' or 'Cruel, be thou my kind'. With regard to the third dialogue, people sometimes react by saying that character B is absurd. In so far as this reaction is justified, it shows that 'morally good' and 'evil' are not perfectly general and that they are tied to a particular kind of morality. If this is so, it would account for the fact that immoralists have sometimes appeared to reject the concepts of good and evil, to go 'beyond' them in the manner of Nietzsche.

Now if we suppose that the general normative words are typical, we shall conclude that one can always 'decide for oneself' what criteria to adopt. That this is false is shown by the existence of specific normative words. On the other hand, if we regard specific normative words as typical, we shall fail to recognize either the actual or the possible existence of general normative words, and we shall conclude that 'a man can no more decide for himself what is evidence for rightness and wrongness than he can decide what is evidence for monetary inflation or a tumour on the brain' (Mrs Foot, 'Moral Arguments' in *Virtues and Vices*, p. 99). The logical possibility of general normative words in our language is sufficient to guarantee our logical freedom to decide for

[1] Balzac's characterization of Vautrin.

ourselves. There is, however, always a constant nisus towards the level of social stability. If a number of people concur in exercising their logical freedom to decide for themselves, they will feel the need to form fresh specific concepts or to new-model old ones. If what purports to be a general word of commendation like 'good' is considered to be tainted by the standard morality, new general words like 'great', or 'noble' or 'fine' will have to be adopted. There is a good example of this process in Tolstoy's *Anna Karenina* (Constance Garnett translation, Part I, Chapter XXXIV, pp. 127-8) where Tolstoy describes Vronsky's world thus:

In his Petersburg world all people were divided into utterly opposed classes. One, the lower class, vulgar, stupid, and, above all, ridiculous people, who believe that one husband ought to live with the one wife whom he has lawfully married; that a girl should be innocent, a woman modest, and a man manly, self-controlled, and strong; that one ought to bring up one's children, earn one's bread, and pay one's debts; and various similar absurdities. This was the class of old-fashioned and ridiculous people. But there was another class of people, the real people. To this class they all belonged, and in it the great thing was to be elegant, generous, plucky, gay, to abandon oneself without a blush to every passion, and to laugh at everything else.

Even in translation it is clear that Vronsky's attitudes involve a reversal of the beliefs of 'ridiculous people' and a refashioning of specific concepts to fit his morality.

But even if this logical possibility is not conceded, there is no need to worry. For just as in the case of general normative concepts we have the freedom of reversibility, so in the case of specific normative concepts, intervening concepts, we have the freedom of rejectability. Acceptance and rejection apply to those concepts whose use presupposes the truth of prior judgements or propositions. The use of an intervening concept presupposes a belief that certain antecedents and sequents are related in such-and-such a way (4.3). Somebody who does not have this belief will reject the concept, that is, he will not be ready to apply the concept in all seriousness and sincerity to anything real or imagined. Thus if I think that people should not be praised for doing things which brave people do, I shall not be prepared sincerely and seriously to apply the word 'brave' to anybody. One may perhaps find an example of this in Naga morality. Some of the Nagas would appear to reject our concept of courage or, at any rate, to come very near to doing so. In von Fürer-Haimendorf's words (*Morality and Merit*, pp. 97-8), 'In Naga warfare valour was always tempered by caution. To die in battle was not considered glorious but was a disaster for the spirit of the dead warrior and a disgrace for his family. . . . A Konyak song praises the fleetfootedness of a band of warriors who had set out to raid a neighbouring village, but being detected by vigilant enemy sentinels ran away so speedily that none of their pursuers could catch them.'

Semi-specific or mixed concepts are more complicated. When in non-moral contexts we call something a good so-and-so, we may merely be saying that it is good for somebody to choose that thing for a certain purpose. For most common objects there is a standard purpose which is presupposed in any appraisal of them. Accordingly one may be said to reject such a concept if one is not prepared to adopt or approve of that purpose. Thus I may reject the concept of a good thumbscrew if I am not prepared to approve the purpose which thumbscrewers use thumbscrews for; I do not accept their presupposition. Alternatively, I may retain the words 'good thumbscrew' and change the purpose with reference to which I am prepared to evaluate thumbscrews. To take another example, suppose I decide that what is ordinarily called a good poison is not a good thing. I may then refuse to employ the expression 'good poison', and this is tantamount to rejection. Alternatively, I may use the expression to refer to those poisons which can be safely used in moderation as opposed to those which are fatal even in small quantities. This is very much like reversing the criteria and so I could almost say 'Bad poison, be thou my good poison'. What I would have done would be to create a new concept, that of poisons which are good-for-leaving-around. It may start life as a deviant concept, but it is logically possible for it to grow into a standard one with 'progress in morality'. Thus with regard to semi-specific normative concepts I can cast off the values encapsulated in them in either of two ways. On the one hand, I can refuse to use the conventional concept categorically and only use it either hypothetically or not at all; on the other hand I can re-anchor the concept to a non-conventional end, thus setting up what is in effect a rival concept of my own. The first alternative is a kind of rejection, the second is tantamount to reversal. Mixed normative concepts, therefore, may either be rejected or reversed.

At this point it may be objected, 'There are clearly some normative concepts which cannot be rejected in this way. Nobody would dream of rejecting the concepts of probability, validity, and truth, if any sense could be given to such a procedure. In any case the concept of truth provides us with an even simpler derivation of a normative from a descriptive utterance "p". Take any so-called descriptive utterance "p". Then "p" entails "it is true that p". But "true" is a normative term and therefore "It is true that p" is a normative utterance. This is a derivation-schema having an "infinite" number of instances, and its very unqualified simplicity proves that you cannot reject the concept of truth'.

This argument, however, falls short of a proof. When we call a statement or a belief true, we are certainly commending it. But things could surely be otherwise. Consider the following fanciful but logically possible situation. Imagine a community of know-alls, people who either know or think that they know everything. If anybody in this community says what is the case, his statement is not commended, but pooh-poohed as 'old hat', 'stale buns', 'trite', 'platitudinous', 'hackneyed', 'obvious', 'trivial', or 'truistic'. Such people would reject the commendatory concept of truth, because nobody amongst them needs to learn from his fellows what he already knows, and therefore to hear it is tedious in the extreme. They try to relieve somewhat the tedium of omniscience by telling one another interesting falsehoods or 'untritehoods'. Of course, if they are truly omniscient they will each know what the other is going to say next. But we may suppose that amusement is derived not from the fact that a certain untritehood is told at a certain time but from the manner of its telling, a manner which can only be savoured by those who are willing to listen. Another apparent difficulty is that the critical comments of which I have given examples will themselves, if justified, be trite. It is, of course, to be admitted that, if anybody in this community says what is the case by uttering a sentence 'q', then 'q' will be trite and 'q is trite' will be trite. However,

although 'q' and 'q is trite' mutually entail one another, saying
'q is trite' to somebody who has said 'q' does have a point,
namely, that of indicating to the first speaker that he should
not continue saying what is the case. Members of this exotic
community may make an exception of meta-linguistic criticisms of tritehood, which they can justify by referring to the
first speaker's infringement of the general ban on saying what
is the case. It would appear, then, that the community of
know-alls rejects the commendatory concept of truth.

But the possibility of rejecting the commendatory concept
of truth need not cause us undue worry. It is only concepts
of truth and tritehood which can be rejected. That which is
the case is as sacrosanct as ever, for 'facts', as Carlyle says,
'are stubborn things'. The expression 'that which is the case',
unlike 'true', is not a normative expression. We have in our
actual language two expressions, one descriptive and the other
normative, which appear on the surface to be logically equivalent. In some of its uses, indeed, the commendatory force of
the word 'true' is minimal and we use it almost as a perfect
synonym of 'the case'. I should remark that the same relation
holds between 'exists' and 'is real' as holds between 'is the
case' and 'is true'. I have shown, then, that it is possible to
reject the commendatory concept of truth, and the same holds
for other concepts of logical appraisal logically connected with
truth, for example, the concept of validity. If even these concepts are rejectable, this strengthens my thesis that all specific
normative concepts are rejectable.

My argument may now be stated as follows:

1. All normative concepts are either general or specific or
   mixed.
2. If they are general, they are reversible.
3. If they are specific, they are rejectable.
4. If they are mixed, each mixed concept is either reversible
   or rejectable.
∴ 5. All normative concepts are either reversible or rejectable.

7.2. I now want to show that the thesis argued for in the first
section of this chapter enables one to restate the anti-naturalist
argument. General normative concepts are acquired via the

speech acts they are used to perform. The speech acts, commendation, recommendation, etc., are inter-subjectively observable and this is why there is no mystery about the acquisition of general concepts. A general-concept judgement (a judgement in which a general concept is predicated of a person or action) can neither be verified nor falsified by an ostensibly brute-factual statement or external normative judgement. This is the cash value of the reversibility of general concepts. No ostensibly brute-factual statement entails a general-concept statement.

By contrast a specific concept is acquired in a complex fashion. Part of the process of acquiring it is via its force and sphere of application. Its force, the speech act to be associated with it, is not always as clear as in the case of general concepts. The sphere or range of application of a specific concept is, of course, always restricted, although there is often some fuzziness about the boundaries of its sphere of application. Thus one can acquire the concept of generosity in part by learning its force, which is favourably appraisive, and its sphere of application, which is concerned with the giving of something valued by the giver. One who has acquired the concept in this way would only have learnt part of what is needful. He would not have learnt how much of value to the giver, if anything, was to be given away. For all the formal part of the lesson is concerned, it might be a good thing never to part with anything one values, on the grounds that it is only a 'fool and his money' which are 'easily parted'.

The remainder of the process of acquiring a specific concept takes place through its antecedents or antecedent determinants (4.3). Thus I could teach somebody what a fair game was through its antecedents or pre-conditions. We call a game 'fair' if and only if the probability, skill apart, of any player's winning is equal. But plainly only a few specific concepts are of this kind. There is no determinate fraction of what a man values such that the giving away of less qualifies as meanness and the giving away of more qualifies as prodigality. The most we are justified in saying of the antecedent determinants of generosity is that something 'sizeable' must be given, where what is sizeable is determined relative to the giver and the occasion. One could therefore rebut the attribution of generosity to a man who had never or seldom given anybody anything which he valued or anything which he had valued very much. This example differs from the example of fairness as applied to games in that the boundaries between 'seldom' and 'often' and between 'valuing a little' and 'valuing a lot' are vague and susceptible to fluctuations, and it is only natural that these fluctuations will often be dependent on who does the valuing. A miser may think of himself as 'often' giving away something he values if he does it, say, twice a year. One thing, however, is clear, that we are in no position to discriminate between, say, meanness, generosity, and prodigality prior to making the appraisals encapsulated in these words. Our appraisal is not something we superimpose on already discriminated features of the world, like spreading butter on toast. It is not, then, open to us to learn the meaning of the word 'generous' from the antecedent determinants solely, as if we could prise the word 'generous' apart from its favourably normative force and make up our minds on some later occasion whether or not we are to praise people for doing what generous people do. Of course we could observe which people and which actions the majority praise for being generous and then make up our minds whether we wish to concur with the majority. In this case our initial discriminations would not be innocent of any normative stance; they would already be 'tainted', as it were, by the attitudes of the majority and parasitic upon them. That many of our specific concepts resemble 'generous' in that they cannot be neatly divided into 'normative' and 'descriptive' constituents is not an argument in favour of ethical naturalism; indeed it points the other way. The applicability of a specific concept of this unsplittable kind cannot follow from the applicability of an ostensibly non-normative part of it. For such parts are *ex hypothesi* not separably identifiable. So anti-naturalism cannot be rebutted by arguments from the existence of un-splittable specific concepts.

Let us now consider those specific concepts which are splittable. The antecedent determinants of such concepts constitute a cognitive kernel. Thus the cognitive kernel of the concept of adultery is 'sexual intercourse of two human beings of different sex, at least one of whom is married to a living third person'. To apply the concept to people while denying the applicability of the cognitive kernel would be almost a contradiction. The reason why it would not be quite a contradiction lies in the elasticity and open texture of intervening concepts. It is open to somebody who uses the standard language of morals to maintain that artificial insemination by donor (AID) constituted adultery or was tantamount to adultery, despite the absence of sexual intercourse. I do not myself consider such a move a desirable extension of the concept of adultery, but in so saying I am taking up a moral position.

The second kind of near-contradiction consists in asserting the applicability of the antecedent determinants and denying the applicability of the intervening concept. The existence of a contradiction here is conditional on the person concerned accepting the intervening concept in question. This is clear from Mrs Foot's discussion of the concept of rudeness in 'Moral Arguments'. So even if the antecedents specified were central and typical cases, there is no logical compulsion to assert the applicability of the intervening concept, for there is no logical compulsion on anybody to accept an intervening concept.

It is true that sometimes those who have rejected specific intervening concepts have only seemed to contradict themselves. When Proudhon said ('Qu'est-ce que la propriété?', *Œuvres complètes*, Vol. IV, pp. 131 ff.), 'La propriété, c'est le vol', this certainly seemed like a contradiction. For the use of the concept of theft presupposes acceptance of the concept of property (private property), just as the use of the concept of adultery presupposes the acceptance of the institution of marriage. A thinker who, like Proudhon, wishes to reject the institution of private property, is going to reason something like this: 'We ought not to predicate "mine" and "thine" of things. To appropriate is to take what does not belong to us. Now those who accept the institution of private property call this "theft". So a dramatic way of rejecting the institution of private property is to say that property is theft. The institution of private property bears the same relation to what ought to be as theft does to private property. All appropriation is misappropriation. Private property ought to be regarded as theft, it is an illicit taking away of what ought to be public property.' The rejection is thus given a rationale amid the appearance of paradox or even contradiction.

The anti-naturalist thesis may now be restated. General-concept moral judgements and specific-concept moral judgements are those in which respectively general and specific moral concepts are predicated of a person or action. No ostensibly brute-factual statement or external moral judgement entails a general-concept moral judgement or a specific-concept moral judgement. Or, to put it in another way, no ostensibly brute-factual statement or external moral judgement is logically incompatible with the reversal of a general moral concept or the rejection of a specific moral concept.

I have argued, then, that whatever the ostensibly brute facts or the institutional facts may be, it is always logically possible to reject or reverse a moral concept without inconsistency. In so arguing I have not been concerned to advocate rejection or reversal, to make an 'Umwertung aller Werte' (Friedrich Nietzsche, *Werke*, Zweiter Band, p. 941). I have stated a purely conceptual thesis from which correct reasoning can derive no normative conclusions. The extent to which it is psychologically or epistemologically possible for us to abandon a given value is another matter. Only a vast epistemological upheaval would cause us to abandon the commendatory concept of truth. The same goes for the concept of probability. It is because we should be so loath to abandon them that these concepts appear to us as hardly being normative at all. They are 'entrenched concepts'. If there were some values which either ostensibly brute facts or institutional facts compelled us on pain of inconsistency to adhere to, we could make some sense of the subjective/objective distinction as applied to values. But since there are none such, this unilluminating distinction is best abandoned.

7.3. One caveat is necessary before I conclude this chapter. It might be thought that in thus restating anti-naturalism I am espousing a kind of liberal individualism. It might seem that I am not merely saying that certain logico-linguistic manœuvres are logically possible but that certain logical freedoms are desirable. Indeed when the word 'freedoms' is thus introduced, it seems plausible to suppose that some kind of value is being discussed and defended. But if one is going to use the word 'freedom' at all, it is as well to make clear that a logical freedom is such that it is *logically* impossible to deprive anybody of it, and in this respect a logical freedom is totally unlike any other. It does not make sense to take sides, as it were, for or against this freedom, and thus it will not do to misrepresent my position as covertly asserting or defending a 'liberal' ideal of freedom of moral thought.

Nevertheless, even though nobody logically can deprive us of this logical freedom, the moral languages of different societies may make it more or less difficult, as the case may be, to avoid participating in the moral values of the society. If a society's language of morals were to contain only specific moral concepts and no general ones, individuals would lack the logico-linguistic wherewithal to express their dissent. If they wished to reject the specific concepts of the society they would have to frame general moral concepts for themselves or fashion fresh specific ones; as a consequence they might find it difficult to make their heterodox views intelligible either to themselves or to others. Nothing that I have hitherto said commits me in any way to saying that a society without general moral concepts would have an inferior language of morals to a society whose language contained them. Indeed it is arguable that *if* a morality was morally good enough, it would be better if its language of morals contained exclusively specific concepts. The analysis I have given in this chapter, however, commits me neither one way nor the other.

One reason why it has been felt that an anti-naturalist position commits one morally is that formally similar positions to those of the naturalist and the anti-naturalist have been debated by thinkers in the Existentialist mode. There is a standing temptation to dramatize philosophical positions, to speculate about the psychological state of somebody who seriously believed that he was only a bundle of sense-data, that he had no knowledge of other minds, that he could infer nothing about the future from his past observations, or that values were completely independent of facts. To act in one's everyday life as if one believed all these would lead to existential nausea, anxiety, and despair. There, but for backgammon, or its equivalent, goes Hume or go I. The Existentialist dramatization of philosophical predicaments is enlightening and amusing, and this is why Existentialist thought is best expounded in novels or plays. But it is, I submit, a mistake to translate the heightened dramatized account of a philosophical predicament back into the pedestrian prose of a philosophical treatise.

Thus the logical possibilities and impossibilities which I have emphasized in restating the anti-naturalist thesis are not logically associated with substantive moral positions. They do not and cannot entail that freedom is a good thing or that reason ought to have no place in moral thinking. Indeed in Part III of this book I shall try to show that reason can play a role in our thought about morals.

8

No Cutting Edge

8.1. It is the purpose of this chapter to show that in any morality unbacked or independent moral judgements cannot be avoided. If I am right, the argument of this chapter reinforces that of Chapter 7 and supports the view that there is no morality which we can be logically forced to accept. I shall argue that there is no equivalent of the concept of objectivity to provide a cutting edge by means of which the moralist can sharply discriminate between what he should accept and what he reject.

There are two ways in which a social morality can be given the appearance of objectivity, first, if there is a common social sanction, and second, if there is a common criterion. In this section I shall consider whether and to what extent the provision of a common social sanction for a morality gives it objectivity in any worthwhile sense and I shall try to show that no social morality can exclude the possibility of deviance.

Let us imagine a society in which reasonably perspicuous rules of conduct are handed down from generation to generation without perceptible change. Perhaps the society of the Icelandic[1] sagas before Christianity began to change it was of this kind. I wish to argue that only a society of robots could conform to the norms of such a society without divergencies. Real human beings would inevitably diverge. There is a perpetual possibility of deviance even within the most static and rigid morality imaginable.

First, no human society can ever provide a set of rules of conduct which can cover all possible cases. This is due both to the nature of human action and to the nature of description.

[1] See A. MacIntyre, *Against the Self-Images of the Age*, p. 143. In point of fact primitive moralities are not as rigid as thinkers like MacIntyre imply. C. von Fürer-Haimendorf writes of the Reddis of Andhra Pradesh, primitive slash-and-burn cultivators (*Morality and Merit*, pp. 40-1) that their community is able 'to modify rules to suit individual cases and to condone conduct which, strictly speaking, is contrary to the law.'

Given any classificatory scheme designed to cover human action, it is always possible to perform a new action and to find a new description for it not available in the established scheme. Just as there is no logical limit to the number of sentences which can be constructed in a language, so there is no limit to the number of differently described actions. When I learn to catch a ball, say, I have learnt how to perform an indefinitely large number of actions, indeed an indefinitely large number of kinds of action. No tidy set of rules, then, can circumscribe the infinite variety of human action. Any. actual set will be essentially incomplete and the members of any society who have to conform to such a tidy set of rules will not be able without making use of their 'private stock of reason' to reach perfect certainty and agreement on how to conduct themselves in new situations.

Second, just because no finite set of rules can cater in advance for all possible situations, it is possible for situations to arise in which there is *de facto* logical conflict between the rules. There is an obvious danger of this in any set which contains a rule allowing the creation of specific obligations. Thus if one rule forbids the killing of relatives and another rule enjoins the performance of promises, the man who has promised to kill somebody who turns out to be a relative is in a situation where he knows what the rules require but does not know what to do. In order for him to resolve the conflict, he must either rely on his own 'private stock of reason' or on the judgement of another, say, a uniquely authoritative and universally accepted interpreter of the rules and their spirit. Even in this last case, where some other individual decides for him how he should act, it is contingent upon the particular person chosen how the conflict is resolved. If the interpreter changed from time to time, then the supposedly static morality could slowly, but nevertheless, suffer change. Such change notoriously takes place in carefully thought out legal systems. *A fortiori*, the diffusely sanctioned rules of morality must be even more prone to such change. Either there is some settled arbitration-procedure in the event of conflict or there is not. If there is not, the individual has no alternative but to fall back on his own judgement. But even if there is some arbitration-procedure, the arbitrators themselves have to make use of their own judgement in applying it.

Third, divergence of interpretation is made likely because the morality of the society is diachronic. Any morality has to be transmitted from one generation to another, in whatever way that transmission may take place. The language of social description employed in the exposition of laws admits of ambiguities and vagueness, and these same ills beset that language when it is used to transmit a morality by means of precept. Indeed a permanent possibility of divergence may exist unrecognized in a concept which encapsulates a confusion. Consider how in moralities of honour the concepts of status and virtue may become so confused that only a rebel against tradition can disentangle them. In the words of Julian Pitt-Rivers '. . . no man of honour ever admits that his honour= precedence is not synonymous with his honour=virtue. To do so would be to admit himself dishonoured. For him there is only one concept, his honour' (*Honour and Shame: The Values of Mediterranean Society*, p. 37). Even more liable to divergence of interpretation is transmission of a morality by example. It is, of course, true that example can be more forceful and effective than bare precepts. But the point of example or of a model is not writ large on it; it may be unclear what aspects of the model or example are intended to be imitated, how, for example, the model is meant to be glossed. Any morality, then, is prone to divergent interpretation in its transmission.

A fourth reason for divergent interpretation lies in the psychological nature of human beings. Human beings are not mass-produced in accordance with a blueprint. They differ from one another in temperament, physique, intelligence, age, and environment. From these differences flow different interests and desires and these provide diverse motives for interpreting a social morality differently wherever there is latitude for divergent interpretation. Where the individual has the right to judge, his own desires will lead him to prefer that interpretation of the social morality which he sees as more welcome to himself.

Fifth, one must assume that the rules of this static morality prescribe what some members of the society would otherwise be unwilling to perform and proscribe other things which they would otherwise be prone to do. Since this is so, the recalcitrant desires of members of the society furnish a standing motive force for divergent interpretation.

It is clear from these five reasons why a perfectly static and rigid morality is impossible for a human society. To construct a society in which divergent interpretation was impossible we should have to stipulate either that its members were Holy Wills or, at any rate, had perfect self-control, or that they were programmed in accordance with the rules, or that the rules never led to conflicts or contradictions, or that the range of possible action was exhaustively determined by the rules. If creatures satisfying these stipulations are imaginable, they approximate to robots. One thing is clear: they would differ from human beings through lack of any spontaneity or any power to introduce novelty. Further, the rules of their morality would not be genuine rules so much as social-scientific laws. (For them deontic logic would 'collapse' into ordinary modal logic.) The absurdity of this construction justifies me in maintaining that no social morality can be so static and rigid as to rule out the possibility of deviance. In a conformist social morality the moralities of individuals, what I shall call their 'idio-moralities', faithfully reflect with minimum differences the social morality of the society. Their relation to the social morality resembles the relation of idiolects to the language of a society. Perfect uniformity is unlikely for the five reasons I have mentioned. As Durkheim puts it: 'Chaque individu, en effet, chaque conscience morale exprime la morale commune à sa façon; chaque individu la comprend, la voit sous un angle différent; aucune conscience n'est peut-être entièrement adéquate à la morale de son temps et on pourrait dire qu'à certains égards il n'y a pas une conscience morale qui ne soit immorale par certains côtés' (*Sociologie et philosophie*, pp. 44-5).

Let us next consider the case where the majority in the society, whatever their covert differences, manifest an overt uniformity in their interpretation of traditional rules and standards. In such a case the deviant individual, when made conscious of his deviance, may react by abandoning his divergent interpretation and adopting an interpretation more acceptable to the rest of his society. But what reason can he have for doing this? Of course, it might be part of the social morality that one should always accept the majority interpre-

tation. But this rule does not admit of an unambiguous interpretation either. For it is unclear whether by 'majority' is
meant a majority of the society at the present time or, say,
over the whole of its past history. Even the majority at the
present time is a fluctuating number. The plague might wipe
out the majority overnight. Moreover, the views of men are
liable to change. Perhaps, however, the situation is simpler.
The social morality may after all designate some one person
or body as a uniquely authoritative interpreter of rules and
traditions. A Hobbesian sovereign would fill the bill. Such a
device would not once and for all exclude the possibility of
deviance, but it would at any rate make it less likely. Plainly,
whenever anybody went so far as to ask himself 'Ought we
to regard this person as a uniquely authoritative interpreter?'
the first step towards deviance would have been taken.

Alternatively, there may be no uniformity in interpretation
of the rules, either overt or covert, and therefore the man
who is conscious of a divergence of interpretations will have
no standard external to himself for calling some one interpretation 'correct' as opposed to the others. He will have no
alternative to thinking his own interpretation 'correct' and
those which differ from his 'incorrect'. He will therefore
regard those who differ from him as mistaken in their thought
and in any conduct which ensues upon their mistaken thought.
In saying that their conduct was wrong, he would not be
making a prediction that their behaviour would be followed
by a socially diffuse sanction. That would be plainly false,
since he knows that he is in a minority of one and is incapable
of originating a sanction. He has not the temerity to say that his
idio-morality, the social morality-of-his-society-as-interpreted-
by-him, *is* the social morality of his society. For the social
morality of his society admits of other interpretations than
that which he happens to give it, interpretations of which
the social morality-as-interpreted-by-him does not admit.
Although he is debarred from saying that his idio-morality is
identical with the social morality of his society, he is not
debarred from saying that his idio-morality ought to be identical with the social morality of the society. But if he uses the
word 'ought' here in this way, he is plainly not saying that
the rules of his society require that his idio-morality should

be the social morality of the society, since the rules do not assign either to him or to his idio-morality any special or privileged status. The rules are after all part and parcel of the social morality. It may be objected (cf. A. MacIntyre, *Against the Self-Images of the Age*, pp. 143-5) that our diverger cannot or even ought not to use the word 'ought', since he has only learnt the use of that word within a context where it is virtually synonymous with 'being required by the rules'. However, even if on grounds such as these we deny our diverger the liberty of using the word 'ought' in an independent fashion, we cannot deny him the use of imperative or optative forms of language. Presumably he may still say 'Would that everybody interpreted the rules as I do!' or even 'Everybody is to interpret the rules as I do'. And it would surely be a natural extension of the meaning of his restricted 'ought' if he made use of the word 'ought' to express his position. If indeed he talks in this way he has already become deviant. While he professes to be talking about and applying the social morality of his society, he is in reality talking about and applying a morality of his own.

A deviant or diverger of this character is, of course, only possible where there is no uniquely authoritative and universally accepted interpreter of the rules, no Hobbesian sovereign on the moral plane. In the absence of such a uniquely authoritative interpreter our deviant will maintain that he himself and perhaps others of his society too ought to conform to the social morality-as-interpreted-by-him. Here he differs from others in his society who think that everybody in the society ought to conform to the social morality but under some different interpretation from his. My attempt to show how our deviant differs from the others has thus revealed a divergence between the deviant's unarticulated premisses and those of the others. If we consider our original example of a perfectly static and rigid morality where no deviance was present, the unarticulated premiss, viz., 'One ought to obey the rules', had the same effect for everybody and because of this its presence was unverifiable.

I conclude, then, that a morality's having a social backing in the form of a common sanction does not give it objectivity in any worthwhile sense. A social morality, however rigid and static it may be, cannot unequivocally determine its own interpretation and thus cannot distinguish with any sharpness between what it appears to the diverger to require and what it really does require. But unless it can do just that, it lacks a cutting edge.

8.2. The second kind of backing which a morality may have is in the form of common criteria. It has sometimes been supposed that the application of criteria is an essential part of the making of moral judgements. On this view, objectivity is provided not by a common sanction but by a common criterion. A common criterion would enable one to reach a 'visible and explicit issue', if not to settle moral questions once and for all. It was this approach which led moral philosophers in the nineteenth century to talk of a 'science of ethics'.

The idea was that if you could identify goodness or rightness as an observable or even a measurable characteristic, morality could be founded on observation and perhaps even on calculation. Hence if 'better', for example, literally meant 'later in the course of evolution', all moral comparisons would depend on the prior establishment of simple biological facts about evolutionary priority. It was views such as these that Moore was attacking in *Principia Ethica* under the name of 'naturalism'. The big advantage of a naturalist view was that it allowed a place both for reason and for observation in ethics; hence the name 'science of ethics'. It was a matter of observation whether one kind of behaviour preceded another in the course of evolution. It was a matter of reasoning that if two kinds of behaviour fell into the same evolutionary period, the same moral epithet would apply to them. If 'good' means 'post-nuclear', and both type of behaviour T_1 and type of behaviour T_2 are post-nuclear, then both alike must be 'good'. This is the cash value of saying that the term 'good' is universalizable. To say that T_1, as so defined, was good, while T_2 was bad, would be to apply the definition inconsistently, that is, given this definition of 'good', anybody who maintained both that T_1 was good and that T_2 was bad would be involved in a contradiction. Again, to take the classical example, let us suppose that Cicero in speaking of Verres' government of Sicilia says

'Verres is a villain', while admitting in private letters that his friend Marcus Brutus in his governorship of Cilicia has done similar things, taken money illegally, imprisoned provincials without trial, executed Roman citizens, and so on. If fully believing all that he has spoken and written Cicero says in all sincerity 'Brutus is an honourable man, he is not a villain like Verres', then he is applying the criteria of villainy inconsistently. Universalizability is, then, a kind of consistency.

It would be a consequence of the wholesale rejection of naturalism that there would be no place for this kind of consistency and inconsistency in moral thinking. But moral philosophers saw that if they were to reserve a place for reason in morals this kind of consistency and inconsistency had to be retained. While they granted that the whole meaning of moral epithets could not be given in terms of non-moral expressions referring to observable properties, they could maintain that we did have 'criteria for the application' of moral terms and this was tantamount to a 'descriptive meaning'. In this way one could have one's naturalistic cake and eat it.

Whether the term 'descriptive meaning' is altogether a happy one might be questioned. But first, it is fairly clear that there is a class of words for which we have criteria of application. These we may call 'supervenient' words. Thus we have criteria for determining whether a man is physically ill, and if these are applicable in one case, consistency demands that we should apply them in another. If criteria were not consistently applied by doctors, we should not call medicine a 'science'. Second, I suggest that all moral epithets are supervenient. If a man deliberately and in all seriousness says what he knows to be false, then we call him 'a liar', and we should be applying the word 'liar' inconsistently if we called one man who did this 'a liar' and another 'not a liar' out of sheer caprice. True, 'liar' is a term of condemnation while 'saying deliberately and in all seriousness what one knows to be false' is not in itself a condemnatory expression. We have not, then, given the whole meaning of the word 'liar' by means of this expression and we should have committed an error worthy of being labelled 'naturalistic' if we thought that we had.

With regard to general words of commendation or condemnation like 'good' in their non-moral uses we plainly have criteria for their application varying with the context. The criteria for calling a cricket-bat 'good' are different from those for calling an apple 'good'. But within each context there is a requirement of consistency. If I call one apple with at least three small bruises 'bad', then I must in all consistency apply the same epithet to any other apple which has the same number of bruises of roughly the same size.

It may be thought that moral uses of the words 'good' and 'bad' and other general words of commendation or condemnation are different. For, it may be said, people differ as to whom to regard as good or bad according to their moral convictions, and therefore, unlike the case of 'good' as applied to cricket-bats or apples, there are no stable criteria for the application of the term. Hitler's idea of what constituted a good man was presumably different from your idea or mine. This objection still would not show that moral uses of the word 'good' were not subject to a requirement of consistency. If for Hitler a good man was one who put the interests of the racially superior people first (whatever his own race might be), then if he thought one such person 'good' and worthy of becoming an honorary Aryan, he would in all consistency be bound to regard another such as likewise good. The consistency of this kind of universalizability is thus relative, and even a subjectivist in morals can admit its importance.

We have seen that whether any terms are universalizable in this way or not depends on whether they have criteria for their application. If, then, there are some moral terms which have no criteria for their application on some occasions of their use, these terms are not universalizable in this sense on those occasions, and so the moral judgements in which they occur could not be called 'universalizable' either. This is what we find to be the case. Even if general terms of moral appraisal are usually employed in such a way that there are criteria for their application in those contexts, yet there must be other contexts in which those criteria are laid down. The 'judgements' in which criteria are laid down are not criterion-applying judgements but rather criterion-positing like, for example, 'The criterion of whether something is right or not is whether it promotes the greatest happiness of the greatest number'. But this judgement is itself a moral judgement; it involves not merely mentioning the word 'right' but using it to commend whatever promotes the greatest happiness. This moral judgement lays down criteria which are applied in other moral judgements and hence does not itself apply any, for it can hardly lay down and apply these same criteria at one and the same time. Therefore such a fundamental moral judgement either applies other criteria or applies none at all. But if it is a *fundamental* moral judgement, there can be no prior criteria which it applies. Therefore there are no criteria at all for the application of the word 'right' in this example. What applies to the word 'right' in this context applies to other general words of moral appraisal when they occur in fundamental moral judgements. Thus there are some moral judgements, namely fundamental ones, which are not universalizable in this sense, and are backed by no prior common criterion.

The kind of universalizability I have been considering is necessarily bound up with the giving of reasons and the application of criteria. In this sense of the term, as Hare puts it (*Freedom and Reason*, p. 5), 'to universalize is to give the reason'. I shall call this kind of universalizability 'criterion-universalizability'. Although not all moral judgements are criterion-universalizable, it is, as we shall see in 13.1, a merit in a morality to have *some* criterion-universalizable judgements; to lack them entirely is a shortcoming which prevents a morality from being rationally discussed and effectively transmitted. However, there is another kind of universalizability which has been discussed in recent moral philosophy. For sometimes when philosophers have talked about universalizability they have not intended to make any mention of criteria. Consider a fundamental moral judgement, say, that promoting happiness is a right-making characteristic. Since this is a fundamental moral judgement, there are, as I have argued, no ulterior criteria for applying the expression 'right-making', and hence this fundamental moral judgement is not criterion-universalizable. Nevertheless it is true to say that any characteristic resembling the promoting of happiness in all morally relevant respects would also be right-making. Maybe there is no characteristic exactly like the promoting of happiness in all morally relevant respects. But it is logically possible for there to be such a characteristic and, if there were, it also would be a right-making characteristic. One suspects, however, that this kind of universalizability is really vacuous; after all, it is fundamental moral judgements which determine just what features of actions are morally relevant. This is indeed borne out by Hare's explanation of universalizability where he explains that the word 'red' is universalizable (ibid. p. 11). 'If a person says that a thing is red, he is committed to the view that anything which was like it in the relevant respects would likewise be red. The relevant respects are those which, he thought, entitled him to call the first thing red; in this particular case, they amount to one respect only: its red colour.' This kind of universalizability is, as Hare appears to see, trivial. But the fact that moral words are trivially-universalizable is important, in so far as it serves to distinguish them from mere expressions of feeling or emotion. When I say 'Damn!', 'Oh!', or 'Ugh!', what I say does not admit of logical appraisal for consistency or inconsistency, while when I use words like 'good' or 'right' or 'ought' what I say does admit of such logical appraisal. It is because moral judgements are used in such a way that they are trivially-universalizable that they exhibit the same logical behaviour as assertions and can be assessed for consistency in a way that expletives and exclamations cannot. Whether we are justified in using them in this way I shall examine in the next chapter. My present argument depends merely on my contention that, since fundamental moral judgements lack criterion-universalizability, a criterion-backed morality must contain some moral judgements which are not themselves criterion-backed.

I conclude that the existence of criterion-backed moral judgements requires the existence of other moral judgements, namely, fundamental ones, which are not themselves criterion-backed. If objectivity is constituted by being criterion-backed, this would mean that so-called objective moral judgements would be derivable from moral judgements which plainly did not possess that kind of objectivity. The objectivity of derived moral judgements would thus be a sham, since apparently *any* criterion would suffice to warrant talk of 'objective' moral judgements. Common or shared criteria cannot, then, provide the kind of objectivity which is required. In any case, even if common criteria ensured that all the moral judgements of a morality were alike criterion-backed, there would still arise the problem of non-uniqueness. For a common criterion could not of itself provide an independent decision-procedure for assessing its own credentials and those of the morality which it grounded, as opposed to those of possible competitors.

We saw in 8.1 that in a social sanction-backed morality the existence of socially unbacked moral judgements was presupposed. The arguments of both sections, then, entitle us to conclude that, whatever kind of morality we are concerned with, independent or unbacked moral judgements are inescapable and are a necessary ingredient in any morality. Neither a common sanction nor a common criterion can yield the desired objectivity or an equally effective substitute. There is nothing, then, in any conceivable morality which can provide us with an equivalent of the cutting edge of objectivity.

9

Morals and Objectivity

9.1. I have tried to show that any morality must contain independent moral judgements which themselves have no backing and are therefore fundamental relative to the morality in question. A social-sanction morality requires a basic belief that certain kinds of conduct ought or deserve to have the backing of a common sanction (8.1). A common-criterion morality requires basic beliefs in fundamental standard-setting moral judgements which are not themselves justified by applying that common criterion (8.2).

It is the logical status of fundamental moral judgements which must be a problem for any normativist, prescriptivist, or emotivist account of moral thinking and language. The difficulty is this. Fundamental moral judgements have the same impersonal form, the form of an assertion, as those moral judgements for which they provide backing or support, and they appear to claim assent in the same way as these do. It is not open to us to justify that form by ascribing to them 'referential' or 'descriptive' meaning, for this kind of meaning requires the existence of prior standard-setting moral judgements, and clearly in the case of fundamental moral judgements no such explanation can be forthcoming. Since fundamental moral judgements are themselves unbacked backers, their impersonal form makes them appear to sail under false colours, by means of which they try to conceal the mere expression of desire. If the procedure of Part I in investigating the logical relationships and status of moral judgements is to be retrospectively justified, I need to show that, despite the inapplicability of the concepts of objectivity and truth to them, fundamental moral judgements are more than mere expressions of desire, that they should be classified with assertions and that they should be credited with the same sort of logical relations as those in which assertions stand to one another.

The difficulties I have mentioned might perhaps be set aside if moral judgements could be grounded outside the individual, even outside society. This could be done if it were shown that moral judgements committed their users to accepting the existence of objective moral properties which moral predicates designate. If this could be shown, it might be sensible to take the Mackie line (J. L. Mackie, *Ethics*) and say that all such judgements are erroneous since there are no such properties. Moral language, however, is a common possession of both objectivists and anti-objectivists and it is implausible to suggest that anti-objectivists have always misused moral language.

Now if objectivist analyses of moral judgements are to be rejected, we need an explanation of why analyses of this type have been so attractive. There are two principal features of moral language responsible for their being so. The first of these is the impersonal form of moral judgements; the second is the double direction of fit possessed by the ordinary run of moral judgements. With regard to the former, the impersonal form of a class of judgements does not of itself imply the existence of objective correlates of our vocabulary. This is recognized by some of the staunchest moral objectivists, who have been disinclined to take an objectivist line about niceness or even beauty, although niceness and beauty manifest some of the same logical behaviour as moral concepts. Thus Kant, for one, in *The Critique of Judgement* (Part I, Book I, § 7, 212-13) says of a man who calls something beautiful that he 'demands the same delight from others. He judges not merely for himself, but for all men, and then speaks of beauty as if it were a property of things'.

The second principal reason why thinkers have postulated an objective moral world to be correlated with our moral concepts is that many or most of our moral judgements have a descriptive as well as a normative direction of fit. Hence the similarity of moral judgements to descriptive judgements has been more conspicuous than their dissimilarity. The development of a particular language of morals with distinctive specific concepts leads to the formation of strong connections between the antecedents and the applications of these specific concepts. At this level, the level which I have called tied, it is typical for terms to have both directions of fit at once. In so far as it

is at this level that rules, standards, and ideals are both promul-
gated and applied, there is inherent in the social structure a
'moral reality' with which our judgements have to correspond
if they are going to be regarded as 'correct'. In our ordinary
use of intervening concepts the primary onus of match is from
the words to the social world. Thus when I apply typical dispositional epithets like 'kind' to somebody, the correctness
of what I say depends on the way he tends to conduct himself. Indeed all dispositional concepts must have a descriptive
direction of fit, for dispositional words are true of somebody
in virtue of what he does. This applies no less to the word
'good' than it does to specific words like 'kind'. The word
'good' in its attributive role is contrasted with the word 'good'
in its mini-prescriptive operator role. Thus it is perfectly
possible for the attributive *agathos* in Homer to mean, as
MacIntyre says it does, 'kingly, courageous and clever' (*A
Short History of Ethics*, p. 6), while at the same time it is
used as a mini-prescriptive operator (meaning '. . . is a good
thing') in the Odysseus speech mentioned in 5.2. If typical
attributive uses of moral terms face primarily in the descriptive direction of fit, it is tempting and natural to construe all
moral language as being similar. However, as we have seen,
the language of fundamental moral judgements is different,
for in it we lay down rules, set standards, and set up ideals.
Here the sole direction of fit is normative, and that is why
such language cannot represent or misrepresent the world.

We must, then, bear in mind and face the consequences of
the truth that fundamental moral judgements have a normative direction of fit only. Any justification of their impersonal
form must lie not so much in the nature of the world we
experience as in the manner in which we react to the world.
We justify the impersonal form of utterances descriptive of
the world by referring to our common intentions in making
statements about the world. For what we intend to do is to
represent the world as it is. Likewise, as I shall contend in 9.4,
we may justify the impersonal form of moral judgements
by referring to our common intentions in making them.

9.2. It is owing to the direction of fit of moral judgements
that the questions we ask about their logical credentials are

different from the ones which we ask about those of factual statements. The concept of objectivity is bound up with the concept of truth, whose primary use is in comment on factual statements. It is to the primary use that Michael Dummett's correspondence principle ('What is a Theory of Meaning? (II)', in *Truth and Meaning*, p. 89) applies, that there is something in virtue of which a true statement is true.

It is patently incorrect to say that the vocabulary of truth and falsity has no place in moral discussion. The words 'true' and 'false' are used of moral and other value-judgements and their use is justified because moral judgements, non-moral value-judgements and non-moral prescriptive utterances have both directions of fit. Consider the following conversation:

A: The train ought to have arrived at Tay Bridge Station at 6.30 a.m.

B: No, that is not true. It was not due in till 6.56 a.m.

Here A is plainly mistaken as to what the accepted rule is and he can be convinced of this if he will but consult the current British Rail timetable. Now consider a second conversation:

A: You ought not to have made that hurtful remark to John.

B: No, that is not true. Somebody had to be frank with him sooner or later for his own good.

In this case A cannot be convinced that he was mistaken by being made to refer to a moral Bradshaw. There may, of course, be a reference to a generally or mutually accepted rule that one ought not, other things being equal, to make hurtful remarks to others. Perhaps everybody was being so squeamish that they were unwilling to tell John the truth about himself through an over-meticulous application of this rule. But B is prepared to argue that John would either benefit from being told the truth or, at any rate, would wish to know it.

Now the concept of truth may be applied in the first conversation in a perfectly standard way. Both the law of excluded middle and the correspondence principle may be used quite unproblematically. We may say, 'Either there is something in virtue of which the train ought to have arrived at Tay Bridge Station at 6.30 a.m. or there is something in virtue of which it is not the case that the train ought to have arrived at 6.30 a.m.' The entry in the timetable '06.30' will justify the first limb of the disjunction, while any other entry will justify the second limb.

The second conversation is analogous to the first only if A and B are taken to be talking either about an objectively determinable social morality or about some anchored morality. However, it is one thing to verify that a rule of the generality of 'Be unselfish' is part either of a given social morality or of Morality$_A$. It is very much more difficult when you encounter such minor moral judgements as 'It is wrong to make hurtful remarks to people'. Further, if we now make use of the law of excluded middle and the correspondence principle, we do say something problematic when we say, 'Either there is something in virtue of which it is wrong to make hurtful remarks to people or there is something in virtue of which it is not wrong to make hurtful remarks to people'. The disjunction is, at any rate, not worthy of acceptance without argument. In my view it is not the law of excluded middle[1] which is responsible for the problematic nature of this utterance, but rather the application of a full-blooded concept of truth that is glossed by the correspondence principle. Since in the case of fundamental moral judgements the direction of fit is normative, the concept of truth can only be applied to them in an emasculated way, shorn of the correspondence principle. It is one thing to apply the vocabulary of truth and falsity to contexts in which rules, standards, and principles are applied. For whether rules, standards, and principles exist or not is a social fact, and in such cases the descriptive direction of fit plays a role, so that talk of their truth or falsity is appropriate. It is quite another thing to apply the vocabulary of truth and falsity to fundamental moral judgements in which rules are laid down, standards set, and ideals set up. For here the sole direction of fit is normative. Hence, in so far as it is useful to apply the vocabulary of truth and falsity at all in such contexts, it should be applied with caution and without the association of the correspondence principle.

We may say that the character of the concept of truth changes with the character of that of which it is predicated. If things were otherwise, it would not be a concept of truth. Hence, if truth is predicated of fundamental moral judgements whose direction of fit is purely normative, its association with the correspondence principle is necessarily precluded.

[1] See my article, 'The Law of Excluded Middle', *Mind*, April 1978.

Consequently, we are here dealing with a minimal use of the concept which has only to satisfy the condition that 'to think that a moral proposition is true is to concur in an attitude to its subject' (Simon Blackburn, 'Moral Realism' in *Morality and Moral Reasoning*, p. 124). Once the correspondence principle and the concept of truth are prised apart, application of the concept of truth ceases to imply objectivity. The concept of objectivity as applied to moral judgements consequently suffers a demise, and it cannot afford to moral judgements a secure ideal against which progress in morals can be judged. If reason is to be applied to matters of morals we must seek substitutes for objectivity such that some, at any rate, of its functions can be handed on to them.

My sceptical position might tempt a would-be objectivist to try to snatch victory from defeat by deriving a normative conclusion from my critique of moral objectivity. 'If', he[2] might say, 'we cannot know objective moral truths, this means that we are not entitled to take up an arrogant and intolerant attitude towards those who disagree with us on moral matters. Surely these sceptical results amount to a vindication of "democratic philosophy" which displays a "deep humility", admitting, as it does, "its own inability to formulate an eternal truth". "Its simple assertion that all men are equal in their ignorance of the final values is the dissolvent of vested interests in knowledge and in social power."' Here, as elsewhere, a normative conclusion indicates the covert presence of one or more normative premisses. In this case the normative premiss is not hard to find. The normative conclusion that we ought not to be intolerant of the moral opinions of those who differ from us can only be derived from my sceptical results if we accept the premiss that nothing but superior moral knowledge can justify moral intolerance, and this is a normative premiss if ever there was one. It is, moreover, one which for myself I feel neither a logical nor a moral compulsion to accept, and much as I would like to vindicate 'democratic philosophy', I have to decline this kind of assistance.

9.3. If the thesis of this chapter is correct and fundamental moral judgements face solely in the normative direction of fit,

---

[2] The objector is based on R. H. S. Crossman, from whose *Plato Today* (p. 205) the double-quoted passages are drawn.

it would appear that no sense can be given to talking, as I have so far, of asserting fundamental moral judgements or of fundamental moral judgements entailing other moral judgements. Let us with Dummett (*Frege, Philosophy of Language*, p. 354) take asserting to be uttering sentences 'with the intention of uttering only true ones'. It follows from this that, as I have denied any sense to talking of 'true fundamental moral judgements', I can likewise give no sense to talk of 'asserting' fundamental moral judgements. Moreover, no two sentences can be justifiably claimed to entail one another in any standard sense unless it is logically impossible for the first to be true and the second false. Consequently, if we cannot provide a sense in which fundamental moral judgements can be either asserted or regarded as true, neither shall we be able to speak of fundamental moral judgements entailing others. But if it were impossible for relations of entailment to exist between moral judgements, we should not be able to find logical holes in the moral positions of others. The power and scope of moral argument would thus be gravely enfeebled. If the positions maintained in this book are tenable, I must, then, respond to the challenge of giving a sense to talk about fundamental moral judgements being asserted and entailing other moral judgements.

My first argument for the possibility of moral assertion I shall call my 'surface' argument, since it concerns the surface structure of moral judgements. In 8.2 I argued that only moral judgements which involved the application of criteria faced in the descriptive direction of fit and that fundamental moral judgements which lay down criteria could not be used to apply these criteria at one and the same time. Consequently fundamental moral judgements cannot face in the descriptive direction of fit or function as ordinary assertions.

This objection to fundamental moral judgements functioning as assertions can be circumvented. In 5.3 I showed how maxi-prescriptive and mini-prescriptive judgements alike could be 'talified', so that they faced in both directions of fit. This device can even be applied to fundamental moral judgements, so as to provide every fundamental moral judgement with a talified transform. Where 'a' is an action-variable and 'O' is a normative operator, every normative judgement 'Oa' has a corresponding talified judgement '*a* is such that O*a*'. Likewise, every fundamental moral judgement, whether it sets up a standard or lays down a rule, has a talified transform which, in virtue of its talified character, faces not only in the normative but also in the descriptive direction of fit. One may compare the relationship between a stipulative definition and its trivially true transform. Stipulative definitions are neither true nor false. Thus when I say, 'I define a straight line as the shortest distance between two points', I am laying down a definition, not stating a truth. However, if I make use of the definition and apply it, I can say 'straight lines are the shortest distances between two points', with or without the parenthetical addition of the words 'by definition'. This latter statement I have to regard as necessarily and trivially true in virtue of my stipulative definition. My definition is not a truth, but it has a trivial transform which is. Analogously when I make a fundamental moral judgement and thereby lay down a moral rule or set up a moral standard, I am not stating a truth. But if I talify the fundamental moral judgement, then the talified transform is trivially true relative to the rule or standard stipulated in the fundamental moral judgement. Consider the moral judgement

(1) One ought to do everything which is ψ

(where 'ϕ' and 'ψ' are ostensibly non-normative predicates applied to actions). When we also accept

(2) Everything which is ϕ is ψ

we feel justified in moving to the ordinary talified moral judgement

(3) Everything which is ϕ is such that one ought to do it.

But the reason why (3) is acceptable is that (2) is accepted as well as (1). Therefore (3) is tantamount to

(4) Everything which is ϕ, being ψ, is such that one ought to do it.

Now we cannot but accept

(5) Everything which is ϕ is ϕ

and hence when we believe

(6) One ought to do everything which is ϕ

there is no non-deep reason why we should not move to (7)

(7) Everything which is ϕ, being ϕ, is such that one ought to do it

and hence also, dropping the parenthetical clause, to (8)

(8) Everything which is ϕ is such that one ought to do it.

By this device any moral judgement can be transformed so as to face in the descriptive direction of fit and thus apparently admit of being asserted or denied. For example, the utilitarian's fundamental moral judgement to the effect that one ought to promote the greatest happiness of the greatest number, i.e.,

(9) For any action a, if[3] a promotes the greatest happiness of the greatest number, one ought to perform a

has the talified transform

(10) For any action a, if a promotes the greatest happiness of the greatest number, then a is such that one ought to do it.

So far my surface argument shows that if it is possible to represent fundamental moral judgements as conditional judgements, their 'then' clauses can be talified. To complete the argument we need to have granted (i) that all fundamental moral judgements may be represented as conditionals, and (ii) that talification, by giving the 'then' clause of a conditional a descriptive direction of fit, confers that direction upon the whole conditional. (i) is not obviously true, although, I submit, the vast majority of ostensibly fundamental moral judgements can be given a conditional form, e.g., 'For all x, for all y (where 'x' and 'y' range over human beings), if x is the parent of y, y ought to honour x'; 'For all x, for all y, for all z, if x is married to y and z is of the same sex as, but is not identical with, y, then z ought not to lie with x'; 'For all x, for all y, x ought not to kill y'. (ii) becomes plausible if we look at examples like 'If you have dug up my seeds, we shall starve' (conditional prediction), 'if you invade Paramania I will cut off your oil supply' (conditional threat), 'if you find the treasure I have buried I promise to share it with you' (conditional promise), and so on.

Once it is granted that fundamental moral judgements admit of being asserted, albeit in some attenuated sense, the concept of entailment may be appropriately redefined or extended. Thus one can stipulate that one moral judgement entails another it it is possible to infer from examination of

---

[3] The 'if . . . then' used is intended to be that of ordinary language and to be stronger than the 'if . . . then' of material implication. Otherwise 'if-iculties' result.

the meaning of semantically related terms in both that it is logically impossible to assert the first and deny the second without contradiction. Thus if we examine the meaning of the terms 'ought' and 'may' respectively in (10) and in (11)

> (11) For any action a, if a promotes the greatest happiness of the greatest number, then a is such that one may do it

we shall find that it is logically impossible to assert (10) and deny (11) without contradiction.[4]

We can also give a sense to moral judgements entailing other moral judgements if the logic of moral judgements has a sufficiently strong analogy with the modal logic of necessity. Now both 'ought' and 'good', maxi-prescriptive and mini-prescriptive operators respectively, resemble other modal operators in being subject to the limitations of referential opacity. Moreover, the logic of 'ought'-judgements can be reduced to alethic modal logic (see 9.5), as Alan Ross Anderson showed (*inter alia* in 'A Reduction of Deontic Logic to Alethic Modal Logic', *Mind*, January 1958, pp. 100-2). Hence if we are justified in talking of entailments in alethic modal logic, we are *pari passu* entitled to speak of entailments between 'ought'-judgements. For my purposes here I shall assume that the use of entailment in applied modal logic is unproblematic. Once this is granted, there can be no objection to speaking of entailments with reference to moral judgements of ordinary language.

9.4. The surface argument, even though it does not prove that fundamental moral judgements admit of assertion, does after a fashion prepare the way for an argument at a deeper level. It does at the very least explain how people who make moral judgements come to think that they are making assertions of a kind. If it does not convince the reader, it does, I hope, soften him up. In my second and deeper argument I shall try to show that what our intentions are when we make a moral judgement are sufficiently like those we have when we make ordinary assertions to warrant our talking of moral assertions.

It is distinctive of ordinary assertion that the sincere asserter intends to represent the world, intends his words to fit or correspond to the world. Someone who makes an ordinary

---

[4] This is subject to the condition that the 'if . . . then' is a strong one.

moral judgement may be taken to have the same intention, provided he is not making a fundamental use of the moral judgement in question. Whether he is or not will often not be at all clear, since even adherents of the same morality differ from one another as to which moral judgements require justification and which are fundamental and need no justification. However this may be, someone who sincerely makes an independent moral judgement which he considers fundamental cannot in the normal case correctly be said to intend his words to correspond to or fit the world. Yet though the speaker cannot be said to intend to represent the world, he can be correctly said to intend the bringing about of a fit or correspondence between the world and his words. One cannot sincerely make an internal or an independent use of a fundamental moral judgement if one intends that nothing shall correspond with it. To 'mean' a moral judgement one must intend, so far as in one lies and so far as one's other moral beliefs permit, that the world shall correspond to one's words. Where the speaker is not disposed to assent to any competing moral judgements, his intention is 'cashed' behaviourally by action to bring about the intended correspondence. Where there are competing moral judgements to which he is disposed to assent, his intention is 'cashed' behaviourally by his taking the moral judgement into consideration together with other appropriate moral judgements in any decision to which they are relevant. The behavioural 'cash value' of the intention may be represented, then, by the speaker-agent's being ready to use the moral 'assertion' in question as a premiss, whether the sole one or one among several, in deliberation about conduct to which it is relevant. As far as other people are concerned, the sincere 'asserter', must intend that they, by recognizing the purport of the 'assertion', shall use it in order to make the world fit or correspond to it, that is, that they likewise shall use it as a premiss, whether the sole one or one among several, in deliberation about conduct to which it is relevant. This will be the intention of the sincere 'asserter' where the fit or correspondence does not yet exist. However, where a fit or correspondence exists already or where moral agents have by their actions effectively precluded correspondence (e.g., by prevarication and letting the opportunity for action irrevocably pass), the intention of the sincere 'asserter' must be that he himself and others shall use the 'assertion' as a premiss in making up their minds what to *think* of the world's fitting or failing to fit the words of the 'assertion'. For where action is precluded, it is only men's thoughts which can be changed; what is possible now is appraisal alone. This is where moral judgements differ from commands and other things which we can do with imperatives. For if acting on a command is precluded, the command does not survive in some other form. Moral 'assertions', on the other hand, when action in conformity with them is no longer possible or in place, may be used to judge or appraise. No one can now prescribe the storming of Troy, but we can judge or appraise what was done by those who stormed Troy.

There are two ways, then, in which the sincere 'asserter' of a fundamental moral judgement intends his 'assertion' to be used, as a premiss in arriving at decisions and as a premiss in arriving at appraisals. This amounts to an intention that people shall take note of the 'assertion' in both a practical and a theoretical manner. It is the 'theoretical' part of the intention which justifies the use of the term 'assertion'. Moral deliberation may conclude in an appraisal as well as in a decision or action. It is likewise the 'theoretical' intention which justifies the use of the term 'belief' as applied to matters of morals. A moral belief, if it is to be a genuine belief and not a mere disposition to behave, must make a difference to what one thinks as well as to what one does. This it can do in so far as it is a reason for appraisal.

This function of moral judgements, even fundamental ones, as reasons for appraisal may be thought of as a kind of logical compensation for their only having a partial resemblance to Dummett's 'quasi-assertions' (*Frege*, p. 357). For the latter have two principal features, first, that they 'require justification' and admit of being classified as 'correct' and 'incorrect', and second, that they 'are to be acted on'. I have already explained how moral assertions are intended to be acted on. But assertions of fundamental moral judgements cannot share the first principal feature of quasi-assertions, since their being fundamental apparently precludes their requiring justification in any ordinary sense. Purported assertions of fundamental moral judgements do not, then, strictly qualify as quasi-assertions in Dummett's sense; at best they are semi-quasi-assertions. However, while assertions of fundamental moral judgements do not have Dummett's first principal feature of quasi-assertions, they do have a substitute feature, for, as I have emphasized, they may be used theoretically, to judge or appraise, as well as practically, to guide action.

9.5. The results of the surface (9.3) and the deeper arguments may now be combined. It is the mark of a genuine assertion that it can figure in both premisses of *modus ponens* arguments. In order, then, for moral judgements in general and fundamental moral judgements in particular to be treated as assertions for logical purposes, they must be able to figure in *modus ponens* without equivocation. Thus, if 'M_1', 'M_2' stand for moral judgements, then in the *modus ponens*

    (i) If M_1 then M_2
    (ii) M_1
∴ (iii) M_2

M_1 must have the same sense both in the 'if' clause and when standing by itself if the argument is to be valid. Now when M_1 occurs categorically in (ii), when it is 'asserted', it is used to perform some speech act, it is used to commend, say, or to prescribe. However, when it occurs in the 'if' clause of (i), M_1 appears to lose its commendatory or prescriptive force, as the case may be, for in order for M_1 to figure in the 'if' clause of (i) it has to be talified and thus, it may be thought, it loses its commendatory or prescriptive force and with it its normative direction of fit. Thus, someone may be tempted to conclude, if M_1 has a different direction of fit in (i) from that which it has in (ii), this is equivocation and hence moral judgements cannot figure in valid *modus ponens*. Were this conclusion correct, fundamental moral judgements would not qualify even as attenuated assertions. This conclusion, however, is based on a misunderstanding of talification. Talification does not destroy a moral judgement's normative direction of fit; rather it gives it the descriptive direction of fit in addition (5.3). That this is the effect of talification can be made evident by two arguments. First, we can, given (12)

(12) *a* is such that, all things considered, you ought to do it,
infer the untalified and clearly prescriptive (13)

(13) You ought to do *a*.

The same kind of inference can be made, *mutatis mutandis*,
with a mini-prescriptive operator. Second, the difference between M_1, as it occurs in (ii), and M_1, as it occurs in (i), may
be expressed in terms of a distinction like that between external and internal uses of expressions. Let us suppose that
we have the following *modus ponens* argument:

(14) If we morally ought not to harm other people then
   we morally ought not to harm any living creature

(15) We morally ought not to harm other people

∴ (16) We morally ought not to harm any living creature.

Let us now symbolize the argument, taking the variables '*p*',
'*q*', etc., as ranging over propositions and representing material
implication by '⊃', logical necessity by 'L', while 'S' is A. R.
Anderson's[5] propositional constant meaning something like
'the sanction is incurred' or 'the rules are broken'. Then the
previous argument is symbolized as follows:

(14f) $L(p \supset S) \supset L(q \supset S)$

(15f) $L(p \supset S)$

∴ (16f) $L(q \supset S)$

Now 'S' can either be interpreted externally or internally. If
'S' is interpreted externally so that it merely means that the
rules of a given system are broken or that the sanction of that
system is incurred, anyone who asserts (14f) and (15f) is
logically committed to (16f). If, on the other hand, 'S' is
interpreted internally, so that it means that the right rules
are broken or that the sanction is justly incurred, this makes
no difference whatever to the cogency of the argument. All
that is necessary to the validity of the argument is that 'S'
refers to the same rules or to the same sanction in every instance of its use. In uttering (15), then, it makes no difference
to the validity of the argument whether the 'ought' is external
or internal. If in uttering (15) we at first merely pay lip-service
to the 'ought's of others and then subsequently come to accept
it ourselves, we do not by this change of heart subtract any-

---

[5] See Alan Ross Anderson, op. cit. and *The Formal Analysis of Normative
Concepts* (Technical Report No. 2, US Office of Naval Research Contract No.
SAR/Nonr-609(16), 1956); also A. N. Prior, 'Escapism: The Logical Basis of
Ethics'.

thing from the meaning of (15); on the contrary, we add our adherence, an addition that cannot in any way impair the validity of the argument.

There is another misunderstanding which hinders the recognition of moral judgements as assertions. It is supposed that there must be some kind of opposition between assertion and what things one does with words. However, with moral judgements it is their full-hearted, internal assertion which shows us what their force is, whether commendatory, censorial, prescriptive, or whatever. When we assert moral judgements internally or independently, we are doing something to the world; we are providing reasons for action or for appraisal, commending, prescribing, laying down rules, setting standards, or setting up ideals. The analogy of promising is helpful here. When I sincerely make a promise, I bring something into existence to which I intend my future actions to correspond and in terms of which I intend them to be judged. Likewise, when I sincerely assert a fundamental moral judgement, I thereby set up or create an ideal or a standard or lay down a rule, to which I intend my own and other people's future actions to correspond and in terms of which I intend them to be judged. It is owing to the creative aspect of moral assertion that we experience moral rules, standards, and values as entities external to ourselves requiring from us appropriate conduct. When we talk about and describe the world, it 'abides' our description, it endures sufficiently long for our words to remain true of it. Were it not to do so, description would not be possible. Similarly when we assert a fundamental moral judgement, when we utter it and bring it into the world, it is not purely ephemeral. In order both to entail other moral judgements and to furnish a standard by which our own conduct and that of others may be judged, it has to endure. Where there are socially recognized rules, standards, and ideals, such enduring entities are conspicuously available. It escapes our notice, however, that each one of us in asserting moral judgements, laying down moral rules, etc., is creating enduring entities, even if these entities are not endued with authority by others (4.2). It is in accordance with or contrary to these, as the case may be, that we act, it is in terms of these that we judge ourselves and others.

We are warranted, then, in speaking of moral assertions for three reasons. First, we have not only a practical but also a theoretical intention in using moral judgements; in making moral judgements we intend to provide not merely reasons for action but also reasons for appraisal. Second, it is because even fundamental moral judgements admit of talification that moral judgements can figure in *modus ponens* without equivocation. Third, it is only when they are asserted that moral judgements are used to perform those moral speech acts with which they are associated.

Finally let us turn to the consequences of taking seriously the normative direction of fit of fundamental moral judgements, rules, standards, and ideals. Given any utterance with a determinate direction of fit, we can indicate this direction by constructing a 'direction-of-fit' sentence, or, as I shall call it, a D. of F. sentence. D. of F. sentences are preferred by me to T-sentences for two related reasons. The first is that T-sentences,[6] being biconditionals, cannot indicate the direction of fit. The second reason is that in any case (as Donald Davidson points out, in 'Truth and Meaning', pp. 316-17) in a theory of truth 'deep differences' do not show; thus, in Davidson's words, 'what is special to evaluative words is simply not touched: the mystery is transferred from the word "good" in the object-language to its translation in the meta-language.' Thus, given a sentence whose primary direction of fit is descriptive, for example 'The snow is white', the D. of F. sentence will run: 'It is correct to say "The snow is white" if the snow is white.' Consider now a fundamental moral judgement whose sole direction of fit is normative. We cannot take the white snow D. of F. sentence as a paradigm and say: 'It is correct to say "Taking life is wrong" if taking life is wrong', for we are speaking now of a sentence whose sole direction of fit is normative and consequently the appropriate D. of F. sentence must be inverted. In the case of 'Taking life is wrong' our D. of F. sentence has to run: 'Taking life is wrong if it is correct to say "Taking life is wrong".' Once having found our D. of

---

[6] According to Tarski-Davidson, it is a requirement of the theory of truth for a language L that for every sentence *s* of L it is possible to prove a T-sentence, i.e., a sentence of the form

'The sentence *s* of L is true if and only if *p*.'

F. sentence it would indicate an excessive obsession with descriptive sentences to press the question when and under what conditions it would be correct to say 'Taking life is wrong'. It would be entirely mistaken to come full circle and look for something 'in the world' both corresponding to this sentence and making it correct. We are debarred from seeking in the world for what 'makes' the sentence correct. We need, then, to seek something to which moral discourse has to respond in our thought or language or in the whole set-up in which intelligent moral agents act on and react with the world. If there are to be constraints at all on our making of moral judgements, it is likely that they will bear an analogy to logical constraints, constraints of thought, rather than to the constraints exercised by facts on what we ordinarily claim to be 'knowledge'. The nature and possible application of these constraints will be the subject of Part III.

PART III
WHAT A MORALITY OUGHT TO BE

Introduction

It is my contention that as moral philosophers we have to take both normativism and rationality seriously. Taking normativism seriously means accepting the consequences of the truth that fundamental moral judgements do not face in the descriptive direction of fit, and so *not* seeking moral facts to which 'correct' fundamental moral judgements have to correspond. Taking rationality seriously means trying to find considerations to which moral judgements have to respond, if they are to be rational. A successful performance of this latter task will help to allay a fear. The fear is that if talk about the objectivity of moral judgements is misguided, as I have argued, moral judgements are logically disreputable and moral discourse is nothing but idle rhetoric. To set this fear at rest moral discourse and thinking appear to need some substitute, even if a modest one, for the notion of objective truth. I shall argue that one such substitute is constituted by the existence of constraints of different kinds.

The constraints on what a morality ought to be are, first, logical constraints, especially those associated with the concept of inconsistency, second, structural constraints, and third, factual constraints, those which are derived from the nature of man and the world he lives in.

What I propose to do is first of all to examine structural constraints and show how some of these may be derived by analogy from logical constraints; second, I shall propose ten structural principles, which I shall deploy in arguments for giving preference to some styles of morality over others. The application of these principles will enable us to determine, albeit contestably, how we ought to talk and think about matters of conduct rather than what ground-level principles of conduct we ought to have. Nevertheless, the question as to how we ought to think about matters of morals is indirectly relevant to ground-level moral questions (see 10.2). Be this as it may, it is no easy task to separate considerations of how one ought to think about morals from considerations of how one ought to behave. This will become apparent in Chapter 15, where in the hope of arriving at some substantial conclusions I apply a combination of structural and factual constraints.

The structural principles at which I shall arrive will serve to discriminate between moralities which satisfy the principles and those which do not. I shall need some epithets to make this distinction and for this purpose I shall press into service the perhaps overworked words 'rational' and 'irrational'. My structural principles will, then, involve extending the concepts of rationality and irrationality. However, before extending these concepts I need to provide some minimal characterization of them as applied to conduct. This minimal characterization is austerely Humean and derives solely from the means-end relationship. Just as in the theoretical field it is a fault of reason if one is inconsistent, so in the practical field there are analogues of inconsistency which enable us to criticize practical judgements.

As far as the means–end relationship is concerned, there is practical irrationality in any situation where the means adopted by an agent are at odds with the end he has in view, either because they do not promote (i.e., conduce to) the end or because they actually frustrate it. Of course, agents may have many ends and there is no irrationality in a person's adopting a course of action which frustrates one of his ends when that course is an effective means to some other end which he considers to be at least as important. Nor indeed is there any irrationality in his adopting a course of action which only temporarily frustrates those of his ends or aims which he considers to be most important, if the occasion for bringing them about has not been rejected but only deferred. It would, however, be irrational to choose a course of action which, by satisfying a subordinate aim, entirely precluded means towards the bringing about of an end which the agent thought to be more important. Such irrational conduct may occur without the knowledge of the agent; in such an event we would not predicate irrationality of the agent, only of the conduct.

A morality is irrational if it commits anybody who holds it to irrational conduct, e.g., to pursuing a given end and at the same time a course of action which frustrates that end. A morality which does not commit one who holds it to irrational conduct is *eo ipso* not irrational and may be called 'rational'. To show that a morality is rational is not to show that it is morally acceptable (i.e., worthy of acceptance); two incompatible moralities can both be rational, i.e., not irrational. Nor does showing that a morality is irrational amount to showing that it is morally unacceptable (i.e., unworthy of acceptance). For to show that a morality is rationally-defective does not indicate that it is morally defective. In general, then, the irrationality of a morality cannot be used as a sifting device to eliminate the flawed morality from moral consideration. Nevertheless, it is in principle possible for some kinds of irrationality utterly to preclude a morality from being a serious candidate for moral acceptability. For example, if a view is shown to be impossible to accept, nobody can plausibly maintain that it ought to be accepted, morally or otherwise. Perhaps this is the message of Mill's 'proof' of the principle of utility (*Utilitarianism*, Chapter IV).

Consider a scientific analogy. No scientific theory is *eo ipso* shown to be false by being shown to be rationally-defective (apart from cases of self-contradictory theories); yet if the defect is sufficiently serious, this may lead to its rejection as surely as if it had been shown to be false. Let us suppose that a statement's being unverifiable and unfalsifiable is such a defect and that of two theories, T_1 and T_2, which are thought to explain certain phenomena, T_2 differs from T_1 in that the former contains a statement, S, which is both unverifiable and unfalsifiable. Somebody may object to eliminating T_2 as rationally-defective and contend that it is surely logically possible for T_2 (including S) to be true while T_1 is false. But this logical possibility is one which is entirely idle; it is a consequence of S's being non-contradictory and does not provide a reason for declining to reject S and T_2 along with it.

Let us now look at the moral case. Consider two moralities, C_1 and C_2, of which the latter, unlike the former, is rationally-defective in that it is logically or empirically impossible to internalize it (a form of unteachability, as shown in 11.4–11.5). Then somebody may object to eliminating C_2 as rationally-defective and contend that it is surely logically possible (i.e. not logically contradictory) for C_2 to be both rationally-defective and morally superior to C_1. This logical possibility, however, is an idle one, for the fact that C_2 is uninternalizable precludes it entirely from being judged worthy of moral or any other kind of acceptance. For if it is logically or empirically *impossible* for people to internalize C_2, i.e., accept it, they cannot sensibly deliberate as to whether C_2 is worthy of acceptance or whether C_2 is more worthy of acceptance than C_1. Nor, of course, since we take normativism seriously, is it open to us to suppose that, despite its being rationally-defective, C_2 may be 'the true morality'. I conclude, then, that it is theoretically possible for a morality to have deficiencies of rationality sufficiently grave to warrant eliminating it entirely. Be this as it may, it is difficult in practice to show of any given deficiency of rationality that it admits in a particular case of this radical employment.

Irrationality, of course, is not logical impossibility. There are certain general purposes which a morality serves, certain general intentions which we have in engaging in moral thought, in using moral language. A morality which neglected these purposes and intentions would not be logically impossible but would be bizarre. It is difficult to know what we should make of moralities which individuals had but societies did not, or which individual kept secret, or which they did not use to judge their past actions or the actions of others, or what we should make of a society in which there was no connection between the social morality and the legal system, in which a person's morality had nothing to do with what he thought about social policy or politics, or with the way he brought up his children or with what advice he gave to his friends. It is these general purposes or intentions which will enable us to specify structural principles in terms of which a moral judgement's or a morality's rationality or irrationality may be judged.

10

Aspects of a Morality:
(1) General

10.1. In 2.2 I tried to show in discussing restrictivism the shortcomings of attempts to say what essentially morality or moral judgements were. It is my contention that these boss-shots at defining moral judgements have been motivated by underlying moral-theoretical beliefs, beliefs concerning the structure which our moral judgements and thinking ought to have. Arguments for these beliefs have been mistakenly couched in the language of conceptual analysis, as if these beliefs were necessarily either tautologies or contradictions. I shall try to show in this chapter that the way in which we discuss such beliefs has to be transformed, for the conflicts between these normative beliefs do not admit of a definitive solution. Rather it is as if we have to arbitrate between the submissions of conflicting litigants, neither of whom has a knock-down case.

Much of traditional philosophy has consisted of attempts to define fundamental human concepts like art, science, language, and morality. Philosophers have claimed to know that art was essentially expression, that science was essentially aimed at predicting the future, or that moral judgements were essentially universalizable. The vast majority of these definitional statements are erroneous, but in saying this we cannot dismiss them. The reason for the tenacity with which such statements are held is that they are not really statements about the meanings of certain words or concepts. Their real role is normative. That there have been constant attempts to make them definitional indicates the immense importance their supporters have given them. Consider how the important normative thesis that sovereignty ought not to be divided appears in Hobbes's work as the thesis that sovereignty is indivisible, that it cannot be divided. Again, in science beliefs about its 'essential aims' have influenced its progress. The

Machian view of science as being essentially an attempt to give condensed descriptions of facts concealed that this was not so much a definition as a programme.[1]

These normative theses, whether masquerading as definitional statements or not, appear often in pairs, sometimes in triads. They exhibit rival aspects of concepts, and the philosopher is required to adjudicate between the rival theses and antitheses. That the concepts concerned give rise to such rival polarities has been noticed by others, notably by Gerald Holton in his *Thematic Origins of Scientific Thought* and Sinclair Gauldie in his *Architecture*. Any attempt to distinguish and adjudicate between rival theses runs into irritating linguistic difficulties. To talk of rival polarities sounds pompous and occasionally even mystical. To talk as I often do here of rival 'facets' or 'aspects' of a concept sounds vague and fails to bring out that the rivalry is between things which are asserted or maintained. On the other hand, the terms 'thesis' and 'antithesis' suggest what is false, namely, that we are only concerned with dualities. I shall choose the coward's way out and ring the changes on several words according to the context of the discussion.

Like the concept of a science or the concept of an art, the concept of a morality has many aspects, only some of which are exhibited by any given morality. Thus there are the social and the individual aspects, the theoretical and the practical, the rational and the intuitive, the retrospective and the prospective, and so on. Particular moralities achieve different resolutions of the tensions between these conflicting aspects, some of them holding the pairs of competing aspects in a harmony of tensions. The aspects appear to come in pairs, although when we study particular moralities we are likely to come across a continuum of cases lying between two extremes. To determine what is essential to the concept of a morality, we have to look at the extremes as well as at the cases which lie between them, for it is at the extremes that we see how much strain the concept of a morality will take.

Typically a moral philosopher examining his own or his society's morality or an anchored morality picks out a salient characteristic, and goes on to argue that it is an essential

[1] See my 'The Aims of Science', *The Philosophical Quarterly*, October 1964.

feature of any possible morality. His activity appears to himself as conceptual analysis, although in reality, as his warm
advocacy may often indicate, he is espousing a moral position.
This parochialism is an occupational hazard of ethical inquiry.
It may be remedied to some extent if the moral philosopher
exercises his conceptual imagination by contemplating a wide
variety of moralities. In this he may be aided by the human
sciences and by writers of fiction. In my view fictional and
anthropological examples are to be preferred to *ad hoc* ones
invented by a moral philosopher solely to illustrate his case.

10.2. One way to avoid these boss-shot conceptual analyses
would be to regard as essential to a morality not the possession
of a particular feature but the possession of some feature in a
certain dimension. Thus if we seek to provide a complete
description of a particular morality, we can attach to it certain
'markers' indicating, say, whether the morality is deontological
or teleological or 'case-by-case'. By so 'marking' a morality
we do not manifest our favour or disfavour; no moral consequences can be inferred from this exercise. But this 'many-
marker' picture is an over-simplification. It gives the misleading impression that every morality must have a place in
every dimension, that every morality must give prominence
either to a given aspect or to its opposite. Indeed, even to see
moralities as necessarily lying between two extremes may
exemplify a one-sided picture of a morality. Such a mistake
would be made by one who, impressed by the two rival
sermons in Iris Murdoch's *The Bell* insisted that every morality
must lie somewhere in between James's rigid-rule morality
and Michael's purpose-geared morality. This would rule out of
account styles of morality which do not lie on the continuum,
like Dora's pursuit of self-realization or the Abbess's commendation of 'perfect love'. The 'many-marker' technique needs
to be used with caution. We cannot be sure without empirical
enquiry that some particular dimension is essential to the
characterization of every morality.

The way in which the diverse facets or aspects of a morality
are emphasized or balanced determines the style of the morality. While they are capable of entering into conflict with one
another, this conflict is not unavoidable. Diverse aspects may

sometimes exist side by side in harmony, and it is often the thinker, examining the ordinary moral consciousness or its reflection in the ordinary use of moral language, who portrays them in stark contrast to one another and thus awakens the dormant conflict.

Much of what has passed as moral philosophy has been devoted to setting out and comparing the different and competing styles. (This is part of what Henry Sidgwick was doing in *The Methods of Ethics*.) The question 'What style of morality ought we to have?' is both normative and meta-moral. On what answer we give *can* depend what moral beliefs we have, but it is tempting to believe that the same morality may be expounded in different styles. Kant's style is very individual, but he does not regard himself as discovering a 'new principle' of morality, only 'eine neue Formel', a new formula (Preface, *Critique of Practical Reason*, 111n). Different styles may well lead to marginal differences within the general framework of an agreed morality. Kant's rigorist style led him to deny that one can ever have a right to tell an untruth. Likewise, Father Joseph Fletcher's situationism (*Situation Ethics: The New Morality*) may lead him to make some heterodox moral judgements within the general framework of Christian Morality. It is round the margins that we encounter the live moral issues of any epoch and it is therefore of moment which style of morality we opt for. If moral philosophy can give us a reason to prefer one style of morality to another, it will have accomplished something of importance.

Any morality exhibits distinctive structural relationships between its concepts. As we saw in 1.6, a morality which has rules, standards, and ideals has a different form, a different conceptual structure, from one with rules only. Again, a morality in which there is perfect correlativity between rights and obligations has a different conceptual structure from one in which a distinction is made between duties of perfect obligation and duties of imperfect obligation (1.3). One cannot infer any necessary connections or necessary disconnections of concepts from the contingent conceptual structure or form of a particular morality. Concepts which have the same extension in one morality may have different extensions in another. Arguments from the actual form or conceptual structure of a particular morality are attractive because they have a spurious conclusiveness at the same time as they engage our interest and concern. Their proponents may treat them as conclusions of logical analysis at the same time as being morally interesting, a feat only possible if they are conceptual falsehoods. It does not follow from this that they should be rejected without more ado. These conceptual falsehoods play a significant role in that they reflect more recondite statements which are indeed conceptual truths. For example, it is sometimes maintained that moral decisions are decisions we take for ourselves. What is conceptually true here is that it is logically possible for there to be a morality in which decisions are only valued if they are made for oneself. From this statement of logical possibility no moral consequences follow. It has little moral interest. But the original statement which masqueraded as a conceptual truth, that moral decisions are decisions one makes for oneself, *is* morally interesting. And just because it is morally interesting it can by a kind of 'take-over bid' transform the ordinary meaning of the word 'moral' so that, for a sufficiently narrow use of the word 'moral', it becomes true by definition that moral decisions are decisions we make for ourselves. In this way an incorrect conceptual analysis may conceal undercover moral prescription.

Such 'take-overs' pose a problem for the would-be moral neutrality of the logic of morals. An honest practitioner of the logic of morals is obliged to report any normative conception or preconception encapsulated in the concept of a morality itself. Thus it could be the case that, because the dominant morality was altruistic, altruism came to be regarded as part of the concept of a morality, while the word 'ethic', say, was reserved for referring to any action-guiding set of principles, whether altruistic or not. Again, to take another example, the word 'good' may at one time have been used as the most general word of moral commendation available for use by moralists of all persuasions. Possibly, however, it has been appropriated by moralists of an altruistic persuasion and associated with the use of their distinctive specific concepts. In this way 'morally good' itself may have come to be used as a specific concept. Thus we could have a schism in the use of such concepts so that while the wider use was given employment by moralists of diverse views, the narrower use was confined to moralists of one particular viewpoint. Linguistic changes of this kind in whichever direction, whether from wider to narrower or from narrower to wider, have consequences for the way we talk, but the occurrence of such changes settles nothing. A change from the narrower to the wider does not establish the moral admissibility of any of the range of conceptions which appear logically consistent. Nor does a change from the wider to the narrower establish the moral inadmissibility of conceptions which have come to be outside the boundaries of the newly narrowed concept. The substantive questions of value remain; all that changes is the language in which these questions are posed. Whether narrower or wider conceptions are adopted, it is always possible to commit the same error, to suppose that conceptual analysis, an analysis of the actual use of concepts, will suffice to answer substantive questions. Consider the use of the word 'good' in which it can be used equally by moralist and immoralist alike, and contrast it with the use of the word 'good' in which it is held that the good man logically must be kind and just. Examination of these different word-usages will not decide anything. Neither use *entails* that the man who is just and kind is worthy of praise. The error I have just alluded to, let us call it 'the conceptualist error', misleads us about the capacity of conceptual analysis. Analysis will often reveal solely what we think to be so. Yesterday's conceptions may become today's concepts. For this reason we may delude ourselves that we are giving a logical analysis of the language of morals when in fact we are giving an analysis of the language of a particular morality. The most useful task for the practitioner of the logic of morals is a study of the common language of moralities, that is, of a comparatively few moral universals. Arguments in support of one style of morality as opposed to another have been used to persuade people that one aspect of a morality or of a moral judgement is more important than another, that one kind of moral judgement is preferable to some other kind. Such arguments cannot in the nature of the case be knockdown ones. Their force is dialectical and persuasive rather than logically compelling, although even so they may provide considerations which help us to delimit the message of moral judgements.

10.3. This comparison of aspects of morality, kinds of moral judgement, styles of morality, has to be a disciplined activity and hence has to be governed by clearly stated principles. Although these principles will be normative, they are intended to have minimum contestability and not themselves to be moral principles, for otherwise I should be moralizing 'about the ways of moralists' (C. L. Stevenson's phrase in *Ethics and Language*, p. 158). The purpose of my principles is to enable us to compare and assess the merits and shortcomings of competing conceptual structures of morality. The principles enable us to make an effective comparison leading either to a preference of one style over another or to a rejection of both in favour of some other distinctive style. The antinomies, if I may so call them, admit of different kinds of resolution. I do not, then, intend to advocate straight syntheses of thesis and antithesis, although, indeed, we may find that our actual working moralities illustrate the cunning of reason and exhibit a harmony of tensions virtually amounting to such a synthesis. A resolving synthesis has in such cases been worked out *ambulando*. In other instances no obvious resolution may present itself. So widely different from one another are the conflicts between rival aspects of a morality that the interest of each resolution will lie in the individual terms on which the resolution is effected.

Completeness is not possible in this area. Even if I wanted to, I could not in imitation of Kant provide a definitive table of all possible polarities and indicate the 'solutions' in advance. The whole area of dispute is essentially contestable. There can be no incontestable decision-procedures and any putative final decision-procedure will be found to have rivals. I shall only be able to arbitrate between opposing conceptions or styles of morality because I am going to stipulate conditions, albeit modest ones, which any rationally acceptable morality has to satisfy. The degree of cogency of my resolutions is relative to my stipulations. The process of stipulation and subsequent arbitration has a necessarily incomplete character. The dialectical process is a continuing one. Hence my argument may be attacked on different counts, first, for either excessive weakness or excessive stringency in my initial stipulation of principles, second, for misdescription of the competing aspects, third, for bias or ineffectiveness in the marshalling of 'pro' and 'anti' arguments, and fourth, for error in specifying the manner in which different aspects or styles or conceptions of a morality meet or fail to meet the initial stipulations.

Aspects of a Morality:
(2) Constraints

11.1. When we are engaging in descriptive discourse we regard it as a fault or defect of rationality if what we say is inconsistent or logically self-contradictory. There is nothing problematic about ascribing such a defect to a sample of descriptive discourse, since the law of non-contradiction is a law of logic which few if any would wish to abandon. In addition to logical laws we have also with regard to descriptive discourse a correspondence requirement that we make only such statements as satisfy the condition that there is something in the world in virtue of which they are true. As we have seen (9.2), this correspondence requirement or principle has only limited application to moral judgements and we must, therefore, look for other requirements or principles to act as constraints on the moral judgements we make, constraints on what a morality ought to be. I shall try, then, in this chapter to derive a number of structural principles which will specify flaws or defects from which rationally acceptable moral judgements or a rationally acceptable morality must be free. I shall contend further that these structural constraints need to be supplemented by factual constraints.

For a start, one might want to lay down a principle that no moral judgement or morality should prescribe the impossible, a principle corresponding to the legal maxim that 'lex non cogit ad impossibilia'. However, while this principle may be applied quite satisfactorily to any particular moral judgements, it is quite another thing to apply it to a morality considered as a whole. One can reject a particular moral judgement on the ground that it commits one to mutually incompatible courses of action. This rejection-procedure cannot be legitimately applied to whole moralities. It is possible for two goods or two ideals to be incompatible. Thus any morality which sets up liberty and equality as ideals is faced with a problem. If liberty is pursued without restraint, the resulting state is likely to be one of inequality. The equality of all can only be achieved if restraints are put on the liberty of at least some. One who subscribes to a morality impossible of complete fulfilment is not *eo ipso* subscribing to something faulty. It is not necessarily a shortcoming in the *morality* that nobody can live up to it perfectly. Rather it is a 'cursed spite' in the world that some of the good things are incompatible. It is not, however, that there is nothing problematic about having incompatible ideals. Having such ideals sets a problem for the moral agent. The problem can in some cases be 'solved' by finding the right blend for the ideals, or by deciding how and in what circumstances the failure to satisfy one ideal may be compensated for.

11.2. One kind of irrationality is that which presupposes what is impossible. Presupposition resembles entailment in that it is logically impossible for the presupposing statement to be true at the same time that the presupposed statement is false, but differs from entailment in that if one statement presupposes the truth of another, the contradictory of the first presupposes the truth of the second too. Thus you cannot contrapose the 'if . . . then' of presupposition. Clearly, then, when one assertion presupposes another, the truth of the second is a necessary condition of the truth or assertibility of the first. A form of presupposition may be applied to moral judgements in virtue of their being semi-quasi-assertions (9.4). A moral judgement presupposes a factual assertion if the truth of the second is a necessary condition of the assertability of the first.

Three kinds of impossibility, logical, physical, and technical, may be distinguished. Prescriptions and appraisals of the logically impossible are absurd. Only what is conceivable can be appraised and the logically impossible is inconceivable. A prescription to perform the logically impossible is always to to be rejected; its shortcoming is irremediable. The prescription cannot have a 'second life' after the defect has been shown up. We cannot say consistently, 'If it were logically possible to do *a* and not-*a*, it would be a good thing', though we can quite sensibly say 'How nice it would be to have the advantages of doing *a* and the advantages of doing not-*a* at one and the same time'. Yet plainly when I commend or recommend what cannot be the case something is amiss no less than when I state what cannot be the case, and this is so whatever the kind of impossibility involved. The man who recommends the impossible or recommends people not to do what is unavoidable is adopting means which fail, and necessarily fail, to promote his end, since his end is unpromotable. His recommendations are therefore 'irrational' in the austere sense I have given that word.

The position I have adopted resembles the Kantian thesis that 'ought' implies 'can'. It is plain that the 'implies' here does not represent the relation of entailment but that of presupposition. For to assert that one ought to and to deny that one ought to both presuppose that the action is possible, logically and otherwise, for the agent. By showing that the action is impossible, logically or otherwise, we may rebut both 'ought'-sentences.

The same goes for prescription and appraisal of the physically impossible. Such prescriptions and commendations, etc., are purposeless or irrational. This shortcoming is not one of falsity nor is it syntactical; it arises out of the way things are or, as perhaps one should say, out of the way things are not. However, prescriptions and appraisals of the physically impossible can have a 'second life', either through their changing their character and becoming less prescriptive and practical, less relevant to decisions about what to do, or through their changing their content. In the first case, we can say quite meaningfully and consistently, 'If it were physically possible, it would be a good thing'; you can *wish*, though not desire or demand, that the laws of nature were other than they are. In the second case, a second life or substitute content is obtainable. Thus where it is physically impossible for us to obey a rule, we may consider ourselves under an obligation to 'do our best to counteract the effect of this physical impossibility' (Macaulay, 'Notes on the Indian Penal Code', *Works*, Vol. VII, p. 555). Macaulay pointed out that it was physically impossible to conform to the rule that trials should be public since the trial chamber could not accommodate all who

wished to attend. This did not absolve one from doing anything about the matter. One could, for example, compensate
for the physical impossibility by publishing the trial proceedings in the press for those to read who were unable to attend.

Prescriptions or appraisals of the technically impossible are
not irremediably faulty. To prescribe or commend what is
only technically impossible might have some point, since it is
not irrational to urge someone to try to bring about the
technically impossible; techniques, unlike the course of nature,
are to a certain extent within our power.

Somewhat more complicated are prescriptions and appraisals of what is at one and the same time impossible, physically
or technically, and yet subsumable under a rule of a social
morality. A (physical or technical) impossibility clearly rebuts
a merely independent or free moral 'ought'-judgement as surely
as a negative instance refutes a generalization. But where we
have an institutional 'ought' or talk of obligations, the rebuttal
is of a less sweeping kind. The pilot who makes a forced landing on a farmer's crops would not be making a felicitous reply
to the irate farmer if he said, 'You mustn't say that I ought
not to have done it. For "ought" implies "can" and I couldn't
help it'. Most people would, I think, agree that it would be
better in every way to say, 'I am awfully sorry for ruining
your crops. I realize that I ought not to have landed there, but
I couldn't help it; it was, you see, a forced landing'. The use
of the word 'realize' shows that the pilot no less than the
general public accepts, or recognizes, the rule of the social
morality that one ought not to harm other people's property.
This is not an independent use of 'ought', for that has been
completely rebutted. Nor is it a purely external use of 'ought';
the pilot is not merely informing the farmer that a rule enjoining respect for other people's property is generally recognized in their society. Presumably the farmer knows that
already. Rather the pilot is making an internal use of 'ought';
he acknowledges that he has infringed a rule, and that is why
he apologizes, but the infringement was unavoidable, and
that is why the farmer cannot rationally blame him.

To sum up, we are entitled to talk of a kind of irrationality
in cases where moral 'ought'-judgements are rebutted by impossibilities. It is, then, quite inadequate to say, as C. L.

Stevenson does (*Facts and Values*, p. 144) that 'it is a psychological fact that people are unwilling to make purposeless ethical judgements' and that that is the reason why we do not proscribe the unavoidable or recommend the impossible. Indeed, we may lay down a meta-moral principle to the following effect:

Any moral judgement which prescribes or commends or commits one to the prescription or commendation of what it is impossible to perform is irrational or pointless (*meta-moral principle A*).

A general caveat is needed here to guard against spurious impossibilities which might lead one to apply meta-moral principle A somewhat too hastily. In everyday life we often come across a kind of practical impossibility. Its spurious character is perhaps recognized by people who call something 'practically impossible' meaning thereby 'almost impossible'. Again, it is sometimes said that a course of action is 'humanly impossible', whereby this is meant that no ordinary human being can be expected to do it. But even what is merely inconvenient may be dignified with the epithet 'impossible'. If I am invited to dine out when I am ill, I may say in excusing myself, 'I can't go because I am not well', or on another occasion, 'I can't go because I have too much work to do', even though neither my indisposition nor my weight of work actually disables or incapacitates me. Often this practical 'cannot' is equivalent to 'cannot without inconvenience' or 'cannot without omitting to do what is more important or higher on my list of priorities'. Now a latitudinarian, making an eristic use of words like 'impossible' and 'cannot', might maintain that a statement of practical impossibility excuses no less than any other statement of impossibility. Thus Machiavelli could maintain that it is necessary for the prince (*The Prince*, p. 99) 'not to diverge from the good if he can avoid doing so, but, if compelled, then to know how to set about it.' But it is a mistake to argue that it is irrational to recommend what is 'practically impossible'; this is a highly contestable claim, for practical impossibility is only very great difficulty, and it follows from the very meaning of the word 'difficult' that it is possible to perform the action if one tries hard enough. Perhaps some substitute for meta-moral principle

A is needed here. If impossibility excuses, one would expect
near-impossibility almost to excuse, or, at any rate, to be a
mitigating circumstance. For there appears to be only a small
gap between impossibility and very great difficulty. This
thought lies behind Macaulay's argument (op. cit., p. 505) that
'it seems difficult to conceive that circumstances which would
be a full justification of any violence short of homicide should
not be a mitigation of the guilt of homicide. That a man
should be merely exercising a right by fracturing the skull and
knocking out the eye of an assailant, and should be guilty of
the highest crime in the code if he kills the same assailant;
that there should be only a single step between perfect inno-
cence and murder, between perfect impunity and liability to
capital punishment, seems unreasonable.' We need, then, to
have an appreciation of the capabilities of human beings and
the feasibility of courses of action. If we are to know what we
may rationally prescribe by rules or set up as standards or
ideals, we must know what sort of people we are laying down
rules or setting standards for, what their characters are, what
the likely effect of our rule-making and standard-setting will
be on them and what they are capable or incapable of. This
was Aristotle's aim, to provide potential legislators with such
knowledge of human character and action as would enable
them to make good and sensible laws.

Clearly when we make moral judgements we are laying
down rules or setting standards or applying rules and standards
for certain organisms. These organisms may or may not be
explicitly referred to, may or may not be the grammatical
subject or the apparent addressees of the moral judgement;
they are nevertheless the target of the moral judgement, the
moral judgement in question is aimed at them. It is they *on
whom*, according to the moral judgement, it is obligatory or
to whom it is permissible or impermissible or *for whom* it is
desirable to conduct themselves in such-and-such ways. It is
they for whom the moral judgement implies that effective
action is possible. They are what I shall call the 'real subjects'
or the 'respondents' of a moral judgement or morality. Consider the moral judgement

(1) Children ought to show respect for their elders.
While the grammatical subject of (1) is children, (1) may be

uttered by a disapproving elder to a particular child's parent who is his target. In this case it is the parent who is both the real subject (respondent) and the addressee of (1) as so used. However, (1) may also be uttered to some other elder likely to disapprove of the child's conduct. In that case, while the addressee is now the other disapproving elder, the real subject or respondent remains the criticized parent. Although the context of utterance of the moral judgement may make clear the identity of the real subject or subjects, this is not invariably so. Thus the sentence

(2) It is obligatory to respect the dead

does not indicate who the respondents might be, whether any human being whatever or only relatives of the dead.

11.3. Let us now consider whether we should rule out as irrational any morality or moral judgement whose real subjects or respondents cannot understand it, where the 'cannot' is of a strong kind, that is, logical or physical or psychological. The case of 'ought'-judgements is the easiest to deal with. It is, I contend, a presupposition of 'ought'-judgements that their real subjects must be capable of understanding them. That we are dealing here with presupposition rather than entailment can be seen if we examine alternative views. In the first place, somebody might maintain that it was part of the meaning of the word 'moral' that a moral judgement, overtly or covertly, has a person as its real subject. But if by 'persons' we mean, to use Locke's definition (*An Essay Concerning Human Understanding*, Book II, Ch. XXVII, § 26), 'intelligent agents capable of a law', capable of deliberation, decision, and action, then whether a given judgement has a person as its real subject is a question of fact, a question of whether that person is capable of deliberation or not. But whether the judgement is a moral judgement or not does not depend upon facts about the non-linguistic world, but on how the judgement is used. Hence it is not part of the meaning of the expression 'moral judgement' that the real subject of a moral judgement is a person and thus it is logically possible for there to be moral judgements whose real subjects are not in fact persons. Somebody might reply, 'Yes, it is logically possible for there to be moral judgements whose real subjects are not persons, but these moral judgements are false ones. Any moral judgement *entails* that its real subject is a person.' But this will not do either. Take a moral judgement of the form 'X morally ought to do *a*.' The real subject of this judgement, viz., X, is necessarily the real subject of the judgement's contradictory, viz., 'It is not the case that X morally ought to do *a*.' Now if we maintain, as I think we should (2.1), that the contradictory of a moral judgement is itself a moral judgement, the judgement 'It is not the case that X morally ought to do *a*' must also imply that X is a person. But what distinguishes the relation of presupposition from that of entailment is that both the presupposing statement and its contradictory imply the presupposed statement. So we may conclude that when we say 'If X morally ought to do *a*, then X is a person', this is the 'if . . . then' not of entailment but of presupposition. When, then, a moral 'ought'-judgement and its contradictory falsely presuppose that their real subject is a person, they are both 'out of place' and should be rejected in favour of a third alternative. What applies to moral 'ought'-judgements applies to other moral judgements also. Indeed, maxi-prescriptions, mini-prescriptions, and commendations can only be effective with those who can understand them. There is something amiss with the issuing of any moral prescription or the making of any moral appraisal whose respondents or real subjects cannot use or could not have used it in deliberation or coming to a decision. This is why we do not pass either favourable or adverse moral judgements on the behaviour of non-human animals. An organism cannot do what is morally wrong if it cannot observe or fail to observe a moral rule, and it cannot observe or fail to observe a moral rule unless it is able to take the rule into consideration in making up its mind, and this, it appears, animals other than man cannot do. It is only intelligent agents who can properly be the real subjects of moral appraisal (2.2).

It is out of place to address a moral recommendation to an organism which cannot understand it and it is no less out of place to pass moral judgement on such an organism. Just as it is out of place to tell a rat 'You ought not to have bitten me' or 'You ought not to bite me', so it is out of place to say of the rat 'It was morally wrong of that rat to bite me'. To say

that such an utterance is out of place relative to a given individual or group or society is not to pass a kind of *moral* judgement on the individual, group, or society concerned. It is
rather to say that the utterance is rationally-defective in that
its real subjects cannot take it into consideration either in
making up their minds what to do or in coming to an appraisal.
Hence arises the legal maxim that laws should be expressed
in intelligible language. The generalized requirement is that
rules should be intelligible to their real subjects. In the case of
the insane, they cannot understand what it is that they are
forbidden or enjoined to do, and so cannot take into consideration to-them-unintelligible rules or standards in making
up their minds what to do. This is why it is out of place to
blame or punish such persons for what they do or omit to do,
and it is because it is out of place to blame or punish them
that it is moreover unjust to do so. A principle of justice is, I
concede, more than is actually warranted by the considerations
I have adduced. What is warranted is the normative but morally
neutral *meta-moral principle B* :
It is irrational (out of place) to make a moral judgement whose
real subject cannot take it into consideration or make use of
it in deliberation.

11.4. There is a third kind of irrationality, concerned with a
third kind of impossibility, the impossibility of accepting a
prescription or appraisal. I shall argue that because of the
close connection between commendation, prescription, etc.,
on the one hand and desire on the other, if it is impossible
for a person or persons to desire a certain state of affairs or
course of action, then it is impossible for them to accept a
commendation or prescription in favour of it.

Let us imagine a community in which no member is able
to desire a certain state of affairs or course of action, either
for its own sake or as a means to some further end. Such a
state of affairs might be, say, the death of all members of the
community. Let us further suppose that an outsider puts it to
them that they morally ought to aim at that state of affairs.
However, they cannot accept this prescription or any appraisal
of similar tenor, for they cannot rationally accept the prescription without being in favour of what is prescribed, and

this *ex hypothesi* is just what they are not. A prescription to such an effect would be 'out of touch' or 'unrootable', it would be out of touch with the desires of the beings to whom it was directed, it could not be rooted in their desires. We may, then, state *meta-moral principle C* as follows:

Any morality or moral judgement is irrational (out of touch) or 'unrootable' relative to a given community if what it prescribes or commends is not capable of being desired by members of the community.

This principle, I concede, might be circumvented. It might be the case that, although it was impossible for any member of the community to perform the action or bring about the state of affairs for its own sake, he might be prepared to behave in this way for the sake of some further end which he greatly valued. This would be a successful circumvention if it were shown that the only way the individual in question could achieve his desired end was by acting on the moral recommendation under consideration. Nevertheless such an individual would not have genuinely and autonomously accepted the moral recommendation, he would only have accepted the necessity of acting in accordance with the so-called 'moral' recommendation for the sake of his further end. This would be the case if he regarded conformity with a moral rule of his society as solely desirable in so far as it was necessary to his desired end. Thus this example does not force a modification on my formulation of meta-moral principle C.

Another putative counter-instance could be constructed on the following lines. It might well be impossible for members of a society to desire some form of behaviour or state of affairs, say, the death of all, without some external sanction, like the fear of God or the backing of tradition, or without some strong inducement or incentive, like the hope of eternal life. Perhaps something of this character is necessary in order that members of a society should desire their own death at all. The existence of tradition poses a challenge to my meta-moral principle as stated. For a rule, say, or an ideal which has been accepted in a community from time immemorial, perhaps for what was originally a good reason, necessarily generates a desire to follow that rule, pursue that ideal. That is a consequence of the internalist thesis of 3.4. But if the desire to follow the rule or pursue the ideal arose in such a way, it would hardly provide us with sufficient warrant for saying that the rule or ideal was free from irrationality of type C. If it did, any custom, rule, or ideal, however anachronistic, could claim to be 'rooted' in our desires, even though the conditions and beliefs which made it acceptable no longer obtained, and could thus escape rejection simply by being entrenched in tradition. To avoid such specious rationality, my meta-moral principle C needs the accompanying gloss that by 'capable of being desired' is meant 'capable of being independently desired'. This gloss is in the spirit of Bentham's attack on all that was obsolete and unreasoned in the Common Law.

11.5. We are now in a position to start listing structural principles which specify constraints on what moral judgements and moralities ought to be. The first two principles are derivable from the meta-moral principles reached in 11.2–11.4.

Principle I (The Principle of Teachability): *It is a defect of rationality in any moral judgement or morality if it cannot be taught to its respondents.* I shall use the expressions 'cannot be taught' and 'unteachable' to mean 'either unintelligible or uninternalizable'. My first principle thus combines meta-moral principles B and C. It says that it is a defect of rationality in any moral judgement or morality if it cannot be understood by its respondents or if what it commends or recommends cannot be internalized by them, that is, desired by them.

Since teachability and unteachability are relations, the fact, if it is a fact, that a given morality or moral judgement is irrational because unteachable must be a relative matter also; if a morality or moral judgement is unteachable relative to a specific class of intelligent agents, then the morality or moral judgement in question is irrational relative to that class of intelligent agents. As far as concerns my application of the principle of teachability in subsequent chapters, I shall only have occasion to use the weaker, 'uninternalizable' part of the principle. Thus in 13.1 I shall try to show that, while a purely particularist morality would be intelligible, its logical structure would preclude its respondents from internalizing it.

A gloss is also needed on what counts as 'teaching' a morality. I contend that *genuinely* teaching any morality involves teaching moral thinking, for the respondent/pupil has to learn how to take the morality into consideration in making up his mind how to act or how to appraise. This involves learning in what distinctive ways he would need to act in order to conform to the morality (Principle VI) as well as learning moral thinking, that is, learning to reason from judgements about acts or people at one time to judgements about the same acts or people at other times (Principle V), to reason from judgements about people's acts to judgements about their characters (Principle VII) and to reason about novel situations in a non-mechanical way by 'detecting' similarities and differences (Principle X). Teaching, to be genuine, must involve imparting the ability to reflect, it must be more than merely programming.

Since the principle of teachability is concerned with the relation between a morality or moral judgement and its respondents, actual or possible, a standard, sincere user of moral judgements will want these respondents to agree with him, that is, to take the morality or moral judgement in question into consideration in arriving at practical decisions or appraisals. But if he wants them to agree with him, it will, in the austerely Humean sense of 'irrational', be irrational for him to put forward a morality or moral judgement which it is impossible for them to share. For it is irrational, other things being equal, for somebody to adopt means to one of his acknowledged ends which he knows to be not conducive to that end. It follows that if somebody wants the respondents of his judgements to agree with him, he must, if he is to be rational (that is, not irrational), put forward a morality or make moral judgements which he believes them to be capable of sharing, that is, capable of being taught.

We must further be prepared to recognize that whether a morality is teachable or not relative to a class of intelligent agents is going to depend not only on the morality in question but also on the nature of the agents. A morality may be unteachable relative to one class of intelligent agents but teachable relative to another and different class. This may be illustrated by a tall story. After many wanderings the tribe of the Children of Abel reach the plains of Thessaly where they decide to settle. Their leader, McAbel, a man of exceptional intellectual brilliance, learns the local Greek dialect and reads widely in the works of wise men. Having decided that his people need to learn a way of life, he ascends Mount Olympus and meets Zeus. Zeus tell him that his people must live in accordance with *Physis*,[1] a concept which McAbel masters by dint of long study. When, however, McAbel tries to teach the new morality to his people, he finds that despite giving them intensive lessons in Greek language and thought he cannot make them grasp what *Physis* is. It would appear that his people have an intellectual ceiling, the consequence of which is that they will only be able to live in accordance with *Physis* so long as he, McAbel, is alive to interpret and spell out how they ought to live. McAbel is aware that teaching them to mouth the words 'Everybody should live in accordance with *Physis*' will accomplish nothing; indeed, it could well be harmful, for the word 'Physis' has so many meanings in ordinary language that those who lack good sense or good will may misconstrue or distort the word's meaning. The morality of *Physis* is unteachable to this people and irrational relative to them. Nevertheless, it is not irrational relative to McAbel. Provided that McAbel excludes his people from the class of the morality's respondents, the morality of *Physis* admits of a logically respectable use. If he, McAbel, is the only respondent of the morality, then relative to him the morality is rational. If this is so, McAbel still has a problem, for if he is sincere in his acceptance of the morality, he must want his people to behave in some ways rather than others either when he is absent and cannot guide them or when he is dead. What McAbel has to do, then, if he really accepts this morality, is to change its style, to teach his people a morality related to his Zeus-given morality, although much more specific and liberated from the unifying but confusing concept of *Physis*.

Similarly, a morality for supermen or angels may well be unteachable (uninternalizable) relative to men. One can indeed imagine somebody who, being the only one of his kind, made a morality for himself which it would be impossible for him to teach to others. Such a one might be the first superman. It would be irrational for him to try to teach his morality to ordinary non-supermen if they were incapable of understanding it. It would not, of course, follow from this that it would

---

[1] Meaning 'nature' in classical Greek.

be irrational for him to live in accordance with his morality. The principle of teachability does not require that any rational morality be teachable to (internalizable by) ordinary men, but that any rational morality be teachable to its respondents. Our aboriginal superman will not fall foul of the principle of teachability so long as supermen are the exclusive respondents of his morality. If he applies his morality to himself alone, he is the sole respondent of his moral judgements and the question of teachability or unteachability will therefore not arise.

Principle II (The Principle of Consistency): *It is a defect of rationality in any moral judgement if it prescribes or commends what it is logically or physically impossible for its respondents to perform or bring about.* While this principle (identical with meta-moral principle A) does not specify any conditions under which it is justifiable to commend, condemn, evaluate, or prescribe, it does stipulate a necessary condition of any justifiable commendation, condemnation, or recommendation, and indeed of any justifiable reward or punishment. Plainly not many moral judgements would infringe this principle, although some moral judgements of what we might regard as 'primitive' moralities would. For example, fourth century BC Athenians apparently thought it right to blame and 'punish' trees and stones if they were causally responsible for fatal accidents.[2] As we saw before (11.1, 11.2), while it is a defect of rationality in a morality as well as in a moral judgement to prescribe or commend what is impossible, what we ought to do about the impossibility is another question. A moral judgement which recommends the impossible needs to be modified or abandoned. In this respect moral judgements resemble descriptive statements. However, when we come across a whole morality which is committed to recommending what is impossible, we have an alternative to modification or abandonment. For we can try to pursue some middle way, some means of doing justice to competing claims or conflicting duties or incompatible goods. It is only if the source of the impossibility is neither competing claims nor conflicting duties nor incompatible goods that modification or abandonment of the offending parts of the morality is in order.

[2] Aeschines, *Against Ctesiphon*, 244-5: '. . . we cast beyond our borders stocks, stones and iron if they happen to fall on a man and kill him.'

Principle III (The Principle of Discussability): *It is a defect of rationality in anything purporting to be a moral judgement or a morality if it cannot be discussed by those of its respondents who accept it and those who do not yet accept it.* This principle can be derived from Principle I, for discussability goes with teachability. Merely to teach somebody to mouth a formula or precept does not constitute the teaching of a morality. For to teach a morality one has to show of a precept how it is to be applied or of an example in what respects it is to be followed. In teaching a morality, whether by precept or example, one has to impart the ability to apply a general rule to new or unforeseen situations. This is necessarily a discursive activity and involves discussion. A morality, then, to be teachable must be discussable by its respondents.

A principle to the effect that any morality should be capable of becoming a social morality will doubtless seem pointless to someone who believes that 'morality' is essentially a social phenomenon. But some principle is required to mark the difference between the standard case of a morality and a personal plan of life which merely embodies resolves and policies and so may barely commit the agent to judgements about the actions of others. It is a defect of rationality in any morality for it to disconnect moral judgements about one's own actions from judgements about the actions of other similar intelligent agents. One might suppose that a principle of social adoptability would in the light of its subject-matter be logically independent, but it too can be derived from the principle of teachability. Suppose that there is some individual morality which violates the principle of social adoptability, that is, which cannot be adopted by people other than the individual whose morality it is, where adopting involves consciously sharing. If people share the knowledge that they share a morality, that is, if they have 'common knowledge' of their sharing a morality, then they have *eo ipso* a social morality. If no class of people can adopt an individual morality, they cannot be brought consciously to share that morality. But if they cannot consciously share the morality, then either they cannot understand it or they cannot desire what it commends or recommends to come about, that is, the morality is unteachable. Thus to be teachable a morality must be socially adoptable, and any irrationality which is a violation of the principle of social adoptability is a violation also of the principle of teachability. The principle of social adoptability is not, then, an independent principle, although because of its importance I shall state it separately. We have, then,

Principle IV (The Principle of Social Adoptability): *It is a defect of rationality in any morality if it is incapable of becoming a social morality for some class of intelligent agents.* Any morality satisfying this principle will be capable of being related to a legal system. This relationship is obvious when you are dealing with a prescriptive morality, but plainly a permissive morality also has a relationship with a legal system in so far as it can lead to or is associated with the repeal of legislation.

Principle V (The Principle of Temporal Link): *It is a defect of rationality in any morality if judgements which differ only in tense have no logical relationship with one another.* This requirement relates to the logical link which exists between moral judgements of different tense. The speaker's or thinker's position in time no more changes the sense of the moral thought than does his position in space. There has thus to be a systematic semantic link between differently tensed statements relating to the same topic and conveying the same message. The topic and the message are time-indifferent. A contemporary of King John's might have said of him, 'King John is a good man.' If after John's death he said, 'King John was not a good man', he would be held to have changed his mind and to be contradicting his previous judgement; if, on the other hand, he said 'King John was a good man', he would be expressing the same judgement. 'Ought'-sentences appear more complicated. With them change in tense indicates a change in speech act. If I say of a future action that somebody ought to do it, I am taken as logically committed, if I have not changed my mind in the meantime, to saying that he ought to be doing it at the time of action and to saying that he ought to have done it when the time for action has passed. Moreover, if I tell you that you ought to perform *a* at a particular time and you do it, I shall be held to have changed my mind or to be contradicting my previous utterance if I then tell you that you ought not to have done it. An 'ought'-sentence referring to the future is used to recommend or prescribe, an 'ought'-sentence referring to the past is used to censure in the standard case, an 'ought'-sentence referring to the present is used both to recommend and censure. (In some cases 'ought'-sentences can be used almost to pooh-pooh as in 'And so you ought to have done it.') A morality which failed to respect this semantic link would be unlike moralities as we know them, it would appear incoherent. We should be unable to determine of these 'moral judgements' what counted as consistency and inconsistency, constancy and inconstancy. One could also argue that a morality which failed to respect the temporal link would be unteachable (uninternalizable); we could thereby derive this principle from the principle of teachability.

My sixth principle is an older one than it looks, although it is none the worse for that. It has an impeccable ancestry and some of its more recent relations have been highly respectable structural principles of theoretical thinking. Because of this kinship it stands on its own amongst my structural principles, although I shall show that it too has a logical connection with the principle of teachability.

Principle VI (The Principle of Sufficient Guidance): *It is a defect of rationality in any morality or in any independently viable element in a morality if it is such that there is no situation in which any deductively rational and self-controlled moral agent could, by taking it into consideration in making up his mind how to act, be led to alter the conclusion of his deliberations and his ensuing behaviour.* This principle is, I think, implicit in the first chapter of G. E. Moore's *Principia Ethica*, where he states (p. 7) that 'propositions about the good are all of them synthetic'. What my principle says is that a morality, or an independently viable part of it, must make a real difference to the decisions and conduct of those who accept it. A rational morality, or a rational element in a morality, must, then, make a 'cash difference' to the conduct of those who genuinely accept it. The principle is plainly related to the kind of pragmatic verification principle appealed to in an undogmatic spirit by C. S. Peirce.

By an 'independently viable element in a morality' I mean such things as moral precepts and judgements, prescriptive or commendatory (even a vision of how things ought to be, if it can be made explicit), in short, anything both assertable and normative, which can be taken into consideration in the course of an agent's practical reasoning. Moral judgements about past events do not qualify as 'independently viable elements of a morality' for two reasons, first, because they are particular, and second, because they require supplementation partly, at any rate, in the light of their particularity. They require supplementation by criterion-stating or standard-setting moral judgements which are not themselves historical. Thus the moral judgement 'King John was not a good man' is particular, and hence, to be in a position to accept or reject it, you need, apart from reliable and adequate evidence of King John's conduct, some prior criterion of what a man must be like to warrant calling him 'good', a prior criterion which can stand on its own feet, which is independently viable. Particular moral judgements relating to the past cannot be acted on although, it is true, one can extract from them with very little ingenuity a recommendation or prescription, for example, 'Don't be like King John', a recommendation unlikely to have much practical relevance to the here and now or to the future. In any case, it is no use knowing that you should not be like King John unless you know the respects in which you should not resemble him, and that involves being acquainted with supplementary moral judgements which are independently viable. Of course, one does encounter moral judgements about the past which are general after a fashion, judgements, say, about the moral failings or merits of feudalism. These judgements, just because they are general, are in principle capable of being extended to apply to the present and future, and consequently are in principle capable of being independently viable.

The expression 'deductively rational' needs to be inserted in the statement of the principle for the following reason. It is logically possible to make deductively invalid moves without actually contradicting oneself. It is, for example, logically possible for a sufficiently illogical moral agent invalidly to deduce a substantive moral conclusion even from a logically necessary premiss. It would, of course, have been easy enough to stipulate that the moral agent had to be 'rational'. This, however, would have led me into an undesirable circularity, since part of the point of the structural principles is to spell out an extension of the concept of rationality, and in any case the term 'rational' would have been too strong for my purpose. On the other hand, the term 'intelligent' would have been either too vague or too weak. All I need is a guarantee that my moral agent has deductive common sense, that, in the deliberations I am concerned with, he makes only deductively valid moves.

One objection to Principle VI does cause some difficulty. As others (e.g., S. N. Hampshire, *Thought and Action*, pp. 207–8) have emphasized, some elements in a morality are concerned with what and how we ought or should do well to think about people and their actions, what sort of attitudes we ought or should do well to take up towards them. These judgements are none the less moral judgements for being about morally appraisable attitudes rather than about morally appraisable actions. There is no reason why the principle of significant guidance should not apply to these moral judgements also. Taking up an attitude is a mental doing, and mental doings are actions, even if their occurrence or non-occurrence is more difficult to verify than clearly physical actions. This objection, then, should not lead us to doubt the acceptability of Principle VI.

Principle VII (The Principle of Act-Character Connection): *It is a defect of rationality in any morality if there is no logical link between judgements about a person's actions and judgements about the same person's character.* It is a fact that we do pass judgements on character as well as on actions, that we praise or condemn not merely actions but also people for the actions they perform ('their' actions, as we call them) and for having a tendency or disposition to perform these actions. This fact is bound up with another fact, noticed by Hume, that a person's past actions enable others to predict his future actions, that there are regularities of conduct just as there are regularities in the course of nature. 'A prisoner, who has neither money nor interest, discovers the impossibility of his escape, as well when he considers the obstinacy of the gaoler, as the walls and bars with which he is surrounded; and, in all attempts for his freedom, chuses rather to work upon the stone and iron of the one, than upon the inflexible nature of the other' (*Enquiry Concerning Human Understanding*, Sect. VIII). But for this regularity and for the universal belief in this regularity, either there would be no moral judgements about the characters of agents at all or there would be a sharp divide between judgements about acts and judgements about character. As things are, we make the distinction between actions which are in character and actions which are out of character. Not all our assessments of character, however, refer to dispositions or tendencies. With regard to murder, theft, adultery, once is enough. However, these concepts are defeasible. One could show that the theft, say, was unwitting, or that the murder was performed under extreme provocation, and hence it could be inferred that the epithets 'thief' and 'murderer' needed qualification.

However, even if the logical tie between judgements of acts and judgements of character were considerably weakened, a minimal logical tie would have to remain if we were to have moral judgements as we know them. Suppose that character was regarded as 99 per cent innate, so that if a man were born kind, cruel conduct, even consistently cruel conduct, on his part would not count against the ascription of kindness to him. Even in this case we would require some kind of explanation of why this should be so, of why his innate kindness failed to express itself. The very fact that we should require an explanation here indicates that even in this extreme case there is a presumptive logical tie-up between judgements about actions and judgements about the character of agents.

There is sometimes a point in maintaining of a person that what he is should be kept separate from what he does. Coleridge makes this move about Southey and others of his friends on whom he does not wish to pass uncharitable judgements. He expresses the hope (*Notebooks*, Vol. I, 1605) '. . . that the Almighty will judge us not by what we do but by what we are . . .'. But there are logical limits to such manœuvres. If nothing at all that Southey does shows what he is, one will be inclined to say either that Southey is not what he was or that he was never what one had supposed him to be.

The eighth and ninth structural principles are very important ones and connect with much everyday discussion of moralities and moral standpoints. In arguments about human affairs people often accuse each other of being 'unrealistic' in their moral positions, while priding themselves on their own 'realism'. The terms 'realistic' and 'unrealistic' are plainly normative terms, but for all that they are not moral normative terms; they are in the broadest sense terms of *logical* appraisal.

Principle VIII (The Weak Principle of Realism): *It is a defect of rationality in any morality, or in any independently viable element in a morality, if it fails to take into account manifest facts.* By a 'manifest fact' I mean general truths or truisms about the situation of human beings which literally nobody doubts 'unless in the grip of some theory'. While the weak principle of realism is a structural principle in that it relates to the structure of a morality and its logical relationship with other judgements, it requires for its application some account of what the 'manifest facts' are. In 11.7 this is what I shall attempt and I shall contend that these manifest facts function as factual constraints on what a morality ought to be, so supplementing and adding teeth to the structural principles of this chapter. By 'taking into account' I mean responding to these facts in an appropriate way. Thus, there are three mutually exclusive but jointly comprehensive possibilities for the relationship between a manifest fact, on the one hand, and on the other hand, a morality or an independently viable part of it. For one may hold that either

(1) the fact provides a good reason for performing a certain kind of action,

or (2) it provides a good reason for not performing a certain kind of action,

or (3) it provides no good reason one way or the other.

To say that a morality should take account of manifest facts is to say that with regard to any such fact the morality should yield one of these three mutually exclusive but jointly exhaustive alternatives. For a morality not to do so is for it to be rationally-defective. This is not to imply that the objective truth must be represented either by (1) or (2) or (3); for, as we saw in 9.2, the consequence of normativism is that fundamental moral judgements are governed by no kind of correspondence principle. A morality does not have to correspond to anything, but the weak principle of realism requires that a realistic, a rational morality must *respond* to manifest facts by placing them in one of the three above-mentioned classes. Now, as we shall see in 11.7, many of these manifest facts are immutable, for example, the fact that all men are mortal. This provides a connection with meta-moral principle A (11.2). For any morality which failed to take into account immutable manifest facts by commending or prescribing what it was impossible to perform would infringe that principle. Immutable facts, whether about people or the world we live in, are fixed points which a morality ignores at its peril. To seek to change or to be committed to changing the genuinely immutable is one kind of irrationality.

Principle IX (The Strong Principle of Realism) is a strengthening of the eighth and states: *It is a defect of rationality in any morality, or in any independently viable part of a morality, if all available knowledge is not taken into account.* This is the moral analogue of the principle of total known evidence in respect of judgements of probability. Like that principle, the strong principle of realism may be used to provide criteria for applying a concept of weight[3] to particular moral judgements. Moral judgements involving the application of principles, rules or standards may be appraised as 'well-grounded' or 'ill-grounded', according as the moral judge makes use of or fails to make use of available factual knowledge.

Principle X (The Principle of Unattainable Ideal Rationality), which we have from 6.3, states: *It is a defect of rationality in any morality or moral judgement if it implies or presupposes the possibility of a complete description of actions or situations.* This principle acts as a corrective to the strong principle of realism, for the latter requires all available knowledge to be taken into consideration. It is tempting to infer from this that 'ideal rationality' would be constituted by somebody who actually possessed all the knowledge available about a given situation, that is, who could provide a complete description of it. Because of the inexhaustibility of description this 'ideal rationality' is a chimera, pursuit of which leads to the kind of 'abstract computational morality' against which Hampshire has recently argued (*Public and Private Morality*,

---

[3] See J. M. Keynes, *A Treatise on Probability*, Chapter VI.

pp. 22–53). It is a consequence of the inexhaustibility of description that no account of moral thinking as being mechanical reasoning from a determinate set of rules can suffice. There can therefore be no definitive and unrevisable moral judgements and it is thus a fault in any morality that it commits one to purely mechanical moral reasoning.

Unlike Principles II–V, the second five principles cannot be derived from the principle of teachability. However, as I indicated in discussing what genuinely teaching a morality involved, some of the principles constitute glosses on what teaching a morality is. Thus with regard to Principle VII, the principle of act–character connection, if a morality infringing it were accepted and the logical link between judgements about actions and judgements about the characters of agents broke down, there would be no restrictions on the extent to which an agent could disown his actions. In such a situation we could give no sense to the idea of either changing or reforming a man's character and the very idea of moral education would fail to get a foothold.

The weak principle of realism can be linked with the principle of teachability but it cannot be derived from it. To try to teach a morality which ignored or neglected 'manifest facts' would not be impossible, but it would be difficult, since they would be a permanent hindrance to the teaching of such a morality. Indeed, in order to teach a morality of this kind people would need to have recourse to special techniques to counteract the effect that knowledge of the manifest facts might have on their pupils. These facts might have to be explained away by *ad hoc* theses, or even in the last resort 'brainwashed' away. These are logical possibilities, even if they are somewhat bizarre, but they suffice to show that Principle VIII cannot be deduced from the principle of teachability.

11.6. I have tried to show that there are certain structural constraints on what sort of morality one ought to have. These constraints have in fact either overtly or covertly operated on moralities, social and individual, throughout the ages and may be regarded as constituting a kind of 'common sense'. This 'common sense' is often embodied in legal maxims, for example, 'lex non cogit ad impossibilia', or the requirement that laws should be known and understood. The famous maxim that ignorance of the law is no excuse is logically connected with this 'common sense'. It is reasonable to have such a maxim if and only if the law is easily known and intelligible. Therefore the law has to be stated in intelligible language and has to be made public. Even Caligula published his laws. 'Caligula published his laws in small characters, but still he published them: he hung them up.high, but still he hung them up' (J. Bentham, *Of Laws in General*, p. 70). In a similar way the American jurist Lon Fuller expounds in his *The Morality of Law* principles which constitute, according to him, 'the internal morality of law'. A typical principle of this kind is that laws should not be retroactive. In my view these principles of his are not moral principles. They rather indicate shortcomings, deficiencies, or flaws, not necessarily of a moral character, the presence of which make a law void or pointless or even crazy. I submit that analogous to this internal common sense of law there is an internal common sense of morality which every rational morality ought to respect. It is this which my structural principles are intended to articulate.

The principles I have laid down are intended to extend our criteria of rationality and irrationality in moral thinking. The austere paradigm of irrationality is that of knowingly adopting means which either hinder or fail to promote the agent's genuine and acknowledged ends. The ten structural principles enable us to extend this criterion and reject as rationally-defective certain logically possible styles of morality which are not 'irrational' in the austere means–end sense. These principles cannot, however, be used to give a knock-out blow to specific moralities; they cannot be used as sifting devices to narrow the range of moral choice, to eliminate moral judgements and moralities themselves. We are not justified in saying of a morality which offends against one of the ten principles that it ought to be rejected, period. For we can have no assurance that the morally best morality must be free from defects of rationality, let alone rationally-superior to any other (see Introduction to Part III). The primary use, then, of my structural principles will be to enable us to discuss the rational merits and shortcomings of conflicting aspects of moralities, to give us reasons to prefer one style of moral thinking to another. They will enable us to determine not what people ought to do but what a morality ought to be.

11.7. My structural constraints, as will become evident particularly in Chapter 15, do not always suffice to determine the preferability of one style of morality to another. In order to circumscribe more narrowly what a morality ought to be I need factual constraints also. These indeed are required by my structural principles themselves, for the weak principle of realism bids us take account of 'manifest facts'. This does not mean that we have to adopt a naturalist theory, for taking account of is different from making deductions from.

The manifest facts which constitute factual constraints on what a morality ought to be are neither concerned solely with the moral agent nor solely with the group to which he belongs nor solely with the world in which individuals and groups flourish. They are facts about individuals in groups in the world, about how human beings are situated in the social and physical worlds. The sum total of factual constraints constitute the human condition or situation. The facts that I allude to must be manifest and unproblematic if they are to be made use of in what purports to be a morally unaligned enquiry. Thus it will not do for me to include as a factual constraint that it is disinctive of human nature to take part in class struggles or that men are God's creatures. These theses may or may not be acceptable, but they cannot be admitted into the select company of unproblematic manifest facts. Nor will it be in order to include an evaluation of the human situation. Whether a right-thinking man sees it as nasty or noble, miserable or blessed, the manifest facts of the human situation remain the same. The truths and truisms of which I shall avail myself constitute a minimal characterization of those unchanging features of the human condition which have been the topic of moralists throughout the ages.

It is a manifest fact that all men are mortal, whatever may also be believed about a life after death. Moreover, men do not in general have a non-intentional knowledge of the length of their lives. The prayer (Psalm 39:4), 'Lord, make me to

know mine end, and the measure of my days, what it is', has
not been made redundant by the growth of human knowledge.
But despite the certainty of death, the life of most of us is
sufficiently long for situations experienced as similar to recur.
While we live, some of us experience extremes of joy and suffering and we are able to react in different ways to the joys
and sufferings of others. Frequently one who has experienced
extreme suffering himself is enabled thereby to feel sympathy
for those who subsequently have similar suffering. Joy and
suffering are brought about by the fulfilment or the frustra-
tion of human desires and wishes. The desires of men often
conflict with one another so as not to be jointly satisfiable.
But even the facts of conflict indicate that an individual's
efforts often do not suffice to achieve his ends without the
acquiescence or the co-operation of others. Indeed there are
some ends which cannot be attained at all without co-operation. Men are interdependent: 'no man is an iland, intire of
it selfe' (John Donne, Devotion XVII). Because of this there
is often agreement as well as disagreement among men as to
what courses of action, what objects of sense-perception and
of human creation, and what human thoughts and statements
are to be valued more highly than others. Whatever diversity
there may be, nearly all men are agreed that *some* of these
things are to be valued more highly than others. Another way
of stating the same facts is to say that there are formal universals roughly corresponding to goodness, beauty, and truth.
It is a manifest fact that each of us seeks to know the truth,
a fact about the human situation which explains why truth is
an entrenched concept (7.2).

Interwoven with the manifest facts I have mentioned is the
great fact of uncertainty. Whatever regularities one may give
credence to, one has to recognize the role played in the lives
of individuals by the contingent and and the unforeseen. We
make both our factual and our moral judgements behind a
real and permanent veil of uncertainty. It is, I suggest, partly
through the operation of the wheel of fortune that the moral
imagination is stimulated, so that the question 'How would
you like it if that were done to you?' exercises leverage. The
uncertainties play a sufficiently important part in our lives to
make role-reversal an ever-present possibility. We have no

need to invoke a hypothetical veil of ignorance behind which hypothetical people rationally contract and decide on principles of fairness (see John Rawls, *A Theory of Justice*).

The highly general factual constraints I have been mentioning have one thing in common. They are permanent features of the human condition. But clearly the situation of human beings in one part of the world or at one epoch of human history may differ significantly from the situation of others in other parts of the world or in different epochs. These variations in the conditions of life embody variable factual constraints. Under those conditions the content of what a morality of a given time and place is and the content of what the same morality ought to be will be influenced, even if not determined, by these variable factual constraints. These constraints will at one and the same time act as causes and reasons, causes of the actual morality of the time and place, and reasons which would be adduced by members of the group for holding the morality they do in fact hold. It is as if the cunning of reason had prearranged a harmony between reasons and causes. Thus the Chenchus, primitive food-gatherers of Andhra Pradesh, value helpfulness as one of the highest virtues because they live in a society 'where no one keeps a store of food and a person unable to go out collecting food must starve unless other members of the small group of families living in the same locality give him a share of the roots they have gathered' (C. von Fürer-Haimendorf, *Morality and Merit*, p. 19). These same conditions of life furnish the Chenchus with reasons for adopting one way of life rather than another, reasons for valuing one virtue more than another. The fact that Chenchus are dependent on one another in this hand-to-mouth existence furnishes a reflective Chenchu with a reason for regarding helpfulness as an important virtue.

Variable factual constraints share an important feature with immutable and constant factual constraints. None of them uniquely determines one particular morality as the only rational morality. The knowledge that we are mortal might make us think that we should try to make others happier in the time remaining to us or, alternatively, it might make us ready to extract the last ounce of personal pleasure from every moment of life. It is clear, then, that even if we attend to factual constraints, our freedom of choice in deciding how we act on this knowledge is not thereby eliminated, for we have the freedom to ignore or neglect even manifest facts. A morality which ignores the constancies of the human condition violates my eighth structural principle and may therefore be called 'unrealistic', while moralities which take the constancies and uncertainties into account we may call 'realistic'.

Constancies of the human condition may be specified by a religion. A religion may be seen as having for one of its objects the answering of Kant's question, 'What may I hope?' (*The Critique of Pure Reason*, p. 635, B833) and, indeed, of the question, 'What may I fear?' as well. The answers to these questions often involve a holistic conception of the human condition and a diagnosis of its ills and advantages, so that fact and value may seem inextricably mingled. Yet it must be possible, if the religion is to be coherent, to specify what it is which is to be hoped for or is to be feared without begging too many normative questions. Since to hope is to think that something which one wishes for or thinks good may or will happen and to fear is to think that something which one wishes not to happen or thinks bad may or will happen, it must be possible to say what it is the existence of which is to be hoped or feared. Thus one may consider with Lucretius (*De Rerum Natura*, Book III) whether there is a life after death and whether there are gods, disobedience to whose commands would bring us suffering. If there are gods who have created us, preserve us, judge us, and have plans which they intend us to follow, these are not things which a moralist can blithely ignore, for they are constancies of the human condition, factual constraints which a realistic moralist ought to take into consideration.

12

Purposes of Moral Language

12.1. In the last chapter I arrived at certain principles which were to enable us to compare and assess competing conceptions, styles, or aspects of moralities. In this chapter I want to show how my structural principles may be utilized in trying to decide what purpose or purposes a morality ought to have. Philosophers have often tried to determine 'the nature of morality' by specifying its distinctive purpose, aim, or object. Some of them were, of course, trying to determine the purpose or object of what I have called 'Morality$_A$' or some other anchored morality; with these I shall not here be concerned. I shall rather be dealing with the purpose or purposes of moral language in general. If it had been possible to find some single distinctive purpose, it would have been tempting to claim that it was *the* essential purpose of moral judgements and the present chapter would have found its place in Part I, but since, as I hope to show, there are at least two potentially conflicting purposes which moral judgements may subserve in their standard use, moralities may be distinguished from one another according as they put emphasis on one or the other of these two purposes. The moral philosopher, then, has to make a choice from amongst these moralities. The choice is primarily of a style of morality but, as we shall see, the style, once chosen, has consequences for what attitudes we adopt to human beings and their actions.

For the purposes of this enquiry I need to make a rough distinction on the same lines as J. L. Austin (*How to do things with Words*) between illocutionary and perlocutionary speech acts. Two kinds of verb referring to speech acts may be distinguished. Verbs of the first kind refer to those speech acts which are typically performed by the first person noncontinuous present tense of the verb referring to the act. Such are 'advise', 'command', 'request', 'commend', and so on. These are illocutionary verbs. In using these verbs in the first person present one performs an action. Verbs of the second kind cannot be used in this way. Rather they refer to the effects of illocutionary acts on the beliefs, attitudes, emotions, and actions of hearers. Such verbs are 'persuade', 'frighten', 'indoctrinate', 'instigate', and so on. These are perlocutionary verbs. Both kinds of verb are used to characterize what one does with words. I may advise somebody to resort to force by uttering the words 'I advise you to adopt a tougher line and to use force'. I may later describe what I did as trying to persuade the man or trying to get him to use force. 'To get to believe', 'to get to act', are, like 'to persuade', perlocutionary verbs. In describing a form of language it is appropriate to mention not only the illocutionary acts it is used to perform but also the perlocutionary acts which a standard speaker of that form of language wishes or intends to bring about. By a 'standard speaker' I understand one who is fully in earnest, not speaking in jest or play-acting or speaking insincerely. Thus a standard speaker of the fact-stating form of language wishes or intends to represent the world as it is, and hence anybody who engages in fact-stating discourse is presumed to wish or intend to represent the world as it is. Because of this we say something important about the fact-stating form of language when we say that its essential purpose is to represent the world as it is. Similarly, as I suggested in 9.4, the standard speaker of a typical moral sentence, an 'ought'-sentence, say, has two intentions, a 'theoretical' and a 'practical' intention, the theoretical one being to get others to believe the judgement made, that is, to be ready to use it as a reason for appraisal, and the practical one being to get others to act on it, to use it as a reason for action. Hence a *standard* speaker of a moral 'ought'-sentence would not make a purely external and non-committal use of the sentence, but a full-blooded internal use. My contention is that all standardly used moral language has at least one of these two essential purposes, getting to believe and getting to act.

That one essential purpose of some standardly used moral judgements is to get people to do what one wants them to do is apparent if we look at second-person moral 'ought'-judgements relating to the present or future. When we prescribe or recommend an action by saying to somebody 'You ought to do it', and the person fails to perform the recommended action, we may well repeat the recommendation, if the time for action has not already gone by, thus indicating that we do not consider ourselves to have achieved our end or purpose. That end or purpose could not have been the prescribing, for that was achieved the first time. It is clear, then, that the prescribing or recommending was merely a means to an end, the end of getting the person addressed to perform the action. One essential purpose of some moral language, then, is to get people to do what one wants, and this is a prospective and practical purpose.

The other purpose of moral judgements is theoretical and retrospective. It is an essential purpose of some moral judgements to get others to believe them, to use them as reasons for appraisal. This purpose is retrospective; we pass judgements on people and their actions with our eyes on their past, not their future. We enquire not whether they need praise or blame as a means of getting them to perform or refrain from performing certain actions in the future, but whether they deserve praise or blame for what they have done in the past. Retrospective moral judgements are judgements in the full sense. Their affinity is not with commands, but with evaluations which involve the application of criteria or standards. Retrospective moral judgements face in both directions of fit. The illocutionary acts which retrospective moral judgements may be used to perform are various kinds of appraisal, commending, condemning, grading and so on. If we wish to know the perlocutionary acts to which these are means, we must seek a perlocutionary act which is to appraisal and grading, etc., as getting people to act is to prescribing, for nobody grades for grading's sake any more than somebody prescribes for the sake of prescribing. We grade, I suggest, because we intend or wish (i) to express our reactions to people and their actions, and (ii) because we intend or wish that others should agree or join with us in these attitudes. What we wish to express in language is what E. Westermarck (*The Origin and Development of the Moral Ideas*, Vol. I, p. 43) calls 'reactionary' and Strawson ('Freedom and Resentment' in *Studies in the Philosophy of Thought and Action*, p. 76) calls 'reactive' attitudes. One may wonder why we should want to express our reactive attitudes and emotions, even if only to ourselves. We need not at this stage of the argument seek a practical justification of this; let it suffice to record that we do achieve some satisfaction in expressing our approval and disapproval, love and hatred, gratitude and resentment.

It appears, then, that there are two essential purposes of standardly used moral judgements, a prospective purpose of getting people to do what one wants them to do, and a retrospective purpose of giving expression to one's reactive attitudes towards people and their actions.

12.2. The descriptive task being done, we have next to enquire whether a purely retrospective morality or a purely prospective morality would satisfy my structural principles of rationality.

First, let us examine a purely retrospectivist morality, a morality in which the prospective purpose of moral judgements plays no part. We might perhaps make it an easier task for our philosophical imagination if we suppose a situation in which moral judgements are made despite the fact that no future lies ahead. Let us suppose that at the end of human life, when the last trump sounds, Rhadamanthys or Minos or somebody like that pronounces a verdict on each man and grades him as good, bad, or merely middling. These judgements can hardly be described as prescriptive; they cannot prescribe for the future, since there is no future to prescribe for. Nor can we say that the purpose of such judgements is to get people to have done what one wants them to have done, for the past cannot be undone. Even this strained example does not do the trick. I invented this extreme case in order to produce a situation where judgements of goodness and badness would have minimal prescriptive force. But even here a residual prescriptive force appears to remain. The mortal judged by Rhadamanthys can infer from the judgement 'You have been a bad man' that if he were, *per impossibile*, to go on living, he ought to behave differently; he can, in fact, infer a counter-factual prescriptive judgement, even though he is not entitled to infer a categorical prescriptive judgement referring to the future. My Rhadamanthys example, then, although the strongest I can produce, is not strong enough, and we shall have to concede that even retrospective moral judgements have a residual prescriptive force. My example appears even more strained if we consider what point there might be in Rhadamanthys's operations of grading and appraisal. If there were to be some kind of afterlife and if our treatment in this afterlife were at issue, there would be some point in Rhadamanthys's gradings. There would be little interest in the operations of a moral examiner, intoxicated by professional zeal. But leaving the underworld, let us consider the consequences of there only being retrospective moral judgements. Users of such judgements would infer from them nothing at all about the future. Hence if somebody in all sincerity told me that it was wrong of me to have beaten my wife last week, I would not be entitled to infer anything about the morality of beating my wife on a subsequent occasion. Further, it could apparently be a matter of indifference to my mentor if my precisely similar conduct were thus repeated. But such 'logical behaviour' contravenes my fifth structural principle, the principle of temporal link, which states that it is 'a defect of rationality in any morality if judgements which differ only in tense have no logical relationship with one another.' For my moral mentor who tells me that it was wrong of me to have beaten my wife last week is logically committed to saying that it will be wrong of me to engage in precisely similar conduct at any future date. It cannot then be a matter of indifference to him if his retrospective moral judgement is not heeded, and I as the moral agent concerned cannot in all consistency accept my moral mentor's criticism of my past conduct without applying it to any precisely similar action I may contemplate in the future. Clearly, then, no rational user of moral judgements can neglect their prospective aspect.

Let us now consider a purely prospectivist morality. The sole purpose of purely prospective moral judgements, if such were possible, would be to get people to do what the users of these judgements wanted them to do. Since such a morality would be oriented towards the future, the notion of desert would have to be dropped and the notions of punishment and blame, reward and praise would undergo a radical change. The sole purpose of favourable moral judgements would be to act as incentives, the sole purpose of unfavourable moral judgements would be to deter. We would not care whether our judgements were deserved or not, but only whether they were effective in achieving our ends. Those who think that the only purpose of moral judgements is to get people to do what one wants them to do tend to have an 'objective', 'spectator' attitude towards other human beings and ought in all consistency to have a similar attitude towards themselves. 'To adopt the objective attitude to another human being', as Strawson puts it ('Freedom and Resentment', p. 79), 'is to see him, perhaps, as an object of social policy; as a subject for what, in a wide range of sense, might be called treatment; as something certainly to be taken account, perhaps precautionary account, of; to be managed or handled or cured or trained; perhaps simply to be avoided, though *this* gerundive is not peculiar to cases of objectivity of attitude'. This objective attitude is often associated with a determinist theory, but here I agree with Strawson (p. 84 n) that 'the connexion between rationality and the adoption of the objective attitude to others is misposed when it is made to seem dependent on the issue of determinism'. In the course of the subsequent argument I shall refrain from taking sides in the determinist controversy. I shall merely make the modest admission that the use of moral language has some influence on human conduct.

The adherents of a purely prospectivist morality would want to change their neighbours' conduct by the use of moral judgements, especially by the use of 'ought'-judgements and mini-prescriptive moral judgements. They would be able to form evaluative judgements by talification, as explained in 5.3. But even their evaluations would be forward-looking. They would say of an action which somebody contemplated doing that it was 'such that he ought to do it' or 'such that nobody ought to do it' or 'such that nobody ought ever to do it', where 'ever' refers to any time in the future. If this is the position of our prospectivist moralist, he will not be satisfied if his respondent (11.2) conforms on but one occasion. The attitude which the moralist evinces is one which does not regard bare conformity as an adequate response. Perhaps the respondent's reason for conformity on this particular occasion is fear or deference or merely the desire to be well thought of. Such a reaction gives the moralist no reason for confidence in the future conformity of his respondent, and that is what causes him anxiety. Reason for anxiety would be removed if his respondent not only conformed to the prescription but agreed (sincerely) with the judgement. A rational user of prospective moral judgements no less than the user of retrospective moral judgements wishes others to agree with him. Without the prospect of agreement moral judgements would be reduced merely to manipulative verbal devices. (Of course, when we say that even the user of prospective moral judgements aims at agreement, one cannot infer from this that he is in any way committed to compromising his own moral position for the sake of agreement. It is one thing to seek a compromise when there is a simple clash between the wishes or inclinations of different individuals; it is quite another to seek for a compromise between conflicting moral beliefs as if they were bargaining positions needing conciliation. The rational user of a prospective moral judgement no less than any other moralist wants agreement with his own moral position.)

A purely prospectivist morality runs into some of the same difficulties as a purely retrospectivist morality, although it has additional ones of its own. First, the word 'ought' is typically used to express rules and standards. While the word 'ought' is prescriptive in its forward-looking use, it is usually censorial as applied to the past. The illocutionary acts which the word is used to perform vary with its tense. But whatever the tense, the uses of the word may be seen as applications of one and the same rule. The language of 'ought' is time-indifferent and so can be used retrospectively as well as prospectively. The actual logic of the word 'ought' requires the existence of rules or standards whose application is time-indifferent and thus commits us to the employment of retrospective language. Of course, a very extreme logical revisionist might maintain that we ought to abandon the actual logic of 'ought', although his extremism will logically preclude him from maintaining that we ought to have abandoned that logic already. Even if we could accept this radical proposal, there would be worse to follow. For since, as we saw before (3.4, 3.5), the sincere use of 'ought' involves desires, any change in the logic of 'ought' will necessitate a corresponding change in the logic of our mental life, if I may so call it. Given constancy as well as consistency, if I express a wish with regard to the future I am committed, when the wished-for action does not occur, to wish that it had. Likewise, if I wish that a certain event had not occurred, and a like event is in prospect, then, given constancy and consistency on my part, I am committed to wishing the second event not to be brought about. Moreover, the evaluations which, as I pointed out, could be formed from maxi-prescriptive and mini-prescriptive judgements are impersonal in their form and can surely not be deprived of the inalienable logical right to tense-modification. It would be a clear infringement of the principle of temporal link if logical relations between prospective and retrospective evaluations were made illicit.

There would be one more serious consequence of a purely prospective morality. As the etymology of the words 'moral' and 'ethical' imply and as is required by my seventh structural principle, the principle of act–character connection, any rational moral judgement has to be connected with judgements of character. Let us take an imaginary example of the kind that Mrs Foot uses so effectively. In a certain society it is a principle that one ought not to tread on the lines between paving-stones. We can only make this intelligible to ourselves, i.e., convince ourselves of the *prima facie* sanity of these people, if we further imagine that members of the society view with deep disapprobation the character-trait manifested by those who deliberately or negligently tread upon the lines. In this society a pejorative term which really hurts is 'line-treader' or 'blurrer'. The more co-operative reader will by now, I am sure, be finding this people's 'ought'-judgement becoming intelligible. Nevertheless even these people would be more rational than the purely prospectivist moralists. For judgements of character are made about people who endure through time and it is in virtue of how people have behaved in the past that we ascribe to them dispositions, virtues and vices. But if our prospectivist moralists refuse to make any retrospective moral judgements, they will preclude themselves from ploughing back moral 'ought'-judgements and making any judgements of character which they can hope to justify. They will not be able, then, to teach their morality by saying of somebody, 'He is a good man.' A purely prospectivist morality would thus infringe the principle of act–character connection and at the same time be faulted, even if not eliminated, by the principle of teachability. It is clear, then, that neither a purely retrospectivist nor a purely prospectivist morality can be rational. So if a morality ought to have both retrospective and prospective aspects, it remains to consider how these aspects should be related.

12.3. Both Morality$_A$ and current social moralities are amalgams of prospectivist and retrospectivist elements. But the influence of utilitarian and determinist theories as well as advances in psychological understanding have brought about a steady erosion of retrospective concepts like those of guilt and desert. In this section I want to determine whether we are entitled to give preference to one of these aspects of moral thinking over the other or whether a rational morality should give roughly equal weight to them both.

We can justify the making of both kinds of judgement. First, the making of prospective moral judgements can be justified in terms of a minimal Humean conception of rationality. The purpose of expressing prospective moral judgements is to get people to act in accordance with them. If that purpose were not often achieved, it would be pointless to use them, but since the purpose is commonly achieved, and prospective moral judgements normally have a non-counter-productive influence on human conduct, it is 'Humeanly' rational to employ them.

Second, the making of retrospective moral judgements and the general practice of expressing reactive attitudes can be justified in terms of the prospective purpose. This is the kind of justification Adam Smith produces when he says of the wrongdoer (*The Theory of Moral Sentiments*, p. 69): 'Resentment would prompt us to desire, not only that he should be punished, but that he should be punished by our means, and upon account of that particular injury which he had done to us . . . He must be made to repent and be sorry for this very action, that others, through fear of the like punishment, may be terrified from being guilty of the like offence. The natural gratification of this passion tends, of its own accord, to produce all the political ends of punishment; the correction of the criminal, and the example to the public.' It is on the whole true that praise encourages and blame deters (although it is also true that occasionally they have the opposite effect). This approximate empirical truth makes it rational to take part in the general practice of praising and blaming. One cannot, however, infer from this the superficial and cynical thesis that each individual expression of praise or blame is solely justified by its effects. It would be superficial because praising and blaming are things we do in our hearts as well as express in words, and the justification of what we do in our hearts cannot lie in the effects their public expression might have on other people. It would be cynical, because in a perfectly good sense of 'justify' we justify praise and blame by more or less agreed criteria in different classes of comparison. Thus we justify awarding a prize in a competition not by the effects giving the prize would have, but by the agreed superior merits of the successful competitor. It is possible to carry out a 'reconciling project' here which parallels Nowell-Smith's reconciliation of theories of punishment (P. H. Nowell-Smith, *Ethics*, pp. 236 ff.). The justification of the general practice of punishment lies in its deterrent effect. On the other hand, the justification of punishing specific individuals lies in the individual's conduct, subject to the proviso that nobody should be punished if he cannot be influenced by punishment. Similarly the effectiveness of the general practice of praising, blaming, and of making retrospective moral judgements lies in influencing conduct in the desired direction. On the other hand, the justification of a particular act of appraisal, praise, or blame, or of other retrospective moral judgements passed on an individual, lies in the individual's past conduct, subject to the proviso that individuals should be judged worthy of praise or blame only if they are capable of being influenced by such judgements.

This proviso is necessary because it is irrational to praise or blame anybody for doing what he cannot help doing. It is a contingent fact that sane people are normally encouraged in their actions by praise and discouraged by blame or censure. Things might have been otherwise. Suppose that it were the case that by blaming or censuring those who had injured us we made them more likely to repeat the same transgression, and that by expressing gratitude to our benefactors we antagonized them and made them less likely to repeat their benefactions. If this had been the case *ab origine*, resentment and gratitude could never have had a *raison d'être*. The very irrationality of expressing gratitude and resentment publicly would have ensured that we never felt them in our hearts. In this imaginary world my telling somebody who had harmed me that he was a 'good man' would have the effect of getting him to change his disposition towards me. Perhaps this is not unlike the way in which dog-owners sometimes say 'Good dog!' to a dog who has been misbehaving, intending these words as an exhortation rather than as a judgement on the dog's behaviour. The consequence of the changed psychology and the ensuing changed use of language would be not merely a sharp divide between the use of retrospective and that of prospective language, but a state of affairs in which it would be impossible to teach retrospective moral language correctly. For if nobody could think of himself as 'good' without resentment, people would tend to think of whatever was called 'good' as objectionable. Thus the word 'good' would take on a pejorative sense. This does not happen in the language of dog-owners in this world, not merely because dog-owners do not normally call themselves 'good dogs', but also because they use the words when the dog is behaving with perfect propriety and not merely as an exhortation.

The use, then, of prospective moral judgements can be Humeanly justified and the use of retrospective moral judgements can be justified in terms of the prospective purpose of moral judgements. It appears that retrospective moral judgements depend for their teachability on the achieving by prospective moral judgements of their present and normal purpose. None of this gives us reason to suppose that retrospective moral judgements are sufficiently dependent or parasitic upon prospective moral judgements to warrant our allocating them a subordinate position. We need a balance of retrospective and prospective aspects in our moral thinking if we are to have a rational morality. For a rational morality cannot regard the actions of a moral agent as entirely discrete and unconnected. People endure through time, and judgements on their actions must connect with judgements on their characters. We need a morality, we need a guide for our conduct, because of necessity we are always moving into the future; but we also have a past which we cannot ignore, either in coming to decisions or in passing judgement on ourselves and others. If we think of ourselves as having unified lives, not for ever being split between our pasts and our futures, then we need also a unified moral language to reflect our unity as individual people. We need both the prospective and the retrospective aspects of our moral thinking and discourse. The unity of the self through time is a necessity for our thought and language. Failure to recognize this unity when thinking about morals leads to lopsided conceptions of what a morality ought to be. An exclusive emphasis on the retrospective aspect of a morality leads to a primary concern with serving people right in thought, word, and deed; an exclusive emphasis on the prospective aspect leads to a primary concern with people as objects to be manipulated. Recognition of the unity of the self through time and of the temporal unity of our moral language leads to our rejection of these two (surely objectionable) alternatives and to our emphasizing the common purposes of all moral judgements. For we saw before (12.2) that users of prospective as well as retrospective moral judgements want others to agree with them as well as to conform to their wishes. If, then, we are to be rational users of moral judgements as they are, we should treat those we address as capable of agreeing with us, or, as Kant might have said, as capable of sharing our ends.

12.4. While we need both prospective and retrospective aspects of our moral thinking, it would be mistaken to suppose that there is only one viable, intermediate, and balanced position between extreme prospectivism and extreme retrospectivism. For one thing it is a fact that even if the general practice of expressing praise and blame, gratitude and resentment can be justified, yet as knowledge of the human mind has advanced, our retrospective moral concepts have been subjected to effective criticism and modification, so that the concept of desert, for instance, has been slowly eroded. But our current morality remains an amalgam of prospectivist and retrospectivist elements, even if it is changing under the impact of prospectivist criticism. We may agree that it is not open to us in practice to abandon what Strawson calls ('Freedom and Resentment',

p. 94) 'the general structure or web of human attitudes and feelings'; if our reactive attitudes are natural and unchangeable, any would-be prospectivist morality which enjoined us either to change them or to ignore them would violate the principle of consistency and the weak principle of realism. Nevertheless, even if a total reweaving of our interpersonal attitudes is not feasible, a piecemeal reweaving is surely possible; the web is not quite seamless. Nothing that we have said in 12.3 would exclude an agapeistic morality as irrational or prevent us from changing the balance between prospectivist and retrospectivist elements. An agapeistic moralist may hold that one ought to love other people sufficiently to preclude condemnation of them as people, however they may conduct themselves. The model for human attitudes and conduct, on this view, would be Job's love for God. A *prima facie* difficulty in such a position may be thought to arise from my Principle VII, the principle of act–character connection. This principle appears to require us to adopt the same or a similar reactive attitude to both action and agent. If an agent performs actions which deserve condemnation, the principle would seem to require us to regard the agent also as worthy of condemnation, if the responsibility for the actions can be ascribed to him. This connection between judgement of the act and judgement of the agent has since Aristotle appeared to be a conceptual necessity and so effectively to block agapeistic moves. However, Principle VII is concerned with the relation between judgements of acts and judgements of character, agents not being mentioned, and so cannot be made use of to preclude an agapeistic reweaving of the web. It is the character, not the agent, which can be identified with the sum of an agent's dispositions within a 'specious present', and it is the agent's character which it is rational to praise or condemn, as the case may be, in the light of his actions. But an agent, it is clear, may change his dispositions and is hence not reducible to their sum. An agapeistic morality cannot, then, be dismissed in advance as irrational.

I conclude that the tension between the prospective and the retrospective aspects of moral thinking admits of a resolution. A rational morality can and should harmonize in some way retrospective and prospective aspects, although the details of such harmonizing cannot be worked out solely on the basis of my structural principles. The only limitation on this harmonizing lies in its being more rational to be concerned with our future than with our past conduct. For we cannot change our past conduct, only our judgements upon it, while the shape of our future lies in our own hands.

13

Reasons in Moralities

13.1. In this chapter I want to deploy my structural principles in order to determine what place reasons ought to have in a morality. It is clear that people differ from one another in their approach to reasons and that this is a difference in their style of morality. Henry James, comparing Mrs Stringham with her friend Mrs Lowder (*The Wings of the Dove*, p. 112), remarks 'The joy, for her, was to know *why* she acted—the reason was half the business; whereas with Mrs Lowder there might have been no reason: "why" was the trivial seasoning-substance, the vanilla or the nutmeg, omittable from the nutritive pudding without spoiling it'. Philosophers who have a vested interest in rationality and the giving of reasons have for long insisted that a moral judgement, to be a judgement, must be backed by reasons. A wag or a cynic, on the other hand, might be tempted to retort that what distinguishes moral beliefs is just that people have *not* got reasons for them.

In this first section I want to consider which is preferable, a morality with reasons or a morality without. To judge the relative advantages of the diverse styles let us compare the extreme cases. There would be strong objections to a morality in which every moral judgement had a reason. For the chain of reasons must either be linear or circular. If there are one or more linear chains of reasons in a morality, there must either be a first reason or none. If there is no first reason, the morality will be a confused mess. Perhaps this was Aristotle's point in the *Nicomachean Ethics* (i, 1094a21) when he said that if the chain of reasons had no end, desire would be 'vain' (*mataios*). But if there is a first reason, the statement of that first reason either is a moral judgement or it is not. If it is not a moral judgement, then those judgements for which it provides a reason can hardly be moral judgements either. But if it is a moral judgement, then, inasmuch as it is not backed by any anterior reason, it falsifies the thesis that all moral judgements have reasons. One may conclude, therefore, that a morality based on a linear chain of reasons must have at least one unreasoned reason if it is to be acceptable.

On the other hand, if one maintained that the chain of reasons was circular, this would provide an entirely illusory means of escape from caprice. That each moral judgement is bolstered up by some other does not mean that they all have a firm foundation. In such circumstances caprice is not eliminated, but attaches to the grand circle of judgements itself. I conclude, then, that to construct a morality in which all moral judgements have reasons either is logically impossible or fails to achieve its object, namely, to eliminate caprice.

Having rejected the all-reason morality let us consider the opposite extreme. We can conceive of a society in which people use moral judgements in order to express their total reactions to whole situations or actions, in much the same way that most of us make aesthetic judgements. A man on seeing a beautiful woman does not 'apply criteria' and after careful deliberation decide that she is beautiful. Likewise in this conceivable society no reasons are given for moral judgements and each person makes them solely with respect to the individual situation. Each case is judged as a whole and non-analytically; similarities and differences are never considered and so no back-references are made to prior principles. Judgements made in this way are irremediably particular and correspond to what Henry Sidgwick called (*The Methods of Ethics*, p. 102) the 'perceptional' stage of intuitionism. My description of the particularist position does not exclude the possibility of some meta-moralist's studying the particularist's judgements and trying to extract from them implicit principles, criteria, or reasons. Such a person might claim that these were the particularist's real principles and that they furnished the 'best justification' of the particularist's moral judgements. A 'moral theory' so produced might from an explanatory point of view shed some light on the hidden structure of the particularist's moral sense, but in so far as it represented the particularist's moral judgements as really based on or derived from general principles it would entirely misrepresent them. For the particularist would not recognize that any two of his moral judgements, being about numerically different situations, could be incompatible, since he himself adduces no reasons. Any reasons which a meddlesome meta-moralist might extract from the particularist's judgements would furnish at best *the* reasons for the particularist's so judging rather than *his* reasons; they would constitute an explanation rather than a justification. While I would claim that particularism is logically possible and, indeed, that the particularist game is sometimes played, there are difficulties in verifying or falsifying this. For there can be no observable difference between the real particularist, whose moral judgements our reflective meta-moralist can explain and predict by hypothesizing a moral sense with a certain structure, and the pseudo-particularist who really has such a moral sense.

However, if, as I have claimed, a particularist morality is logically possible, it would violate my structural principles. For since the particularist makes no universal judgements, the content or message of his morality cannot be imparted or taught. Nor, since he lacks reasons for his judgements, would anything recognizable as argument with such an individual be possible. It would thus violate my third principle, the principle of discussability. A particularist style would thus be saddled with several connected faults. A morality with such a style could not be taught or discussed and so could not become a social morality.

Application of the weak principle of realism yields the same results, since it requires that manifest facts, when relevant, be taken into account. But the only way this can be done is if there are fundamental judgements laying down which facts are relevant to which decisions, which facts are to be counted as reasons for doing (or not doing) what. Thus for the weak principle of realism (and *a fortiori* for the strong principle) to be satisfied, a morality must contain reasons.

If, then, we want a morality which we can think about and talk about, a morality which can be taught and discussed, a morality which can respond to factual knowledge and be modified accordingly, we need reasons; this is what we in fact have. We should therefore prefer such a morality to a similar morality without reasons. This is not an *a priori* necessity to be detected by pure reason, a logically essential feature of any morality, but a reasoned preference adopted in accordance with the structural principles of 11.5.

We have now fulfilled the promise of 8.2 that we would show that it is 'a merit in a morality to have *some* criterion-universalizable judgements', to have some judgements for which we have reasons. A stronger thesis than this would not be justifiable; it is not open to us to maintain that we ought to give reasons for all moral judgements, for, as we have seen, some unreasoned moral judgements are unavoidable in any morality.

There are, however, merits, strong points, in the particularist style of thinking which can be absorbed by a rationalist approach. The particularist who insists that we should judge each situation in all its particularity need not necessarily be construed as recommending the suspension of all reason and deliberation. On the contrary, it is just because situations need to be examined in all their particularity that a strenuous use of reason is required; it is just because there are an indefinitely large number of ways in which the same action can be described that both the moral agent and the moral critic experience difficulty, the one in knowing how to act, the other in knowing how to judge. It is a consequence of the inexhaustibility of description that someone who made light of such difficulty and ignored the possibility of further aspects under which a proposed course of action might be regarded would be importing a simplistic style into moral thinking. Those who espouse such a simplistic style often talk as if there were only one correct description of a given action, attainable by all men of good will and good sense. Accordingly, they find communication and dialogue with those who disagree with them difficult. The necessary conditions for arriving at agreement are absent, and even where there is the appearance of agreement the difference in style precludes genuine communication. This is certainly the situation between Fleda and Mrs Gereth in Henry James's *The Spoils of Poynton* (p. 160) where at one point Fleda bursts out: 'You simplify far too much. You always did and you always will. The tangle of life is much more intricate than you've ever, I think, felt it to be. You slash into it . . . with a great pair of shears, you nip at it as if you were one of the Fates!'

Somebody who taught his children that definitive and final descriptions of human actions were forthcoming would have imparted a simplistic style which violates my tenth principle; he would have failed to teach his children genuine moral thinking, he would merely have taught them how to reach decisions from standardized descriptions and clearly defined precepts. Oliver Wendell Holmes jun. once said (*The Common Law*, p. 1) that 'the life of the law is not logic but experience'. A variant of that maxim has application to the moral life. To apply standardized descriptions mechanically to new situations is a quasi-legalistic form of moral reasoning which is only appropriate where morally similar situations recur. However, we can only be in a position to judge whether new situations are similar, morally speaking, to the old if we have been taught non-mechanical moral reflection. A command of non-mechanical moral reflection is, then, essential if we are, as moral agents and thinkers, to be able to distinguish between those situations which do and those which do not admit of mechanical moral reasoning.

13.2. While a morality with reasons is preferable to one without, it is not just any reasons which will suffice. In this section I shall try to show the shortcomings of certain kinds of reason which have sometimes been proffered.

There are some monolithic moralities in which there is one and only one fundamental moral judgement which stipulates as a reason for action the *ipse dixit* of some person or institution. These moralities I shall call, for want of a better name, 'open-cheque moralities'. These are moralities in which the fundamental moral judgement is not an axiom or postulate from which other moral judgements of the same form may be deduced, so much as a moral-judgement-generator. Such fundamental moral judgements are 'One ought to do whatever God/the State/the Church/Il Duce commands'. Moralities based on such fundamental moral judgements are guilty of what Bentham (*Works*, ed. Bowring, Vol. VI, p. 240) ridiculed as 'ipse-dixitism'. Open-cheque moral judgements can only be cashed, as it were, when they are supplemented by statements specifying what in fact is commanded or commended by God, the State or some other sovereign source of moral judgements. Of such statements we can ask not only 'Why did — command that?', but also 'Was — right to command that?', whether the

'——' is filled by the name of a person or an institution. The source of our discomfort when faced with such purportedly fundamental moral judgements does not lie in the illegitimacy of importing singular terms or proper names into fundamental moral judgements. That is not the root of the trouble. It is because the moral-judgement-generation specified in the open-cheque judgement is itself subject to moral appraisal that open-cheque moral judgements are unsuitable to rank as fundamental moral judgements in a morality. It is always open to us to question the goodness of the commander and the rightness of what the commander, be it a person or a group, has commanded. Cudworth's 'Things are what they are not by Will but by Nature', while related to my criticisms, does not suffice to give the *coup de grâce* to open-cheque fundamental moral judgements. As our moral judgements are, we judge the goodness of a commander by the goodness of his intentions and the rightness of his actions. Therefore an open-cheque moral judgement is unfit to be a fundamental moral judgement since it needs to be supplemented by other moral judgements concerned with the character of the agent, as required by Principle VII. These are to the effect that, say, the commander in question has good intentions, that his commands have in the past led to good consequences and that his present commands are made in awareness of the moral nature and quality of the likely consequences.

An open-cheque moral judgement, while unfit to be a *fundamental* moral judgement, can be made intelligible when seen as a fragment of a larger system in which 'ought'-judgements are associated with judgements on the morality of actions and of agents. This does indicate a restriction on the topic of moral judgements and hence on what can count as fundamental reasons in a morality. Something can only be a felicitous moral judgement if it either is, or is associated with, or is intended to be associated with, a judgement about people and their actions. Thus when obedience to God comes to be justified in terms of gratitude or obedience to a creator or on some such lines, an intelligible morality can be constructed around it, although, of course, the open-cheque judgement itself can no longer be the foundation of such a morality.

13.3. The argument of the previous sections has concerned moral judgements in general, whether independent or not. In 13.1 I argued that some moral judgements must be accepted without a reason. For, even if it is desirable for us to give reasons for our moral judgements whenever possible, yet unless the chain of reasons came to an end, we should never be able to learn a morality at all or even to make a start in discussing it intelligently. Inevitably, then, in any morality there are unreasoned moral judgements which are its foundations and furnish the premisses for moral deliberation, providing, as they do, the reasons which we employ in moral reflection. This position is substantially identical with that of Hume (*A Treatise of Human Nature*, Book III, Part I, Sec. I) that 'the rules of morality, therefore, are not conclusions of our reason'. Later in 13.1, still concerned with moral judgements in general, I argued that a morality with reasons was to be preferred to one without. I wish now in the light of these considerations to attempt to decide where the reasons in a reason-giving morality ought to come from. The question is whether in our moral deliberations we should give priority to the deliverances of our individual consciences, or to the more or less clear rules and standards of the dominant social morality, or to whatever traditional or anchored morality has our allegiance.

On the first view, the view of the 'individualist', as I shall call him, it is maintained that genuine moral judgements are those one makes independently, and that a social morality is a mere construct from the independent though, of course, related moral beliefs of individuals. In Bentham's words (*Fragment on Government*, Preface to First Edition) 'Whatever *now* is establishment, *once* was innovation' and it would be misguided to adhere blindly to the moral beliefs of our ancestors. Indeed, on this view, 'to accept a traditional moral standard unreflectively is to fall short in human dignity, which is only fully achieved by individuals who accept only those standards that they consciously approve of for themselves and others' (H. B. Acton, 'Tradition and Other Forms of Order', *Proceedings of the Aristotelian Society*, 1952-3, p. 25).

The second and third views have seldom, if ever, been clearly distinguished by their adherents, and for this reason I shall in the first part of this discussion class them together as 'traditionists'. Both alike question the legitimacy of making independent moral judgements (4.2). Of course, they do not deny that some moralists make independent moral judgements. They contend, however, that these moralists have been misguided and that they have raised spurious questions through their failure to appreciate the 'essentially' social nature of morality. On the traditionist view, all legitimate moral judgements are made at what I called in 4.1 'the level of social stability'. The traditionist urges that in coming to moral decisions we should take our departure from established forms of social order and give priority to existing institutions, existing moral rules, rather than work out the content of 'morality' from scratch. As Burke put it (*Reflections on the Revolution in France*, p. 83), 'No discoveries are to be made in morality', and again (p. 84), 'We are afraid to put men to live and trade each on his own private stock of reason; because we suspect that this stock in each man is small, and that the individuals would do better to avail themselves of the general bank and capital of nations and of ages.' Our rules and institutions may not be perfect, but that is no reason to 'new-model' them or to abandon them entirely. It would be far better, the traditionist argues, to promote gradual improvement. In the course of time imperfections will be weeded out and institutions which are unfit to survive will of themselves decline or wither away. The alternative, as the traditionist sees it, is moral chaos. Apparently unique categorical imperatives are merely the illicit projection of our own 'fancies and wishes' (F. H. Bradley, *Collected Essays*, Vol. I, p. 122), and 'the world of our fancies and wishes, the home of absolute categorical imperatives, has no place in legitimate speculation.' The individualist moralist, on this view, is both arrogant and blind; he is arrogant, for he thinks himself, or wishes to be 'better than the world' and that is to be 'already on the threshold of immorality' (F. H. Bradley, *Ethical Studies*, p. 199); he is blind, for he attempts to determine or calculate what is moral by some especially contrived decision-procedure, oblivious of the moral world in which he is all the time living, 'for morality exists all round us' (ibid. p. 187).

I have dwelt on the exposition of these rival views because rarely has an issue of such importance been at once so influential in determining the conduct of moral philosophy in our time and yet so neglected in the lists of philosophical debate. Before Oakeshott's work[1] it was only in Bradley's review of Sidgwick's *Methods of Ethics* (*Collected Essays*, Vol. I, pp. 71-128) and Prichard's posthumously published lectures on Green (in *Moral Obligation*) that there was much more than a hint at arguments capable of exercising leverage on one side or the other. Because the debate on this issue was scarcely even rehearsed, different styles of moral philosophy for long flourished side by side in mutually neglectful coexistence. The traditionists discussed rights and obligations in society, the individualists the right and the good. The individualists were indeed so obsessed with their own point of view that they were led to give independent uses to such patently social words as 'obligation', 'duty', and 'rights'. Hence in some of their writings 'ought', 'duty', and 'obligation' admit of easy inter-translation. Consequently, when Oxford moral philosophy moved into its analytical phase after 1945 there was, to begin with, an excessive preoccupation with the ordinary employment of moral language in making independent moral judgements and, in particular, with the use of the most general words 'ought', 'right', and 'good'.

It is sometimes assumed that purely conceptual arguments could settle the issue one way or the other. Thus, on the one hand, it is maintained that an individual's moral judgements should override the social morality and the traditional morality, since the so-called moral judgements in a social morality, which are accepted as part of a tradition through indolence or deference, are 'ossified' and so normatively dead or 'hollow'. The argument breaks down because it assumes that a judgement reflecting an ossified standard must be normatively or prescriptively dead. But what distinguishes an ossified standard is not that it lacks normativeness or prescriptiveness, for plainly it can be acted on no less than a non-ossified standard, but that it lacks a rationale and has become detached[2] from the reasons which originally made it appear acceptable.

On the other hand, it is doubtless true, as Hart suggests

---

[1] See Michael Oakeshott's *Rationalism in Politics*, pp. 1-36.
[2] In Hare's words, it has 'extreme descriptive rigidity' (*The Language of Morals*, p. 143).

('Legal and Moral Obligation' in *Essays in Moral Philosophy*,
p. 100) that we can only understand the morality of the individual 'as a development from the primary phenomenon of the
morality of a social group'. Some thinkers have apparently
wanted to go further and actually to infer from this that the
social morality or the traditional morality of a society should
always be given priority over the independent moral judgements
of individuals. This does not follow. Granted, we have learnt
the concept of a morality with reference to the moralities of
groups. This chronological priority in the acquisition of concepts does not necessarily generate a moral priority. Indeed,
there is no necessary chronological priority either. It would
have been possible for individuals to think and to behave in
certain ways and for their conduct to be consciously or un-
consciously imitated by others until it became the norm. But it
is surely also possible for a social morality to take its rise from
the conscious decisions of individuals (that the latter would not
be *called* a 'morality' is irrelevant). Even in a theocratic society
certain moral rules are recognized because of specific moral
decisions allegedly made by a God or an inspired legislator, a
Moses perhaps, who puts the fear of God into those who
appear unwilling or unfit to make moral decisions for themselves. Moreover, it is surely logically possible for individuals
to have independent moralities of their own, specifying how
they are to behave to others, anterior to the existence of any
social or traditional morality. Such people might not have the
concepts of obligation and rights, but they would be able to
make intelligible to one another their possibly differing conceptions of how members of a society should live. The myth
of a Natural Law holding sway in a state of nature is a
shadow cast on political theory by this logical possibility.

Conceptual analysis, then, does not and cannot suffice to
decide which of the three kinds of morality we should give
preference to as the source of reasons. To answer this question we need in the second, explicitly normative, stage of the
argument to treat separately the three contending views as to
which kind of morality should be the dominant and principal
source of reasons. The resolution of this triangular conflict
will be in two parts, only the first part of which can be contributed in this chapter. I shall argue that a part-resolution

can be achieved through the dialectical interplay of the three moral elements I have mentioned.

Each kind of morality has advantages and disadvantages which affect its capacity to act as the primary source of reasons. The advantages of an individual morality are clearly exhibited in its interactions with a social morality. The very diversity of individual moralities and the individual's capacity for moral reappraisal in response to changed circumstances serve to protect social moralities from immobility and unrealism. Were these advantages not offset by countervailing disadvantages, individual moralities might be capable of providing dominant reasons for action. The principal disadvantage lies in the vagaries of the individual conscience. For there appears to be nothing which can act as a check on the individual conscience which may arrogate to itself the authority to legislate for all. A check is needed, because there are in the case of moral beliefs, as is argued in 9.2, no moral facts to which the moral beliefs have to correspond. There is thus no onus on the individual to match his moral beliefs to moral facts. Any check on the individual's morality has, then, to come from some other source, and since the individual conscience's sphere of operation is social, that check must come either from the shared social morality or from the shared traditional or anchored morality.

The principal advantage of a social morality is that it ensures that moral thinking does not take place completely *in vacuo*. Otherwise each one of us would be like a moral Descartes starting from scratch. The raw material of our moral thinking is provided by the customs we are brought up in, by the precepts we are taught, by the picture of human life handed down to us; unreasoned moral judgements are transmitted to us in the form of traditions and Burkean prejudices. A social morality left to itself is certainly teachable; the letter of its precepts can be learnt and the conclusions of its practical syllogisms can follow like logical clockwork. Here again, the advantages are clear to see and one might be tempted to conclude that the moral agent ought to give priority to the social morality of his time and place as a source of reasons. This would be mistaken, since the hazards are serious. For unless the members of the society have acquired skill in non-mechanical moral reflection, they will not have the means to cope with any social changes unenvisaged in the precepts they have learnt, nor will they know how to discuss their social morality with the deviant interpreter we considered in 8.1. In a social morality no procedure is provided for the deliberate change of moral rules and precepts; change is dependent on prior changes in the moralities of individuals. A social morality is protected against the related hazards of immobility and mechanization because it is subject to a double critique, first, a critique which arises from the diversity of individual moralities, and second, a critique from the point of view of an anchored morality, in the light of which it may be found wanting. It is in the appeal to an anchored morality that the Antigones of this world (2.4) may find protection against the tyranny of the dominant social morality of their time and place.

Like the other two elements, an anchored morality has its inherent hazards and advantages. There are two principal hazards. First, the traditional or anchored morality may be treated as if it were actually complete in that it is expected to provide an answer to every moral question or problem. If individuals attempt to achieve this completeness by perfect articulation of the anchored morality, the result is a kind of moral *rigor mortis*, the construction of a casuistic encyclopaedia resembling eighteenth-century treatises of Natural Law, which would preclude the possibility either of non-mechanical moral reflection or of moral change. Second, it was stated in 2.4 that the content of a traditional or anchored morality depended in part on the attitude of those who attempted to identify it. But if this is so, an anchored morality cannot exercise a genuinely independent check on individual or social moralities, for the very nature and extent of its content may already have been influenced or determined by the prior moralities of the identifiers. Unless both these hazards are overcome, it will be impossible for an anchored morality to act as a genuinely independent source of reasons for moral agents. Only, then, if we can find an anchored morality which can overcome these two hazards, will it be capable of acting as an independent source of reasons.

Such an anchored morality is forthcoming, if the characterization of Morality$_A$ in 2.4 is correct. I claimed there that

Morality$_A$ was relatively schematic and stated only the most abstract and general principles of conduct. However, even if Morality$_A$ is not sufficiently schematic to avoid moral disagreement about its content, for the purposes of our present argument we are only concerned with the minimum content or core of Morality$_A$, namely, altruism. Then, since the determination of the minimum content of a traditional morality (the common content of the social moralities of different generations) depends hardly if at all on the attitude of its identifiers, Morality$_A$ or its minimum content or core is vulnerable to neither of the principal hazards I have mentioned. It is this fact which makes it possible for the minimum content of Morality$_A$ to exercise leverage as a genuinely independent source of reasons. This constitutes only a part-resolution of the triangular antinomy, for we have still to argue that Morality$_A$, or its minimum content or core, not merely can but ought to act as a dominant source of reasons. Such an argument will have to wait until Chapter 15. The coda of this section, then, has given us a picture of our moral world as constituting a system of checks and balances, a division of moral powers, which affords it coherence and stability at the same time as it facilitates orderly moral change. The remaining part-resolution will consist in showing that the minimum content of Morality$_A$, namely altruism, has and ought to have a presidential role to play in this system.

13.4. The triangular antinomy is not the only unfinished business of 13.3. For I spoke there of 'the individual conscience which may arrogate to itself the authority to legislate for all.' This hazard incidental to the individual conscience is not a mere quirk but arises from the logical features of moral judgements as we know them. Indeed, it was partly by appealing to this supposedly essential feature of moral judgements in 9.4 that I argued that moral judgements were a kind of assertion, albeit semi-quasi-assertions. However, it is surely possible for somebody to criticize this feature of universal legislation as morally objectionable. 'Surely', an objector may say, 'it is one thing to make decisions for oneself, to set up a rule or to set a standard for oneself to live by, but it is quite another thing to become so intoxicated with the power of universal legislation that one arrogantly legislates for others'. This objection gives rise to a new antinomy between the universal-legislative aspect and what may be called the strict-autonomy aspect of a morality. It would be superficially attractive to deploy my structural principles and adjudicate in favour of the universal-legislative conception. For if people did not legislate for others, there would be no kind of a morality to teach or for a society to discuss or to adopt. But surely, it might be objected, this would be because I have rigged the structural principles in favour of a universal-legislative conception and have assumed without argument that moral judgements are essentially universal-legislative, thus making a matter of definition what is a subject of normative dispute.

This objection can be surmounted, since the universal-legislative nature of moral judgements in general can be vindicated. This is possible because the strict-autonomy view is self-refuting. For the strict-autonomy view has to allow some limited applicability to the universal-legislative conception, since the strict-autonomy adherent, in order to be effective, has to legislate for others. The strict autonomist does not object merely to himself legislating for others, he objects to the arrogance of other people legislating for others. In so objecting he is doing what he objects to. Thus the universal-legislative aspect of moral judgements, if rejected at the ground level, reappears at a higher level. We saw in 6.6 that whatever takes precedence over a moral judgement functions as or actually is a moral judgement. But the strict autonomist's higher-order judgement about the arrogance of his own or others' universal legislation is intended by him to restrict and take precedence over any ground-level moral judgements which he or others may make. It would appear, then, that the strict autonomist's higher-level judgement is a virtual moral judgement which cannot in all consistency be applied to itself. This suggests that the strict autonomist's thesis is likewise concerned with the application of ground-level moral judgements and not their logical character. The intention of the thesis is not to deny their universally legislative character, but solely to recommend that all moral judgements apart from itself have a truncated application.

All that the above argument does is to vindicate the universally legislative nature of moralities; it does nothing to resolve the antinomy on matters of substance, for my structural principles are not strong enough either to support or to rebut the view that moral judgements ought not to be applied to others. However, this does not mean that no conclusions at all may be reached, because when the triangular antinomy has been resolved, some rational means will emerge, as I hope to show (16.3), for constraining the universally legislative character of the individual conscience.

14

Two Higher-order Antinomies

14.1. The antinomies which I shall be dealing with in this chapter are of a more complex and subtle kind than those I discussed in Chapters 12 and 13. Their special character challenges the very feasibility of the kind of enquiry undertaken in this book and that is why their consideration must not be shirked.

In Chapter 1 I said that while it was my aim in my exploration of the nature of moralities to cultivate and maintain moral neutrality or non-alignment, this moral neutrality was highly precarious, there being a standing danger that, infected by the occupational disease of moral philosophers, I would surreptitiously import significant but unacknowledged moral beliefs into my analysis. What at that stage I chose to ignore was that the very activity I was engaged on, the analysis of moral language, carried with it a particular conception or picture of the nature of moralities, from which the moral philosopher can find it difficult to liberate himself. It does not suffice for him to fortify himself against this picture with a few self-conscious and hyper-cautious caveats. Extensive distortions are caused in the logic of morals if moral thinking is pictured as essentially and necessarily a matter of dispassionate spectators surveying standards and ideals, rules and reasons, principles, plans, and policies, issuing categorical prescriptions and making sober calculations whenever they happen to have a cool hour. It may be a true picture of much moral thinking, but it all sounds dauntingly formal and austere, and very far removed from the real world of real human beings, torn by conflicting passions, uncertain which are the promptings of moral principle and which the promptings of the dear self, and too emotionally involved to be able to judge whether they are having a cool hour or not. Unless the logical anatomist recognizes that he has, in a first approximation, as it were, painted a biased and lopsided picture of what a morality is, he cannot evade the just criticism that he is morally aligned for all his pretensions, protests, and defensive arguments. Nevertheless he can evade the criticism if by a kind of 'semantic ascent' he rises to a higher level and with parity of logical esteem critically compares two things, first, the picture which his erstwhile analysis appeared to presuppose, and second, genuine alternative views antithetical to it. I shall try to do this and so compensate for the distorted picture of its moral subject-matter produced by the analytical enterprise itself. There are two such distortions which I shall try to put right in this chapter by an unbiased application of my structural principles to the two antinomies which are uncovered.

14.2. The first antinomy arises in this way. Moral thinking may be pictured not in terms of the subsumption of particular cases under general principles and rules, but rather as the following out in practice of a vision of the world. A large-scale *Weltanschauung* or the impact of a charismatic individual or an inspiring book (say, *De Imitatione Christi* or Mao's *Thoughts*) may lead people to experience a *gestalt*-switch, to see themselves and their lives differently, to have a consequent change of mind or heart leading to a different way of life. Perhaps similar effects are achieved by encounters with a work of art, like *Guernica* or *Anna Karenina*, but more importantly by the first-hand experience of suffering. Perhaps this is the point of the Aeschylean theme that the doer must suffer and by suffering learn, where by 'learn' is meant seeing one's life with new eyes. It is wrong, on this view, to take blind and mechanical obedience to learned precepts and rules as a paradigm of rationality, for precepts and maxims separated from a general vision of man to give them sense and direction are morally lifeless. The followers of such precepts and maxims may, according to their lights, be acting rightly but, lacking a guiding and all-embracing vision, have no real understanding of what they are doing. It is, I suppose, that sort of person, followers of 'The Pilgrim's Scrip', whom George Meredith ridicules so savagely in *The Ordeal of Richard Feverel.*

Now if, indeed, as I have suggested, there are changes in people's vision, there must be prior visions from which these changes are made. These visions are intellectual and emotional frameworks in terms of which their adherents, if I may so call them, understand and react to the world in which they live. Such frameworks have been provided most notably by the great religions. The visions they have expressed and imparted have not been merely personal, concerned, say, with how an individual sees his place in society, but are holistic, concerned with how the whole physical and social world should be re-garded. A man with a holistic vision may see the world not merely as 'the totality of things', but as the totality of things arranged and directed in a particular way, perhaps even with a managerial presence to keep it to its allotted path. Human history to him may be more than a mere succession of events, it will exhibit a discernible pattern, not necessarily enabling one to predict the future but rather to make sense of the past in the way, perhaps, that an aerial photograph can help one to understand the history of a landscape. I have not meant to imply that a holistic vision necessarily involves a belief in theism. A man might after all see the totality of things as lacking an inner purpose or any comforting managerial presence and being no more than 'a tale told by an idiot, . . . signifying nothing.' Others still may have a vision of the social world as inexorably governed by economic and social laws, so that the history of man has to pass through certain determinate stages before it issues in some millennarian but earthly utopia. So much in general terms to indicate some of the diversity of which holistic visions admit.

Visions of the kinds I have mentioned contain, for the most part, a mixture of factual, metaphysical, and normative ele-ments. In that mixture lies their peculiar strength. Because of their factual elements they appear to be amenable to some form of verification or, at any rate, empirical illustration; because of their metaphysical elements they appear immune to any empirical falsification, and because of their normative elements they appear practically relevant and provide a pro-gramme for social action from an apparently rock-solid base. The metaphysical and the normative elements are closely connected; like Kant's Ideas of Reason it is because the meta-physical elements are immune to empirical falsification that they admit of a regulative function as ideals.

While personal visions differ from holistic visions, they may occur either with or without them. An individual may have a vision of his place in society or the world, he may see himself as having a distinctive mission or, even more grandly, a destiny. Or he may see himself as a very ordinary person whose task is solely to attend to his 'station and its duties'. Alternatively, he may see himself as someone very special, as someone entitled to privileges because of his sex, class, caste, position in the family, age, education, intellectual brilliance, or, perhaps most commonly, because as the inevitable centre of his own consciousness he naturally feels special to himself. Many people are hardly aware of what their own personal visions are, although they may become aware of them in retrospect and by contrast, when through disaster, humiliation, or deep suffering they find their whole way of looking at themselves and at others radically and pervasively changed. Certainly this is what happens to Maggie Tulliver in George Eliot's *The Mill on the Floss* (IV. iii), when at a critical point in her life she reads from the work of St. Thomas à Kempis. In George Eliot's words 'it flashed through her like the suddenly apprehended solution of a problem, that all the miseries of her young life had come from fixing her heart on her own pleasure, as if that were the central necessity of the universe; and for the first time she saw the possibility of shifting the position from which she looked at the gratification of her own desires—of taking her stand out of herself, and looking at her own life as an insignificant part of a divinely-guided whole'.

To distinguish, as I have done,[1] moralities of vision from moralities conceived in terms of precepts and choices is a descriptive task, one which it would have been natural for me to undertake in Part I, where I was purporting to deal with the logic of morals. My reasons for postponing consideration of this distinction until the present stage are twofold. First, the analytic method itself appeared to favour one conception of morality as opposed to the other, and therefore the analytic task of distinguishing the two flowed naturally into a comparative and normative study of the conflict or antinomy between the two conceptions. The second reason is that this antinomy has a peculiar higher-order and reflexive character.

[1] See further the symposium 'Vision and Choice in Morality' by R. Hepburn and I. Murdoch, *Proceedings of the Aristotelian Society*, Supp. Vol. XXX.

For we have to consider whether the conception of moral thinking as consisting of precepts and choices is in any way to be preferred as rationally superior to the conception of moral thinking in terms of a vision and its application. It appears that we have to make a choice between two visions, a vision of moral thinking as vision-dominated or a vision of it as choice-dominated.

Let us not worry about this double reflexiveness, which is unavoidable, but proceed to the critical comparison. Consider a morality of precepts and maxims. We saw in 13.1 that a morality consisting solely of particularist precepts would be defective. Here a vision could come to the aid of a situational morality and this in fact happens. Where there are no universal rules or principles, a vision of something or other, be it love or ideal justice or the pursuit of perfection, could make a morality minimally teachable. Indeed, even a morality of clear and crisp rules and principles could be made genuinely teachable by the articulation of a vision in the absence of which it might have been defective. If, for example, a morality appears to be just 'a heap of unconnected obligations', a vision would have a place as providing a principle of unity and connection. It thus imposes a kind of rationality on one's decisions and choices, it provides a coherent rationale and for that very reason enables what is primarily a morality of choice-guiding precepts and maxims better to satisfy the principle of teachability. A vision that sustains and pervades precepts and maxims enables the spirit as well as the letter of a morality to be transmitted, for genuinely to teach or transmit a morality involves not the mere mouthing of a formula, but the imparting of an ability to apply a rule or precept to new or unforeseen circumstances.

Let us now turn to the conception of a morality as being entirely in terms of a vision and its application. Here we shall need to apply both my first and sixth principles, the principles of teachability and of significant guidance. If a vision is to be teachable or transmissable it must be such that adherence to it makes a difference to the way one behaves. A rational vision must be such that its genuine adherents do not always behave in the same way as adherents of a different and apparently incompatible vision. We must, then, have a criterion for applying

the expression 'the same vision', a criterion which must indicate how the genuine adherents of a vision will tend to conduct themselves as opposed to non-adherents or to adherents
of an entirely different vision. But if the availability of such
a criterion is necessary in order that a vision may both be
teachable and satisfy Principle VI, this is tantamount to supplementing the vision by precepts or maxims. For the behaviour or conduct which counts as a criterion of somebody's
acquisition or possession of a vision cannot but be conduct
which is in some sense required or, at any rate, encouraged
by the vision, and this is tantamount to supplementing the
vision by precepts, maxims, etc., which recommend conduct
of one sort as opposed to conduct of some different sort.

Without supplementation by precepts, etc., a vision is
likely to have an open-endedness or indeterminacy which
Kant complained of in the case of the concept of happiness
(*Groundwork of the Metaphysic of Morals* 418, in *The Moral
Law*, p. 85). Consider the vision which the Abbess puts before
Michael in Iris Murdoch's novel *The Bell* (p. 235). She con-
cludes her speech with the words, '"God can always show us,
if we will, a higher and a better way; and we can only learn to
love by loving. Remember that all our failures are ultimately
failures in love. Imperfect love must not be condemned and
rejected, but made perfect. The way is always forward, never
back."' Is this vision of perfect love an adequate substitute
for some specific advice in a desperately complex situation?
Whatever the novelist's intention the last words of the chapter
(p. 236) point to the uselessness of this vision for Michael in
his situation. The Abbess's 'exhortations seemed to him a
marvel rather than a practical inspiration. He was too tarnished
an instrument to do the work that needed doing. Love. He
shook his head. Perhaps only those who had given up the
world had the right to use that word.'

The Abbess's general message, 'Do what perfect love requires' expresses a striking vision and has the form which a
precept or maxim might take. But in so far as it has this form,
it sails under false colours, it is a bogus precept. Michael does
not know what perfect love is or in what direction the way
'forward' lies. There are many different forms of love and they
pull Michael in different directions. The defect of rationality

in the Abbess's speech is that she imparts only the name of the vision. A vision to be teachable needs to be fleshed out in precepts and maxims capable of satisfying the principle of significant guidance. Without such precepts and maxims a vision can be taught only nominally, and that is no teaching at all. Without the constraining force of clear and specific precepts, rules, principles, maxims, standards, and ideals, there would be no determinate limit to what might count as acting in accordance with one's vision, say, of perfect love. (The truth of the previous sentence is even clearer if one takes account of special pleading and its necessarily distorting effect on the moral agent's interpretation of his vision.) To conclude, then, a morality conceived solely in terms of a vision will be compatible with any kind of conduct and will therefore violate the structural principles of teachability and of significant guidance.

To sum up my critical comparison of the two conceptions of moral thinking, an exclusively precept-and-choice morality is not perfectly teachable, in that its teachability can only take the form of literal and mechanical transmission. On the other hand, a morality expressed solely in terms of a vision is teachable only in name, that is, not at all, and clearly violates the principle of sufficient guidance. While, then, both extreme conceptions of moral thinking are to be rejected, the precept-and-choice conception has taken 'less punishment', as they might say in the ring. The comparative situation of the two rivals bears some analogy to Plato's comparison of the relative merits of pleasure and virtue in the *Philebus*, in which, while both fail to make the grade as the Supreme Good, virtue has a higher place than pleasure at the final prize-giving. Likewise with these two rival conceptions of moral thinking, application of my structural principles shows the rational superiority of a morality based on precepts, maxims, etc., and the necessity in any rational morality for the presence of maxims or precepts. Nevertheless, both vision and precepts are important elements in a rational morality. A rational morality needs a pervasive vision to give unity, connection, and direction to diverse and perhaps unconnected precepts and maxims. On the other hand, it needs clear and specific precepts, maxims, standards and ideals to flesh out a vision. One might say, parodying Kant in an entirely different context, precepts without vision are blind, vision without precepts is empty.

14.3. The second antinomy posing special difficulties of a higher-order character is a very ancient one; it is the supposed antinomy between reason and emotion. I tried to show in Chapter 6 that a morality was constituted by an individual's or group's master-concerns and that these master-concerns themselves both sprang from and sought to regulate all those emotions which people are necessarily conscious of as playing an important role in human life. In that chapter I was still concerned with questions of definition, and hence I was not yet prepared to consider the relative merits of a morality primarily based on reason and one primarily based on emotion. The reason why this antinomy poses special difficulty is that Reason appears both as judge and litigant, if one may dramatize and personalize a little. The best procedure is to delineate the two rival conceptions of what a morality ought to be and then try to determine in the light of our structural principles how we should adjudicate. For the adjudicating Reason, unlike the litigant, is represented by the structural principles of 11.5 and by nothing else, unless the advantages of theft over honest toil have utterly suborned me.

There is a style of moral thinking which is carried on as if human beings were solely embodiments of practical reason. If there are any human beings who approximate to such embodiments I do not envy them, but I will not insult them by denying even their logical possibility. There is, however, a standing temptation amongst twentieth-century philosophers to picture all human beings on this model, especially if one has behaviourist tendencies (I do my best to struggle with mine). If emotions are reduced merely to logically complicated desires, and desires are reduced merely to tendencies to action, the inner life comes to be pictured as so attenuated and impoverished that men are nothing but 'intelligent agents' in the minimal Lockean sense. A style of morality consonant with this picture of man's inner life can certainly be taught. A morality would, on such a view, be a matter of taught precepts and behaviour patterns and could be handed down from generation to generation with an almost military precision.

In the best of all possible worlds everything would be what it ought to be and there would never be an emotional hitch in the movement from universally agreed premisses to the inevitable conclusions of practical syllogisms. Deontic logic would provide a reliable description of human social life, and the Kingdom of Nature and the Kingdom of Ends would celebrate their happy but contingent identity.

Something, however, would be wrong. It is not merely that life would be uninteresting without evil or intentional deviance. The purely cerebral kind of morality which I have been ridiculing is certainly logically possible. This perhaps was the great flaw in the education of John Stuart Mill (4.4), that he had been taught a morality of this kind so that, unless his potentiality for feeling and emotion was developed, it was only to be expected that he could feel no 'joy and happiness' in envisaging the realization of the greatest happiness of the greatest number. Fortunately for him he was able to cultivate his emotions, albeit at a late stage. Otherwise he would have been as Dickens pictured the children of Thomas Gradgrind in *Hard Times*, living in accordance with the philosophy of Gradgrind, forever eschewing 'Fancy' both in name and reality.

The teaching of such a purely cerebral morality, however morally admirable the precepts and ideals might be, would nevertheless be rationally-defective. For the new generation, while morally programmed to perfection, would not have been taught any non-mechanical moral reflection. Hence they would be incapable of arriving at reasoned decisions on matters not covered by the traditional precepts or on the interstitial task of filling up the gaps between the precepts which they had so effectively learned. Their reactions would bear some resemblance to those of Dr Who's enemies, the Daleks, who faced with a borderline-case by the Doctor exclaimed only 'We . . . do . . . not . . . know . . . what . . . to . . . do' and suffered the metallic Dalek equivalent of a nervous breakdown.

Perhaps a legal analogy might be helpful here. There is a conception of a legal system which works fairly well for the run-of-the-mill magistrate. According to this conception, the work of lower courts is simply and solely a matter of applying general rules to particular cases. It is all a matter of what some lawyers call 'logic'. At best this conception caters for

statute law expressed in language whose open texture has been
duly compensated for by foolproof stipulative definitions.
Quite apart from this being an unattainable ideal for human
framers of statutes, the conception fares ill in application to
a common-law system, where precedent plays a significant part
and the role of 'logic' in the narrow sense is restricted. At
some time some judges in some courts have to consider
whether a case sufficiently resembles others already decided
and whether these previous cases should be treated as containing binding precedents. For this task non-mechanical legal
reasoning is required. If a law student under a common-law
system knew to perfection *solely* the exact wording of every
statute and judicial judgement, and all four figures of the traditional syllogism, we should not regard him as having been
properly taught to reason on legal matters. It is likewise, I
suggest, with moral reasoning. Non-mechanical moral reflection involves something more than deductions from taught
precepts. This, indeed, is the point where the two antinomies
of this chapter meet, for if a general vision is transmitted to
provide a unifying framework for the precepts, there is hope
that the moral agent will be able to decide for himself what
the situation demands. In this way hyper-cerebral moralities
of the kind I have described can be avoided.

Let us now consider the antithesis of this, which I shall call
the hyper-emotional conception of a morality. A morality,
on this view, is a matter of gut-reactions. The only moral
thinking is 'with the blood'. A social morality, if one is really
necessary, is arrived at by induction from the gut-reactions of
the majority or, at any rate, of a sufficient number of individuals. If it so happens that there is no uniformity in gut-reactions, then this either has to be accepted as an unfortunate
fact or, perhaps, the gut-reactions of the stronger may be
imposed on the weaker.

The legal analogue of this is, I suppose, the theory of 'free
law' (see W. Friedmann's *Legal Theory*, p. 245) which was in
vogue in Germany in the Nazi era when judges imposed
penalties on those convicted of crimes 'in accordance with
"the healthy instinct of the people".' Men can quite clearly be
trained to proceed in the courts on lines such as these but, as
Lon Fuller has emphasized in *The Morality of Law*, structural

principles, what he calls 'the internal morality of law', concerned with what sort of legal system one ought to have, principles such as 'nulla poena sine lege', will plainly be breached. Likewise, I think, a gut-reaction style of morality can in a sense be transmitted or taught in that the younger generation can be told to make moral judgements in accordance with their gut-reactions. But no *specific* morality with this style could be taught, for the teachers rely on their students to produce 'the right' gut-reactions, whatever these might be. Since the guts of individuals can hardly be trusted to turn out 'right', the teachers would presumably, in order to be assured of producing the morality which coincided with their own gut-reactions, have to make use of techniques of behaviour therapy. This, however, would be 'teaching' only in the crude sense in which a psychological experimenter teaches a rat to run a maze. It is one thing to teach reactions in this way, but what is at issue here is not the teaching of behaviour patterns but the teaching of moral thinking and, if this is to be non-mechanical, it must involve something more than conditioning, reinforcement and so on. Any conception of moral thinking must be able to account not only for the man who routinely subsumes actions and people under general rules, the moral subsumer, but also for the existence and the success of the moral reformer. Moreover, a gut-reaction conception of a morality would make moralities undiscussable, so infringing the principle of discussability. A moral disagreement, on this conception of a morality, would be just a matter of my gut against yours, neither of which can furnish the materials of even an uncogent argument. One could go on to show how both these extreme conceptions infringe other of my structural principles, but I see no virtue in overkill. Enough has been said to show that both extreme conceptions of a morality are rationally-defective, since each fails to satisfy at least one of my structural principles.

A rational morality must, in order to satisfy my structural principles, contain both cerebral and emotional elements. This can be seen if we examine the methods of reasoning not of the routine but of the revolutionary moral thinker. In the course of the Sermon on the Mount Jesus of Nazareth said to his audience (St. Matthew, 5.43): 'Ye have heard that it hath been said, Thou shalt love thy neighbour, and hate thine enemy', presumably alluding to ordinary Mediterranean morality. As a moral reformer Jesus aimed to make his hearers leap to a new consensus, one which involved loving one's enemies also. The art of the reforming moralist has to join up an old morality with a new one. He can do that by appealing to traditional beliefs and to elements in the old morality which furnish an analogy to the new, and by appealing also to emotions which he can expect his audience to share with him. Rabbi Hillel and others[2] had already smoothed the way for Jesus. Consequently Jesus's audience had their hearts prepared, if indeed they had listened to Hillel. Hence Jesus is able to proceed smoothly: 'But I say unto you, Love your enemies, bless them that curse you, do good to them that hate you, and pray for them which despitefully use you, and persecute you; That ye may be the children of your Father which is in heaven: for he maketh his sun to rise on the evil and on the good, and sendeth rain on the just and on the unjust. For if ye love them which love you, what reward have ye? do not even the publicans the same? And if ye salute your brethren only, what do ye more than others? do not even the publicans so? Be ye therefore perfect, even as your Father which is in heaven is perfect.'

This section of the Sermon on the Mount is effective in appealing at once to the head and the heart, for while Jesus's basic premises are firmly based on the Hebrew tradition and therefore appeal to his audience's strong feeling for that tradition, he deploys or takes for granted several plausible moral theses and conceptual or quasi-conceptual truths which facilitate his transition to the new morality. In order to appeal to the head Jesus had to give reasons; just his say-so would not have been enough.

I have extracted two related arguments which seem to me to be suggested by the passage quoted above. They are intended to illustrate how the reforming moralist may act on

---

[2] Cf. the following from Rabbi Joshua ben Nehemia (quoted by the Revd. William Barclay in *The Gospel of Matthew*, pp. 174-5): 'Have you ever noticed that the rain fell on the field of A who was righteous and not on the field of B, who was wicked? Or that the sun rose and shone on Israel, who was righteous, and not upon the Gentiles, who were wicked? God causes the sun to shine both on Israel and on the nations, for the Lord is good to all.'

his audience's minds and sensibilities in moving from an old consensus to a new one.

Argument I

    (1) Anyone who is perfect loves all his children/brothers. [Old consensus.]

    (2) The evil as well as the good are God's children. [Malachi 2.10: 'Have we not all one father?']

    (3) Your enemies as well as you are God's children. [An acceptable application of (2).]

∴   (4) Your enemies are your brothers. [From (3).]

    (5) You ought to be perfect. [Matthew 5.48.]

∴   (6) You ought to love your enemies. [From (1), (4), and (5).]

Argument II

    (7) God is perfect. [Old consensus.]

    (8) God's enemies are evil. [Old consensus.]

∴   (9) God loves his enemies. [(1), (2), (3), (7), and (8).]

  (10) All conduct which is exceptionally good and possible is meritorious. [Quasi-conceptual truth.]

  (11) No one who is perfect omits to do whatever is meritorious. [Plausible moral thesis.]

  (12) All conduct of a perfect being towards other persons is exceptionally good. [Plausible moral thesis.]

∴ (13) To love one's enemies is exceptionally good.

  (14) To love one's enemies is possible.

  (15) To love one's enemies is meritorious. [From (10), (13), and (14).]

∴ (16) No one who is perfect omits to love his enemies. [From (11) and (15).]

  (17) You ought to love your enemies. [From (5) and (16).]

Note 1: I have not attempted to do justice to the references either to reward (*misthos*) or to the publicans.

Note 2: The Greek word *perissos* in this context means 'out of the ordinary', 'exceptional', and is not far from the meaning of 'great' in modern colloquial English.

The arguments rely for their persuasiveness on a common vision of the children of Israel as God's children. This vision is important both as illuminating the 'oughty' precepts or imperatives and filling in the notion of perfection. Listeners might well be reminded of, say, Deuteronomy 18.13: 'Thou shalt be perfect with the Lord thy God', the same Greek adjective *teleios* being used in the Septuagint translation as in the Sermon on the Mount as reported by St. Matthew. Exhortations to be like God in holiness appear in Leviticus (e.g., 19.2). It would be conceptually profitable to look further at the acceptability of the premisses about meritoriousness and the nature of 'works of expectation', deeds which you would be blamed for not doing but not praised for doing. But this would take us too far astray from the theme of this section which is to emphasize that the reforming moralist does not merely instruct, he enkindles, and the enkindling is an essential part of the lesson. When Jewish and Christian moralists exhort people to love one another, they do not add a Kantian gloss: 'Please remember that we are speaking of practical love not pathological[3] love.' True, emotions cannot be summoned into existence at will, but they can be cultivated, if educators believe them to be worthy of cultivation, and they can be neglected, with a consequent impoverishment of the whole life and personality. Even a stern moralist like St. Paul has a place for the emotions. Whatever one may think of his views about women or wit, one cannot deny that he exhorts the Christian faithful in Philippi to hope and joy (Philippians, 4.4: 'Rejoice in the Lord alway: and again I say, Rejoice').

The moralist, then, unless he is merely a trotter-out of traditional moral platitudes, has to act on the will through the head and the heart. That is the reason why he needs the knowledge of the psychologist and the art of the orator, and that is why a rational morality needs both cerebral and emotional elements.

14.4. Although I have offered resolutions of both the higher-order antinomies which are the main subject of this chapter, I have as yet not even tried to give a coherent and convincing account of how changes of vision (which I treated in 14.2) can be rational, and how the moralist's appeal to the heart (treated in 14.3) can also be rational in some sense of 'rational'. In this concluding section I shall try to determine whether

[3] See Kant, *Groundwork of the Metaphysic of Morals* 399, in *The Moral Law*, p. 67.

such an account is possible, and then see what conclusions can be drawn from the success or failure of this enterprise. If the going here is hardest, it is partly, at any rate, due to the nature of the terrain. We have little hard and fast knowledge about human nature; we do not even know that there is such a thing. It would be highly tendentious for me to seek in current psychological controversy some fixed points, some incontrovertible truths about human nature upon which my argument could pivot and which would enable me to arrive at comforting conclusions about the rationality of the kind of thinking here in question. There are no easy answers, and whatever conclusions I may eventually reach will be highly tentative and hesitant without, I hope, being woolly or obscure.

An entry into our discussion may best be found by considering an analogy drawn from the philosophy of science. Philosophers of science used to maintain that there was such a thing as a crucial experiment which, once found, would decide once and for all for or against a particular physical theory. More recently, philosophers of science have been more sceptical and have interpreted the crucial experiment not so much as providing a definitive refutation of a theory as discovering an anomaly too difficult for the theory in question to accommodate or explain at that particular stage in a research programme.[4]

I suggest that analogously there are crucial moral experiences. In the light of recent scepticism about the effectiveness of crucial experiments in physics it would be rash to suggest that we have good prospects for giving an account of crucial moral experiences capable of indicating the superiority of one moral stance over another. My initial contention is that individuals or even groups may undergo certain experiences, which appear to them incompatible with and inexplicable by the corpus of moral and other beliefs which they have previously held, and that they are consequently led to abandon a cherished belief or to see themselves and the world they inhabit in a radically different light. An encounter with a charismatic personality, the loss of a loved one, great personal suffering, or even a disaster befalling the whole group of which one is a member, may lead to a sudden change in moral vision. Nothing

---

[4] See the work of Imre Lakatos, *passim*.

in what I have said provides any guarantee or, indeed, the slightest reason for supposing that the views or vision adopted under the influence of the crucial experience will be either morally or otherwise superior to the beliefs previously held or the vision previously dominant. At this juncture I do no more than indicate that such changes occur. Nor is it necessarily moral beliefs rather than factual or metaphysical ones which one might be led to change. There was once a woman who, her son being dangerously ill, prayed to God that he might recover. When he died, she said, 'There is no God, otherwise my son would have lived'. That she so reacted is intelligible to us, but it was only one of a number of possible changes of belief by which she could have come to terms with her grief. She might after all have said, 'God is bad' or 'God must have intended death as a good thing for my son' or 'God does not answer all prayers' or, perhaps, 'One should not make use of petitionary prayer.'

If we can take it as true that experiences such as extreme suffering sometimes produce a change in moral vision and belief, this is all I need to continue my argument. As premisses for my argument I must appeal to facts about human suffering which I mentioned in 11.7, first, that human beings sometimes experience extreme suffering, and second, that one who has experienced great suffering is more likely than others are to feel sympathy for those who experience similar suffering. True, it is possible for some people to react differently; they might feel generally envious of the good fortune of others and in an excess of *Schadenfreude* actually rejoice that others also have to suffer. I hope that it is not wishful thinking on my part to suppose that such people are rare and that, where they do exist, there are special circumstances which explain their to me unenviable condition, say, the desire for revenge, as in the case of the central character of Balzac's *La Cousine Bette*. I hope, then, that I can take it as agreed that sympathy is a natural emotion for human beings to experience.

Not all of us by any means experience the kind of extreme suffering I have mentioned. However, if we do not feel it at first hand, we may experience it vicariously or by proxy. We may know and love somebody who has had such an experience, and sympathy would be a natural emotion for us to feel because of our love for that person. At one further remove, we may know people whom we love who know people whom they love who have had experiences of this kind, and so on. Or, if we have a sufficiently educated imagination, we do not need to have actual knowledge but can imagine, albeit imperfectly, what it would be like for us or those whom we love to undergo experiences of this nature. But perhaps the imagination of some individuals would find this too difficult a task to perform unprompted. In that event we can get help from others. This is where the moralist or the moral theologian or the novelist or the dramatist or the painter or the musician or, indeed, any other artist may find a role to play. It is certainly true, even if we cannot generalize about all artists, that some have tried to win sympathy for the deepest suffering from those who have had no experience of it themselves.

This, after all, is what the actor does. 'What's Hecuba to him or he to Hecuba, That he should weep for her?', but weep he does in our presence and by his weeping induces sympathy in us. The artistry is to win our sympathy for individuals who are after all mere 'might-have-been's' for the sake of those individuals who have been, to make us conscious that 'there but for fortune' go you or go I. The novelist has to write with sufficient conviction and realism for us to feel that we actually do know and care about his or her characters. This was George Eliot's purpose in the writing of her novels. For her (*The George Eliot Letters*, Vol. VI, pp. 216–17) they were 'a set of experiments in life', studies of different kinds of egoism and self-absorption. Since each one of us has a tendency to egoism (isn't that what original sin is?), what we see in the George Eliot novels is not, for the most part, impossible ideal characters whom we could admire but never come to know or love, but by 'a willing suspension of disbelief', lifelike people, people who react as we might in their kind of situation, people whom we could come to know and love, people who, in words philosophers should surely permit us to use, we might have been. George Eliot's purpose was not to make people experience a kind of diffused sympathy for others in general, but to have a genuine understanding and sympathy for 'individual suffering and individual joy' (ibid., Vol. II, p. 403). The educational danger of our sympathy being aroused for the individual joy and suffering of evil men or, at any rate, of undesirable characters was, of course, one of Plato's fears. The justifiability of this fear need not concern us; the important point is that the novelist or other artist can educate the emotion of sympathy so that we extend it more widely to take in other individuals different both in character and in situation from ourselves.

It would seem (and these words are intended to indicate a tentative assertion) that any human being is susceptible of feeling some sympathy for the extreme suffering of others (and perhaps, but to a lesser extent, for the joy or pleasure of others). There are tales of woe which, given sufficient powers of imagination in an individual, can almost be counted on to touch his heart. On the other hand, even if this is so, one cannot be perfectly sure that a man so moved would react in the same way in the world of his own affairs. But it is, I suggest, no accident that the word 'human' functions as a term of commendation and connotes the readiness to be moved by the suffering of others and to act appropriately. From such a linguistic fact we can, of course, infer nothing whatever about what is right or wrong, although we can infer that sympathetic attitudes tend to dominate our moralities and to influence the use of common terms accordingly. There is a widely prevalent expectation that great suffering will receive sympathy from an impartial observer. Two thousand years ago there was, as now, much savagery amongst so-called civilized men; yet the poet Virgil emphasizes the natural expectation of encountering sympathy amongst human beings as opposed to, say, fictional Cyclopes or Harpies, when Aeneas brought by a storm to the shores of Carthage is reassured by the story of Troy depicted on the murals of the rising city and exclaims[5] (I translate freely): '[Here too] things make men weep and misfortune touches human hearts'.

It is remarkable that fiction can often engage human sympathies more than real suffering. While we may see this as a perversion, it is a perversion for which there is a good explanation. 'Our friend, the bad man' (to use Oliver Wendell Holmes's phrase) is not likely to feel much sympathy for his victims. If he did, we should see it as sickening hypocrisy. But it is not

[5] Virgil, *Aeneid* I, line 462: 'sunt lacrimae rerum et mentem mortalia tangunt'.

unknown for a man whom many would regard as a 'moral monster' to be moved by the misfortunes of a stage character, when he has sent myriads to their death without a qualm. The story is told of the Sicilian tyrant, Phalaris, who would weep at the performance of a tragedy, after cheerfully roasting his enemies in a brazen bull. We cannot assume that the natural emotion of human sympathy is entirely lacking in a man because he behaves like 'a moral monster' to those towards whom he feels personal animosity. The stage character has this advantage over the tyrant's enemies, that the tyrant is unlikely to be biased by self-interest in his reaction to the character's misfortunes. The tyrant sees the tragic character through the dramatist's eyes and reacts as the dramatist would have him react.

It is clear, then, that if the moralist wants to act on the heart, mind, and will of 'our friend, the bad man', he must avoid putting to him general cases, where 'the bad man's' sensibility may not become engaged. Again, he must avoid putting to him particular cases where 'the bad man's' self-interest may pervert his judgement. The way to the heart of a 'bad man' must be through particular cases, but particular cases the connection of which with his own interests are entirely hidden from him. Such cases can be looked at by him as an outsider, and for this reason can elicit from him both a sympathetic reaction and a disinterested judgement.

A brilliantly effective way to the 'bad man's' heart is demonstrated by Nathan in 2 Samuel, 12. King David, having committed adultery with Bathsheba, wife of Uriah, sends Uriah into the front line of battle, giving instructions that he should be abandoned to face death from the enemy. Chapter 12 begins after Uriah's death becomes known. 'And the Lord sent Nathan unto David. And he came unto him, and said unto him, There were two men in one city; the one rich, and the other poor. The rich man had exceeding many flocks and herds: But the poor man had nothing, save one little ewe lamb, which he had bought and nourished up: and it grew up together with him, and with his children; it did eat of his own meat, and drank of his own cup, and lay in his bosom, and was unto him as a daughter. And there came a traveller unto the rich man, and he spared to take of his own flock and of his own herd, to dress for the wayfaring man that was come unto him; but took the poor man's lamb, and dressed it for the man that was come to him. And David's anger was greatly kindled against the man; and he said to Nathan, As the Lord liveth, the man that hath done this thing shall surely die: And he shall restore the lamb fourfold, because he did this thing, and because he had no pity. And Nathan said to David, Thou art the man.' Nathan's psychological insight enables him to trap David into self-condemnation. In order to appeal to David's moral sensibility David has to be morally distanced; that is what the irrelevant detail of the story achieves. On the other hand, the story has to have concealed within it common features which David is likely to see as morally relevant when the parallelism between the rich man's deed and his own is pointed out. Nathan is trying to get David's head and heart to work together, to persuade David to generalize from the story, to see the same universal in both particulars. After Nathan has morally distanced David, the words 'Thou art the man' utterly annihilate the moral distance so cunningly contrived and force David to apply his disinterested moral judgement to his own case.[6]

Nathan was lucky. David was only half bad, he resembled that city of Aristotle's which had good laws but did not use them. He was a moral lapser (5.5), and that is why he needed a Nathan. Nathan would have had much less success with Hitler or Stalin. We have to reckon with the possibility that, natural though sympathy with individual suffering is, there are other vastly different human passions. These can form the motive power for moral principles which gentle readers of works of moral philosophy would find horrifying or repellent. Unlimited ambition or plain hero-worship may be the source

---

[6] The rationale of Nathan's technique is well expressed by Pope in one of his self-edited letters (*The Correspondence of Alexander Pope*, Vol. III, pp. 418–19): '. . . the best Precepts, as well as the best Laws, would prove of small use, if there were no Examples to inforce them. To attack Vices in the abstract, without touching Persons, may be safe fighting indeed, but it is fighting with Shadows. General propositions are obscure, misty, and uncertain, compar'd with plain, full and home examples: Precepts only apply to our Reason, which in most men is but weak: Examples are pictures, and strike the Senses, nay raise the Passions, and call in those (the strongest and most general of all motives) to the aid of reformation. Every Vicious man makes the case his own; and that is the only way by which such men can be affected, much less deterr'd.'

of a *Macht*-morality in the light of which emotions like sympathy, pity, and compassion would appear to be the mark of men who are 'too full of the milk of human kindness'. Courage, toughness, and strength are also valued amongst the heroic virtues, and there are passions which go with them, say, the emotion of manly pride which somebody feels whose maxim is 'nemo me impune lacessit'. We have no guarantee that the man who possessed Gyges' ring (Plato, *The Republic*, Book II, 359 f) would derive his principles from the sympathetic passions.

However natural and near-universal the sympathetic emotions may be, this fact does not enable us to use them as a sifting device to eliminate all other moralities associated with opposite emotions, which may be just as natural and almost as universal. Nor do we have any guarantee that crucial experiences cannot work in the reverse direction and change a man from being full of compassion to being pitiless and revengeful. Imagine a man of noble ideals, dedicated to helping the poor, healing the sick, comforting the bereaved, a devoted husband, a loving father, a dutiful son, a faithful friend. Suppose that such a man is convicted of a crime he did not commit on a trumped-up charge by perjured evidence and is condemned to a slow, painful, and ignominious death. Let us suppose further that in his hour of need he is deserted by all his erstwhile friends and only survives because he is removed prematurely from the place of execution and by good luck cast on to a heap of leaves as if dead. If the warmth of his surroundings enabled him to revive and slowly recover enough strength to forage for himself and begin a new life far from his false friends, we would not, I think, be surprised if the terrible experience he had endured sadly changed him from the man he was. We may suppose that now he sees human beings as being all irredeemably bad, and the singleness of purpose, which in his pre-execution life he used so benevolently, is now directed solely towards the carrying out of a terrible revenge. The primary duty of each man, as he sees it, is to become a genuine *Mensch*; man for him is now 'essentially' a power-seeking animal, and a man can only achieve true human dignity when he realizes himself and attains power over others. The nearest parallel in fiction is, I suppose, Dumas's

Edmond Dantès in *Le Comte de Monte-Cristo*. The case I have depicted is logically and, I maintain, psychologically possible. If this is so, it is clear that crucial moral experiences can lead to the dominance of passions other than the sympathetic ones. The moral traffic resulting from crucial experiences is not necessarily one-way only, and hence we are unable to differentiate between veridical and non-veridical crucial experiences merely by inspecting the direction of moral 'conversion'. The hope of distinguishing rational from non-rational changes of vision cannot then be realized.

The concluding section of this chapter has been more tentatively exploratory than any other chapter of the book, and it has at the same time been more personal and almost moralistic. No apology is needed for this; there has been no real departure from the general guidelines about moral non-alignment which I laid down for myself at the beginning of this enquiry. I have nowhere, I think, insinuated my own moral beliefs, although I have made certain assumptions about the kind of moral position which readers of this chapter are likely to hold. If, however, anybody thinks that I have departed significantly from my self-imposed 'rules of the game', let him take comfort that the negative result of my argument clearly indicates that what in my own eyes would have been an intellectual crime does not pay. The upshot of this section has been quite clearly defeat, but a defeat from which we can extract a lesson. In the course of the argument I made use of two highly general facts about human suffering. That I was not able to use them to arrive at any dramatic conclusion is no argument against making use of other facts about the human situation to give greater 'bite' to the structural constraints I have up till now deployed. In the next chapter I shall try to use both kinds of constraint to justify the altruistic core of Morality$_A$.

15

The Emergence of Altruism

15.1. In 13.3 I began examining a triangular antinomy involving three elements, the moralities of individuals, the contemporary social morality, and some anchored morality. At that stage I was only able to offer a part-resolution of the antinomy. This part-resolution consisted in showing that a schematic anchored morality, like Morality$_A$ or its altruistic core, was capable of providing moral agents with independent and dominant reasons. In this chapter I want to complete the resolution and, by deploying both structural and factual constraints, to show that it is self-interestedly rational to be altruistic and that therefore Morality$_A$'s altruistic core ought, where there is conflict, to be given preference over individual and social moralities as a source of reasons. In this way I hope to justify our calling one particular morality 'Morality' and one particular point of view 'the moral point of view'.

This enquiry will be a recognizable attempt to answer the seventh principal question of moral philosophy (1.1) concerned with whether one ought, or whether it is in one's interest, to be moral. The traditional conception of how this question should be approached bears some resemblance to the traditional conception of how to justify belief in an external world. In epistemological theory one was supposed to start with belief in one's own existence and move inferentially to belief in an external world. In moral theory one was supposed to start with the belief that caring for oneself was rational and move inferentially to the belief that caring for others was rational. The rules of the game, as it were, forbade the unargued assumption that the sympathetic emotions were part of the nature of man. For if they were, the sympathetic nature of man would be a fixed point and self-interested rationality would of itself involve caring for others. Since we have taken rationality to be merely a matter of finding means appropriate to ends, then were the welfare of others to be one of those ends, it would be self-interestedly rational to promote that welfare. If, however, as I admitted in 14.4, the sympathetic emotions are not necessarily dominant in man, then self-interested rationality has to be interpreted more narrowly.

The argument will have two stages. First, I want in this section to consider the antinomy between egoism and altruism and to see how far we can get towards resolving that antinomy by the application of structural constraints only. Second (15.2–15.4), I shall import factual constraints, taking as my point of departure the existence of co-operative goals and arguing for the rationality of co-operation. The prisoner's dilemma will be examined and it will be contended that the human situation is structured like a transformed prisoner's dilemma. Four means of transforming the prisoner's dilemma are considered apart from extension to more than two persons, external coercion, internalized sanctions, conditional strategies, and iteration. All four are operative in real life and hence the human situation is formally analogous to the prisoner's dilemma as transformed by these four devices. On this basis, it is argued, a strategy of conditional co-operation is rational although precarious. Finally, I shall argue (15.5) that it is rational for people not only to behave as if they were altruistic but also actually to internalize altruism and be altruistic.

The antinomy between egoism and altruism may be expounded as follows. On the one hand, it might be said that moralities are essentially concerned with other-regarding considerations and that therefore (a) morality ought to be altruistic. The whole point of (a) morality is to set limits to man's natural egoism; it is its task, on this view, to give reasons for rejecting egoism, not to countenance or, what would be worse, include it. By contrast, the view is sometimes taken that egoism provides an entrance into (a) morality, furnishing one of 'the methods of ethics'. Consequently, in order for a morality to be accepted, it must be rational even for the purely self-interested individual to choose it.

My structural principles do not enable me to reject any form of egoism or altruism. Thus while extreme forms of egoism and altruism are difficult to teach, we cannot show

that any are impossible to teach and hence the principle of
teachability cannot obtain a purchase. Let us consider first
an extreme form of particularist egoism such as is held by
Gwendolen Harleth in George Eliot's *Daniel Deronda* (Book
I, Chapter VII) who says, 'My plan is to do what pleases me'.
Plainly such a 'plan' or way of life, or whatever one cares to
call it—and whether one calls it a morality or not does not
matter—is open to the objection that it is imperfectly teachable. Perhaps her mother did teach her other children a par-
ticularistic altruism expressed in the words 'Everybody ought
to do what Gwendolen wants.' The *prima facie* arbitrariness
of such a dictum makes it defective like other open-cheque
moral judgements (13.2). The dictum can carry conviction
and so be genuinely taught only if people can be convinced
that Gwendolen is of such a character that others are justified in treating her as 'special'. Neither Gwendolen Harleth
nor any other individual can make mere reasons of his or her
self-interest weigh with other people or exercise leverage on
them without proved specialness. Those who wanted to argue
that one ought to do what the State demands had to persuade
others of the truth of a metaphysical theory to the effect that
the State was something over and above individual citizens,
that it was something more worthy of respect if not of worship.
Plainly, too, theological moralists would say that God was
special, that we are required to love God especially, the love
of God neither being identical with nor being of the same kind
as love for one's neighbour. Consider any two people, A and
B. If by nature considerations of B's self-interest weigh most
heavily with B and considerations of A's self-interest weigh
most heavily with A, in the absence of proof of specialness
A and B will each find it equally difficult to convince the other
of the superior weight of considerations of his own self-interest.
In order for a morality to be *perfectly* teachable it must embody more than considerations of a particular individual's
self-interest. One way of achieving this is by universalizing
egoism; this is the tribute which egoism pays to impersonality.
A universalizing egoism which maintains that each and every
person should pursue his own self-interest will give each person
the same amount of leverage as any other.
Universalizing egoism, however, runs into difficulties in its

turn. These difficulties always arise when a morality values what I shall call 'relational' goods or values. Sometimes we value not merely some attribute but a relationship of a person with other persons or things. Egoism, altruism, and all kinds of loyalty including patriotism come under the heading of relational goods or values. A man is patriotic if he is loyal to *his own* country, a man is egoistic if he is 'loyal' to *his own* interests, a man is altruistic if he looks after *other* people's interests. From the point of view of relational goods, if you look after your own interests, you are not doing the same thing as somebody else does if he is looking after your interests.

Let us, in order to think more effectively about egoism, consider difficulties which arise in giving a description of patriotism. Two types of patriotism may be distinguished, particularist patriotism and universalizing patriotism. The particularist patriot will hold that the interests of *his* country are paramount and ought to be paramount for himself and everybody else at all times, since he believes his own country to be special. The universalizing patriot, on the other hand, will have to face a conflict. He believes that everybody should defend the interests of his *own* country, whichever that may be. He thus denies himself the ruthlessness of the particularist patriot who can sincerely welcome the treason of an enemy country's national. For he values not merely patriotism, the relational good, but the state of mind from which this good arises. He therefore cannot condone his enemy's treason, although in all consistency his patriotism leads him to work for that very end. Plainly there is conflict here, but it is a real and tenable position. He encourages what he believes to be bad, he fosters behaviour which he despises, namely, treason. The universalizing patriot may in justification of his behaviour appeal to other goods apart from patriotism. He may, for example, argue that his country is morally good while his enemy's country is morally evil. Alternatively, if he does not see the conflict as one between good and evil, he may be content for the whole clash to be settled by force of arms. His attitude may then be expressed as follows: let each look to himself and accept the arbitrament of battle. In such circumstances he might deem everything fair except maybe the attempt to suborn one of his opponents. I say 'maybe' because it is possible to envisage a wide range of attitudes and approaches here, all compatible with a universalizing patriotism.

Let us turn back to the universalizing egoist. What we can learn from the case of the corresponding kind of patriot is that the conflict need not be seen as a straightforward contradiction, as some have argued (see Brian Medlin's 'Ultimate Principles and Ethical Egoism' in *Morality and Rational Self-Interest*). The universalizing egoist believes that everybody ought to look after his own interests. If he believes this, he must believe that, when other people's interests conflict with his, *they* would do right in struggling against his interests while *he* would be doing right in defending them. If they acted in his interests he would presumably despise them for so doing, although he would welcome their action from his own personal point of view. Being a universalizing egoist, he has to hold that the world would be a better place if each and every person tried to look after his own interests. If conflict results, this he accepts as part of the better world. But the resulting conflict is not of merely theoretical interest, it is conflict which causes him to suffer accordingly. For if everybody else looks after his own interests, his (the egoist's) interests are likely to suffer. Therefore he can most effectively look after his own interests by persuading others of the incorrectness of his universalizing egoism. This internal conflict is the price he has to pay for abandoning the all too simple ethic of the particularist egoist. Some have seen this conflict as an inconsistency affecting the whole coherence of the egoistic view. But only the egoist who refused to condone conflict is open to objection on this score. It should come as no surprise that egoism involves the condonation of conflict, for Hobbes's war of all against all in a state of nature is a consequence of systematic egoism. One thing is clear. To be committed to conflict is not the same as to be committed to inconsistency. Hence the universalizing egoist cannot be logically faulted for condoning conflict.

Interestingly, the altruist's position encounters similar difficulties when he attempts to teach his altruism to his children. In so far as he is an altruist, he cares for their best interests, but if he teaches them what he believes, he will be teaching them principles which may not be in their best interests; if they live in accordance with his principles, they will not be putting their own interests first. While his children are 'others' for their altruistic parent, they are not 'others' for themselves. The quasi-logical difficulties for the altruist, no less than for the egoist, are due to the token-reflexive terms 'one's own' and 'others', terms whose reference varies with the speaker or thinker.

The quasi-logical difficulties which I have mentioned cannot be used to eliminate forms of egoism and altruism for two reasons. First, they are merely difficulties in expounding and teaching, and not impossibilities, and second, the difficulties are symmetrical and apply to both egoism and altruism; they cannot therefore be exploited in order to eliminate one to the advantage of the other. Despite the difficulties both egoism and altruism are coherent.

15.2. Application of a structural constraint, the principle of teachability, has not resolved the antinomy between egoism and altruism, since we have been unable to eliminate even the extreme cases as irrational. We shall need, then, to deploy factual constraints too in the hope that they will have more bite.

It cannot be (self-interestedly) rational for the egoist to treat other people's desires as reasons for action on his part whether or not others behave likewise. If others do not behave in this way, he has no reason of self-interest to behave so. 'For he who should be modest, and tractable, and perform all he promises, in such time, and place, where no man else should do so, should but make himself a prey to others, and pursue his own certain ruin' (Hobbes, *Leviathan*, p. 103). On the other hand, even if all others behave altruistically, the egoist has every incentive to take a 'free ride' at their expense. From the point of view of individual self-interested rationality, however other people may behave, the only rational course is egoism. The result is that everybody loses out. This is illustrated by the kind of society depicted by E. C. Banfield in his *The Moral Basis of a Backward Society*, where he shows how the families of a Southern Italian village condemn themselves to economic backwardness by eschewing mutual aid and co-operation.

Systematic egoism lands its adherents in a human dilemma. I shall try to show that this human dilemma can be represented

as analogous to the well-known prisoner's dilemma. Apart
from the fact that most societies contain more than two
people, we shall need to refer to three important truths (11.7)
in our consideration of the human dilemma, first, that most
men have co-operative goals, second, that human life is sufficiently long for situations experienced as similar to recur, and
third, that most men do not know either of themselves or
others when they will die.

   In order to show that the 'game of life' is sufficiently like
the game of prisoner's dilemma, I need the first truth that
most or all men have some co-operative goals. There is a class
of human goals which we require the assistance of others in
achieving. These I call 'co-operative goals', following Mrs
Ullman-Margalit's terminology in her book *The Emergence of
Norms*. There (pp. 130–1) she defines co-operative goals as
follows:

A *co-operative goal*, with respect to a certain group of agents, is a goal
G such that
   (1) it is in the interest of each agent that G be attained;
   (2) G is attainable by none of the agents alone;
   (3) G is attainable by all the agents together, given appropriate plan-
       ning and division of roles among them.

I wish to borrow this definition with only slight modification
to the three clauses. It is not necessarily in the *interest* of an
agent that a co-operative goal be attained. It suffices if each
agent wants or wishes G to be attained. Further, G may be
attainable by one of the agents alone, but only slowly or with
difficulty. Again, G does not necessarily need conscious planning or the deliberate allocation of roles. All that is necessary
is that each agent adjusts to the goal-seeking activity of others
and the adjustment may be of a tacit and inexplicit nature.
Planning and role-allocation would be one explicit means of
mutual adjustment. Hence the revised definition will run: 'A
co-operative goal, with respect to a certain group of agents,
is a goal G such that
   (1) each agent wishes or wants that G be attained;
   (2) G is attainable either by no single agent alone or by no
       single agent in its entirety or by no single agent with
       ease or speed;

(3) G is attainable by all the agents together, given co-ordination or mutual adjustment.'

One kind of co-operative goal is the enjoyment of public goods. A public good may be defined with P. A. Samuelson ('Pure Theory of Public Expenditure and Taxation' in *Public Economics*, p. 108) as a good 'that enters two or more persons' utility.' Thus clean air, parks, roads, and national defence are public goods in this sense. The enjoyment of some private goods is a co-operative goal too if the co-operation or the acquiescence of others is necessary for their production. The variety of co-operative goals does not concern me here. All I need to assume for the purposes of my argument is that there are co-operative goals in the sense defined and that all human beings desire the attainment of some co-operative goals; in default of achieving these individuals lose out.

With regard to some co-operative goals there is what Amartya Sen[1] calls an 'assurance problem'; while each person wishes for the goal in question, he is only prepared to make the effort to work towards that goal if other people are prepared to do so too. The factory-owner who, living in an industrial city near his own factory and others, prefers all factory-owners to invest in smoke-prevention appliances, is prepared to do so himself *if and only if* the other factory-owners do likewise. The problem here is to have correct beliefs, assurance about the conduct of others, and subsequently to co-ordinate activity towards the co-operative goal. If all men had identical interests, the assurance problem would be the only hurdle. But as things are, desires, preferences, and interests may be diametrically opposed and thus people are often unwilling to contribute towards a co-operative goal even if everybody else is doing so; indeed, they may be unwilling *because* everybody else is doing so. The assurance problem is then compounded by the tempta-tion to be a free-rider. It is this more complex and less tract-able situation typical of the human condition which may best be studied in the prisoner's dilemma.

15.3. The story of the prisoner's dilemma is as follows. Two prisoners, A and B, held separately and incommunicado, are

[1] For the assurance game see A. Sen, 'Choice, Ordering and Morality' in *Practical Reason*, pp. 59–60; and 'Isolation, Assurance and the Social Rate of Discount', *Quarterly Journal of Economics*, Vol. lxxxi, 1967, p. 122.

accused of a major crime. Without a confession from one of them there is insufficient evidence to convict and so each is given an incentive to confess by being informed of the following pay-offs. If the one confesses while the other does not, the former will go scot-free, while the other will get the severer sentence of ten years. If they both confess, they will each receive five years' imprisonment. If both refuse to confess, they will be convicted on a minor charge and will only receive one year of imprisonment each. The following game-theoretical matrix represents the situation, where disutility is indicated by negative integers corresponding to years of imprisonment:

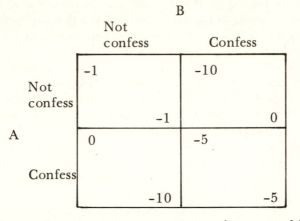

The matrix represents a non-co-operative game which has only one rational solution, the lower right cell. By 'rational' is meant 'rational relative to the end of satisfying one's own desires only', and it is assumed that each prisoner desires either to be free or to be imprisoned for as short a time as possible. Only the strategy of confessing produces a situation which in game-theoretical language is 'stable'. One cannot do better than by confessing, whatever the other prisoner does. If the other confesses, one cannot rationally not confess oneself, while if the other does not confess, one cannot rationally let pass the opportunity of going free. This reasoning applies even if the prisoners have entered into a prior bargain, for it will pay each to break the bargain. Perfect self-interested rationality on the part of each prisoner will earn them five years' imprisonment each. Yet the optimal outcome for them jointly is for them both to refuse to confess, in which case each receives one year's imprisonment only. Plainly there is something amiss with a game in which a pursuit of rational strategies leads to a less than optimal outcome. There is a temptation to say, as Luce and Raiffa put it (R. D. Luce and H. Raiffa, *Games and Decisions*, p. 97): '"There should be a law against such games!"' The thought behind this is that it is rational to try and transform the game into one which will yield an optimal outcome.

The game can be so transformed by means of four devices. First, we can change the relative pay-offs (and thus the game) by imposing external sanctions for betraying one's fellow prisoner. Thus if the prisoners know in advance that reprisals after release for having informed on one's fellow prisoner will be equivalent in disutility to six years' imprisonment, this amounts to changing the superior pay-off in the upper right and lower left cells from 0 to –6. In this event the strategy of not confessing becomes the rational strategy for each prisoner, and the non-co-operative game is transformed into a co-operative game with a 'stable' solution. Second, the pay-offs can further be changed if either sympathetic emotions or a sense of honour or of loyalty act on the prisoners' minds to 'punish' them for defection. Third, account can be taken of conditional strategies like 'I will co-operate if you will'. A player's adopting a conditional strategy in ordinary prisoner's dilemma does not induce a co-operative solution (i.e., the upper left cell). To decide on the strategy 'I will co-operate if you will' will be of no avail in obtaining an improved solution, since (a) in the ordinary prisoner's dilemma no communication takes place, and (b) if it did take place there would be no means of knowing that it was truthful. Verification that a given conditional strategy really was the strategy of the other player could only take place after a sequence of trial situations in which the issue of one trial affected that of the next. Hence to supplement the third we need a fourth transforming device which will change the game from one-off to repeated prisoner's dilemma. In such a game information about players' conditional strategies would be inferred from their conduct in individual prisoner's dilemma (PD) situations. It is tempting to assume that in the repeated game ratting on the other prisoner would not be to the long-term advantage of either, since each runs the risk of reprisals from the other, as a consequence of which he would always be saddled with a less than optimal outcome. But this would hold only if the number of individual games either were unknown or were infinite. For if a player knows that a given game is the last, it is rational for him to treat it as an ordinary prisoner's dilemma and so not to co-operate. But if the players know that their last game will be played as ordinary prisoner's dilemma, it will be rational for them to treat the penultimate game in the same manner, and so on by a kind of backward induction[2] until one reaches the first game. It is a condition, then, of a co-operative solution's being possible in repeated prisoner's dilemma that the number of individual PD situations to be encountered is not known.

Later I shall discuss how the game so transformed provides a model of the human situation. But before that I want to determine to what extent our condition is like that of the two prisoners in the untransformed game. There are some co-operative goals such that a typical agent A from a purely egoistic point of view has the following order of preferences among states of affairs:

   (i)   Everybody but A promoting the goal;
  (ii) Everybody promoting the goal;
 (iii) Nobody promoting the goal;
 (iv) Nobody but A promoting the goal.

Because it generates a prisoner's dilemma situation I shall call this order of preference a 'PD-order'. Now it will not do to say that there are some goals with reference to which every-body has a PD-order of preference. For with reference to any co-operative goal there may always be individuals to whom the cost of co-operation is greater than the benefit accruing therefrom. For example, the cost to a factory-owner of eli-minating the smoke from his factory chimneys may outweigh the benefit he receives from living in a smokeless zone. Perhaps he would rather take his chance in a free-for-all in which nobody aims at smoke reduction than have to behave in this particular other-regarding fashion, that is, he may prefer (iii) to (ii). Hence from a bargaining point of view he always has the upper hand over somebody who has the PD-order. The

---

[2] For this regress argument see Luce and Raiffa, ibid. pp. 98–9.

best they could agree on is state of affairs (iii); the factory-owner's antagonist cannot persuade him to accept a mutually advantageous move to (ii), because for the factory-owner (ii) stands lower than (iii). The asymmetry is thus to his bargaining advantage. Indeed, there may always be some people who because of their relative strength or invulnerability are in a better bargaining position than others. Let us suppose that Matthew,[3] a partially deaf trumpet player, and Luke, a highly sensitive pianist, are neighbours in adjacent flats with acoustically 'transparent' walls. Each of them desires to arrange his musical recreation time so as not to be disturbed by the other, but as it happens the only hour available for either is between 9 and 10 p.m. Then the fact that it is only Luke's loudest chords which will disturb Matthew means that, when Matthew negotiates with Luke in order to decide which days each should play on, he will do so from a position of strength.

Matthew's neighbours and the factory-owner's neighbours have no leverage unless there are co-operative goals other than noise reduction and smoke reduction which Matthew or the factory-owner needs the co-operation of others in promoting. As long as we describe the situation in terms of a particular co-operative goal, as long, say, as we describe the factory-owner as conforming or failing to conform to a clean-air norm or rule, there is an asymmetry in the bargaining situation. If, on the other hand, we describe the factory-owner and the trumpeter as conforming or failing to conform to *some* other-regarding norm or rule, then both the factory-owner and his neighbours, both Matthew and Luke become more on a par with one another. For everybody will need the co-operation of some others in the achievement of some goal, even if there are relatively few things which everybody wants everybody else to co-operate in achieving. Each of us stands to benefit from some other-regarding rules and stands to lose if others ignore some other-regarding rules. What I am saying here is that everybody has some other-regarding rules which it pays him that others should observe. With respect to conforming to other-regarding rules or behaving altruistically, the PD-order of preference holds, I submit, for each agent from a standpoint

[3] The example is adapted from R. B. Braithwaite's *Theory of Games as a Tool for the Moral Philosopher.*

of purely self-interested rationality. His order of preference is:

   (i) Everybody but him behaving altruistically;

  (ii) Everybody behaving altruistically;

 (iii) Nobody behaving altruistically;

 (iv) Nobody but him behaving altruistically.

Because men are interdependent, if A is dependent on B's co-operation for attaining a co-operative goal G_1, there is likely to be another goal G_2, such that B is dependent on a third person's co-operation for its attainment. By living in society men ensure that they will encounter PD-like situations. Only by becoming completely self-sufficient and desocializing himself can a man avoid PD-like situations or opt out of 'the morality game'. But this is not a live option. True, there are misanthropists, bizarre characters who appear to lack the desire to co-operate with others. But it is not that they do not want to co-operate; misanthropists are not so much non-co-operators as disillusioned co-operators, they object not to co-operation, but to their fellow humans whose co-operation they are expected to seek. Co-operation, then, despite the existence of occasional misanthropists, is a universal focal end. In the satisfaction of basic needs and desires each man is dependent upon a measure of co-operation from others.

The human situation resembles transformed many-person prisoner's dilemma. It has the following principal features. First, there is an element of coercion. I argued in Chapter 6 that moral matters are concerned with what we think to be most important. Some of these moral matters we think to be so important that we are unwilling to leave them to the workings of men's conscience or good nature or even to their fear of the diffuse and informal sanctions of social morality. The coercive framework of law is thus needed and this is why even in the most primitive societies those parts of a morality which are thought to be most important and binding are backed by legal sanctions. The effect of legal sanctions is to change the pay-offs so that the game is transformed from being a non-co-operative to being a co-operative one. As far as the legally enforceable part of a morality is concerned, at any rate, the human situation is no longer formally analogous to the game of ordinary prisoner's dilemma.

With regard to the remainder of a morality, we have to rely on the second, third, and fourth devices to counter the inherent instability of isolated and independent PD situations. With regard to internal sanctions, it is the aim of what we call 'moral education' to produce an internalized altruism which, were such education perfectly successful, would transform the game into a co-operative one. Coercion in this event would be rendered superfluous. The third and fourth transforming devices (conditional strategies and iteration) may be taken together. That the repeated prisoner's dilemma is an appropriate model of the human situation is ensured by two of the highly general factual constraints of 11.7, first, that human life is sufficiently long for situations experienced as similar to recur, and second, that in general no one knows the length of his life. The first fact makes it possible for men to communicate to one another their conditional strategies (e.g., 'I will play ball with you, if you play ball with me') and to have time to assure themselves of each other's good faith. It will thus be possible for defectors to be repaid in kind in the next PD situation, the next round of 'the game', and for them to be confined to a less than optimal solution, namely, that represented by the lower right cell of the prisoner's dilemma matrix. However, the first fact would not of itself suffice to make co-operation rational. For, as we saw before, if in repeated prisoner's dilemma it is known when the last game will be, it becomes rational to treat the last game as an ordinary prisoner's dilemma with the consequence that by backward induction the iterated game disintegrates into a many-stage game of ordinary prisoner's dilemma. This is where the second fact comes in, for if no one knows the length of his life, a man will not know when his last PD situation will be and he will therefore avail himself of opportunistic gamesmanship at his peril.

There are exceptions to my second fact. First, at a time of acute famine, devastation, or plague death may become almost certain. This can be driven home by reading Thucydides' graphic first-hand account of the Athenian plague at the beginning of the Peloponnesian War and its effect on moral attitudes (*The History of the Peloponnesian War*, II, 53, in Sir Richard Livingstone's translation, p. 122): 'They reflected that life and wealth alike were transitory, and resolved to live for pleasure and enjoy themselves quickly. No one was eager to persevere in the ideals of honour—it was so uncertain whether they would be spared to attain the object; present enjoyment, and all that contributed to it, was accepted as both honourable and useful. Fear of gods or law of man were no restraint. They thought that it made no difference whether they worshipped God or not, as they saw all alike perishing; no one expected to live to be brought to trial for his offences, but each felt that a far severer sentence had been already passed upon them all and hung over their heads, and before this fell it was only reasonable to enjoy life a little.' The second exception arises from the decision to commit suicide at a particular time. A potential suicide who has made such a decision has an 'intentional knowledge' of his own death. We should not find it surprising or irrational if a man who had such knowledge resolved to 'eat, drink, and be merry' and ignore the needs of others. But for most men at most times the second fact holds and the veil of uncertainty remains in place. For them our argument goes through.

The first fact, then, ensures that there is more than one choice-situation, that more than one 'game' is likely to be played and that therefore the iterated, not the ordinary, prisoner's dilemma is a plausible model for the human situation. The second fact, on the other hand, ensures that since we all judge behind a veil of uncertainty, we cannot know when long-run considerations will cease to be relevant, and it is therefore rational to treat long-run considerations as relevant, unless we have good reason to suppose the opposite. It is rational, then, to behave as if we were involved in a game of iterated prisoner's dilemma.

There are important consequences of taking the game of iterated prisoner's dilemma as our model. First, unlike the one-off prisoners, in real life we communicate with one another. Life is sufficiently long for situations experienced as similar to recur (11.7), for us to ascribe to others and ourselves to manifest 'known dispositions'. We communicate by deeds and not by words alone. For our conduct does not consist entirely of discrete episodes, pin-pointed in time, but has duration. Honouring one's parents, tending the sick, relieving the poor are nexuses of action betokening, for others to see, steady and continual dispositions. An observed constant refraining or an observed constant manifestation of a readiness to behave altruistically functions as a communication of the agent's attitude, a communication which in most cases makes an exchange of verbal vows or contracts unnecessary. In a large society bargaining on the game-theoretical model would be impracticable. The mutual observation of each other's constant readiness to behave altruistically suffices.

Second, in a repeated PD situation it is rational for each person to adopt conditional strategies. It is rational for each person purely from the point of view of egoistic rationality to act on the strategy, 'I will co-operate with A. N. Other in situation n if he co-operates with me in situation $n-1$' (where situation $n-1$ precedes situation n in time). However, in a situation of mutual distrust it will never be rational for any particular person to make a start and so trigger the conditional strategies of others. Suspicion makes one man say, 'After you, Jimmy', just as suspicion makes the other say, 'No, after you, Leonid'. But it is also rational, in order to obtain mutually beneficial outcomes in the long run, for somebody to start, although the nature of the situation is such that whoever starts takes a risk. If, then, somebody believes that there is a prospect of others behaving likewise, it will be rational for him to take the risk and, of course, he can make that risk suitably small by adopting a policy of escalating risk, such as is common in international negotiation. The dilemma is reduced to an assurance problem.

Alternatively, the conditional strategies of all concerned may be co-ordinated. Such co-ordination may be achieved by institutional means (in the manner, say, in which contracts are exchanged through the medium of a solicitor in conveyancing). Once the Blood Transfusion Unit[4] of the National Health Service was in operation the conditional strategies of blood donors were triggered. It would be useless for only one person to have been a blood donor, but *somebody* had to make a start. While from a purely egoistic point of view it would be rational for me to take a free ride at the expense of others, if everybody reasoned in this way, everybody would be worse off. It is rational, then, to want it to be the case that

[4] See R. M. Titmuss, *The Gift Relationship: From Human Blood to Social Policy.*

somebody takes a risk which, considered in itself and apart from its effects on others, is irrational. But nothing ventured, nothing gained. The altruist, then, lives dangerously. He makes a leap of reason and at the same time a leap of trust. Hobbes's sharp break between the state of nature and the civil condition reflects this leap.

The transforming devices, although they mutually reinforce one another and make rational co-operation possible, cannot guarantee us a solution which is both optimal and stable. The stable solution is not optimal and the optimal solution is not stable. The repeated prisoner's dilemma has an 'unstable' optimal solution for, as Luce and Raiffa (*Games and Decisions*, p. 98) express it, 'any loss of "faith" in one's opponent sets up the chain which leads to loss for both players.' Fortunately, the instability is symmetrical, for any access or gain of faith or trust in one's opponent sets up the chain which leads to possible gain for both players. This chain cannot be assured but it can be facilitated by legal sanctions, institutionalization, and moral education.

Moreover, the very factors which make altruism precarious serve to make the lone egoism of others less dangerous. It is a well-attested fact[5] that the more people interact in any situation, the less noticeable will be the lone free-rider, the less damage he will cause to the mass of conforming altruists. In a large society the consequences for an individual of other people's free-riding are in general only serious if the number of free-riders is large in proportion to the size of the society. Since it is difficult to overlook the defection of a relatively large number, the situation contains within itself a modest remedial mechanism. That a large number of others take a free ride makes it rational for me too to revert to free-riding.

I should conclude this section by a caveat as to the kind of altruism the rationality of which I am trying to show. A consideration of the extreme altruist's dilemma[6] will help here. The story is told of two extreme altruists in a desert, who in their zeal each to sacrifice a cup of water to the other pass it between them until, all the water having evaporated, both die of thirst, a result which neither of them wanted.

---

[5] See Mancur Olson, *The Logic of Collective Action.*
[6] For this see Mrs Ullmann-Margalit, *The Emergence of Norms,* p. 48 n.

The aim of each altruist is to satisfy the other only, and hence one judges the rationality or irrationality of their actions relative to that aim. Each altruist's order of preference is the PD-order:

   (i) The other drinking and himself not;
  (ii) Both drinking;
 (iii) Neither drinking;
 (iv) Himself drinking and the other not.

Clearly, then, the pay-off matrix will be the same as in the prisoner's dilemma.

It appears, then, that if the ends of an individual are wholly self-directed or wholly other-directed, he will not achieve his ends as effectively as if he counts the ends of others equally with his own. Extreme egoism and extreme altruism lead alike to PD situations, situations which are irrational in the sense that those locked into them preclude themselves from obtaining an optimal outcome. Plainly the rational course is to avoid getting into that situation, if possible, or if one is in such a situation, to seek to transform it as soon as practicable. Trust and co-operation are the means by which one may avoid getting into PD situations in the first place. They are the cornerstones of a sober altruism which avoids the fanaticism of our extreme altruists by means of Bentham's dictum, 'everybody to count for one, nobody for more than one'.

15.4. The result of 15.3 is that it is self-interestedly rational in the long run to adopt conditional co-operative strategies and thus to behave as if one were altruistic, provided that and so long as everybody else behaves likewise. I want in this section to set out the relevant facts differently and so produce variant arguments which lead to the same result and which may then be generalized. If it is a datum that everybody wishes for co-operation from others, then every rational egoist will have the following PD-order of preference, where (i), (ii), (iii), and (iv) are situations:

   (i) Everybody but him conforming to the rule requiring co-operation;
  (ii) Everybody conforming to the rule requiring co-operation;
 (iii) Nobody conforming to the rule requiring co-operation;

(iv) Nobody but him conforming to the rule requiring co-
operation.

Self-interested rationality makes him prefer (i) to (ii), the
datum makes him prefer (ii) to (iii). Situation (i) gives him all
the advantages of being a free-rider. Situation (ii) deprives
him of these advantages but precludes others from taking a
free ride at his expense. (iii) involves nobody co-operating,
and consequently in this situation the agent can neither bank
on the advantages of a free ride nor be protected from the
detrimental consequences of others' non-co-operation.

Consider now a group or society of average rational egoists
in which it is a datum that each person wishes for co-operation
from others. Let each express his preference-ranking as before.
Then R(ational) E(goist) No. 1's order of preference-ranking
will be:

(i)′ Everybody but RE.1 conforming to the co-operative
rule;

(ii) Everybody conforming to the co-operative rule;

(iii) Nobody conforming to the co-operative rule.

Likewise RE.2's order of preference-ranking will be:

(i)″ Everybody but RE.2 conforming to the co-operative
rule;

(ii) Everybody conforming to the co-operative rule;

(iii) Nobody conforming to the co-operative rule.

RE.1 will, however, prefer that everybody conforms rather
than that (i)″ holds. For if (i)″ holds, RE.2 will be taking a
free ride at his (RE.1's) expense. Hence RE.1 will rank (i)″
lower than (ii). Likewise, RE.2 will rank (i)′ lower than (ii),
and so on.

By parity of reasoning, each situation in the (i)-series, as
one might call it, is preferred to (ii) by only one member of
the group. Consequently, no member of the group can get
other members of the group to agree to prescribing his own
first preference as part of the morality of the group. So long
as they remain rational egoists, a proposal of this kind will
meet with universal opposition. His first preference will be
intelligible to his fellow rational egoists, but will not be acceptable unless we make additional assumptions about our group
of average rational egoists, say, that some of them are singularly devious or engage in private deals, or that some of them

are not genuinely egoistical or not fully rational, or are not average but recognized as 'special' by their fellows. But, provided that we make no additional assumptions and lay down that our group is composed of *ex hypothesi* average rational egoists, no prescription of the (i)-series can be accepted by more than one member of the group. Thus by the principle of social adoptability all states of affairs which are members of the (i)-series will be eliminated as unfit to be prescribed. Hence if an average rational egoist wants others to co-operate with him in the pursuit of co-operative goods, he can rationally prescribe giving priority to the (ii)-situation over the (iii)-situation. Since it is a truism about the human condition that people have co-operative goals and want others to co-operate in their pursuit, we may drop the 'if'-clause and state categorically that an average rational egoist can rationally prescribe giving priority to the (ii)-situation over the (iii)-situation, that is, that it is rational to prescribe co-operation. The role of the factual constraint in this argument is to entitle us to assert a categorical rationality-statement.

We may make other rationality-statements with differing degrees of confidence according to the degree of certainty of the factual constraint deployed. For example, it is a fact of the human situation (11.7) that, other things being equal, we all want to know the truth, and hence want to be told the truth by others. An argument of a similar form will then go through, which by application of the principle of social adoptability leads to a categorical statement asserting the rationality of prescribing that everybody should tell the truth.

One would be able to reach a similar categorical rationality-statement about using people only as means to ends if there were an incontestable truth of the human situation that everybody wished to be treated as an end in himself and not merely as a means. Were this accepted as a fact about the human situation, it would plainly have enormous potential. True, some people might be prepared to acquiesce in *some* of the consequences of being treated solely as a means to the ends of others, but I submit that nobody would acquiesce in *all* the consequences of being treated solely as a means. For one thing refusal genuinely to co-operate with somebody is a consequence of treating him as a means solely, although it might be difficult to spell out what genuine co-operation amounted to. Perhaps the best way to approach this topic is through the notion of doing something for someone else's sake. One may think of the norm, prescribing that others should not be treated solely as means, as expressed in the words 'Do things for the sake of others'. Then the four situations to be compared are:

(a) Everybody but the agent doing things for the sake of others;
(b) Everybody doing things for the sake of others; .
(c) Nobody doing things for the sake of others;
(d) Nobody but the agent doing things for the sake of others.

One could imagine somebody taking up the following position: 'I don't care whether people do things for my sake; all I care about is whether they deliver the goods, the co-operative goals which I need their co-operation in attaining. As long as they behave as if they were altruists, it doesn't matter, as far as I am concerned, whether they really are altruists or not.' That it is possible for somebody to take this line indicates that I may have shown the self-interested rationality of behaving as if one were altruistic, but that this is still some distance from justifying (moderate) altruism itself. In the next section I shall try to take this further step.

15.5. I want to argue that it is rational for people not only to conform to but also to internalize moral rules with an altruistic message. Let us, then, start again from the fact that we have co-operative goals. It is a fact that, in general and other things being equal, we all want others to co-operate with us. Given this, I must, if I am rational, want others to co-operate with me even when they do not want to or when it is not in their interest for them to do so. But in order for them to co-operate they must either have a sufficiently strong natural inclination to co-operate with others or have a rule-induced desire to do so (3.4). Since no such natural inclination can be attributed to rational egoists (and, indeed, if there were such we should have no need of tortuous arguments of the present type), I must, if I am rational, want others to have a rule-induced desire to co-operate. From this it follows that, if I am rational, I must want there to be a rule of the society/

group through the acceptance of which by others a rule-induced desire will be derived. Moreover, since I want others to co-operate with me even when they think they have reasons for not doing so, I must, if I am rational, desire that the rule in question be a moral rule, for if it is a moral rule it will require conformity to itself in preference to other considerations not themselves derived from moral rules (6.5). Thus given that a man has co-operative goals, it is rational for him to want there to be a moral rule of the society requiring co-operation. For an internalized rule has a superior efficacy to an uninternalized rule, that is, other people are more likely to act in accordance with a moral rule if they regard it as a good rule than if it is not a moral rule for them and they merely conform for extraneous and contingent reasons. If I am rational, I shall want other people to regard the moral rule requiring co-operation as a good rule, that is, I shall want other people to internalize the moral rule and so to have the disposition to give relative priority to the rule prescribing co-operation when making up their minds what to do. The argument so far does not show the rationality of internalizing altruism, only the rationality of wanting others to internalize altruism. To reach the stronger conclusion we need to take account of other people's assurance problem. The fact, if it is a fact, of the superior efficacy of an internalized rule is available to others as well as to me; consequently for them to solve their assurance problem, for them to have assurance that I shall co-operate, they need to be assured that I also shall internalize the rule requiring co-operation. The possession of such assurance is necessary for it to be rational for them to internalize the rule and for that reason makes it more likely that they will in fact internalize the rule in question. Thus if it is rational for me to want others to internalize the rule, I must, if I am rational, want others to be so assured. But the best way, logically speaking, for them to have such assurance is by their believing truly that I have internalized the rule. Therefore, given both the superior efficacy of the internalized rule and shared knowledge of this, I must, if I am rational, want myself as well as others to internalize the rule in question, that is, to internalize altruism.

As might be expected in view of the connection between

truthfulness and co-operation, an argument of the same form may be constructed with respect to truthfulness. In general, other things being equal, we all want to know the truth (11.7). Given this, I must, if I am rational, want it to be the case that others tell the truth, and that they do so even on occasions when they are disinclined to or when it is not in their interests to do so. But in order that they should tell the truth under these conditions, it is necessary that they should either have a sufficiently strong natural inclination to tell the truth or have a rule-induced desire to tell the truth (3.4). Since there would appear to be no such natural inclination, I must, if I am rational, wish that others have a rule-induced desire to tell the truth. From this it follows that, if I am rational, I must want there to be a rule of the society through the acceptance of which by others the rule-induced desire will be derived. However, since I want others to tell the truth even when they think they have reasons for not doing so, I must, if I am rational, desire that the rule in question be a moral rule, for if it is a moral rule, it will require conformity to itself in preference to other considerations not themselves derived from moral rules. Thus, given that a man desires to know the truth, it is rational for him to want there to be a moral rule of the society requiring truthfulness. As I pointed out in the previous argument, an internalized rule has a superior efficacy to an uninternalized rule, and so if I am rational, I shall want other people to regard the moral rule requiring truthfulness as a good rule, that is, I shall want other people to internalize the rule and so to have the disposition to give relative priority to the moral rule requiring truthfulness when making up their minds what to do. To show the rationality of everybody's internalizing the rule prescribing truthfulness, I need to extend the argument by taking account of other people's assurance problem and proceeding as in the previous argument. The fact of the superior efficacy of an internalized rule is available to others as well as to me; consequently for them to solve their assurance problem, for them to have assurance that I shall tell the truth to them, they need to be assured that I also shall internalize the rule requiring truthfulness. The possession of such assurance is necessary for it to be rational for them to internalize the rule and for that reason makes it likely that they will in fact internalize the rule in question. Thus if it is rational for me to want others to internalize the rule, I must, if I am rational, want others to be so assured. But the best way, logically speaking, for them to have such assurance is by their believing truly that I have internalized the rule. Therefore, given both the superior efficacy of the internalized rule and shared knowledge of this, I must, if I am rational, want myself as well as others to internalize the rule in question, that is, the rule requiring truthfulness.

In 15.3 I argued that it was self-interestedly rational to behave as if one were altruistic. In 15.4 I have extended this thesis by arguing for the rationality of the moral dispositions to give mutual aid and to tell the truth. It is rational not only to behave as if one were altruistic but also to *be* altruistic. In this way I have given a justification of the altruistic core of Morality$_A$ and put myself in a position in which I can complete the resolution of the triangular antinomy of 13.4. The part-resolution offered there claimed to show that Morality$_A$'s altruistic core was capable of exercising a genuinely independent check on individual and social moralities. The justificatory argument in favour of Morality$_A$'s altruistic core, henceforth referred to as altruistic morality, now gives us reason to say that it is in each moral agent's interest to be altruistic and that therefore it is rational in a reason-giving morality to give preference to reasons drawn from altruistic morality. Nor does it matter now if there are other anchored moralities besides Morality$_A$, for they can share the authority it has won, if they share its altruistic core. The leverage which altruistic morality gains from the justificatory argument is genuinely independent, since it is derived neither from individual nor from social moralities. Consequently it is capable of playing and ought to play a dominant role in its dealings with both social and individual moralities. Although there is a division of powers between the three elements, the status of altruistic morality is quasi-presidential. The unreasoned moral judgements which comprise it are, as I said at the beginning of 13.3, the foundations for, and furnish the premises and reasons for, moral deliberation. Altruistic morality constitutes an Archimedean point which guarantees us the possibility of an independent criticism of individual and social moralities.

Moderate altruism, it seems, has emerged from the argument as a rational attitude, while egoism is unfit to be adopted as a social morality. The key to the argument has been the factual constraints, in particular, the desire for co-operation. We have found a fixed point in the social nature of man.

16

Altruism and Beyond

16.1. The justification of altruistic morality in Chapter 15 has of its nature two limitations. The first of these is that the justification was purely in terms of self-interested rationality (16.1, 16.2), while the second concerns the inadequacy of the altruistic core to the derivation of the rest of Morality$_A$ (16.3) and its kindred.

It is a consequence of the first limitation that the justification itself, seen from the moral (altruistic) point of view, appears squalid. The altruist, the moral (in the commendatory sense) man, surely does not ask for the justification of the moral point of view, any more than the man of common sense asks for a justification of his belief in an external world; for him such a question can only be asked outside the framework of his beliefs. Morality, he may say, is surely more than a bargain, even a good bargain, more than a balance of trade-offs, a method of conciliating the cunning and the self-seeking. That Morality$_A$ should avail itself of a justification of this kind is like a woman at once beautiful and virtuous decking herself out with the meretricious adornments of the courtesan. Moreover, this justification has the apparent effect of making Morality$_A$ and its kindred into sets of hypothetical imperatives, nothing more than Hobbes's 'theorems concerning what conduceth to the conservation and defence' of men (*Leviathan*, p. 104).

There are good reasons for making this objection. First, one must concede that Morality$_A$ (including altruistic morality) does serve the purpose of releasing people from or allowing them to avoid PD situations. However, from this it does not follow that the only reason for being an altruist is derived from self-interested rationality. Of course, the 'evils', the things to be avoided in the PD situation, are evils, moral evils, from the moral point of view, for unless the standing temptation to be a free-rider and the associated mutual distrust find a remedy, the 'moral situation' (that is, the situation in which people co-operate) will by reason of its inherent instability revert to a PD situation. To prevent deterioration towards PD-like situations we need the emotion of resentment and the virtue of justice, which have a negative and prophylactic role. The precepts associated with justice may be looked on, if not as Kantian hypothetical imperatives, at any rate as assertoric imperatives like 'As you want to avoid PD situations, you ought not to be a free-rider at the expense of others.' These resemble 'convenient articles of peace'. The temptation to be a free-rider has to be overcome in one's own case and one needs assurance that others will not yield to that temptation either. This area of morality, which seeks to preserve the moral situation, I shall call 'prophylactic morality'. It is in this area that the virtues of temperance, honesty, and justice are supreme.

The switch to the moral (altruistic) point of view is like an orbital jump. At the moral level, virtues and emotions are made possible which have no *raison d'être* at the PD level. At the latter level, for instance, there can be no such thing as genuine friendship, only temporary coalitions to achieve jointly desired ends. A similar point was made by Aristotle in the *Nicomachean Ethics* (viii, 1155a26), when he said that if we have friendship, we have no need of justice. Justice is only the stuff by means of which we compensate for the lack of friendship. Thus within moralities of the Morality$_A$ family there is a contrast between the negative, purely prophylactic, virtues and emotions on the one hand, and on the other hand, those virtues and emotions which only emerge at the moral level and from the moral point of view. The latter are the positive emotions of love, affection, and disinterested gratitude.

Once people start to play the morality-game for its own sake, the consequent transformation of men's hearts leads to all kinds of new, essentially non-competitive, relationships, the nature and range of which are explored by novelists, dramatists, and poets, as well as by moralists and men of religion. There are a number of ways in which the moral level gives rise to new virtues and values. First, it is at this level that man becomes truly a social being without losing his individuality. Amiable virtues, like kindness, cannot be interpreted as purely prophylactic, having the role solely of averting PD situations. The person who performs a genuine and unsolicited kindness without thought of repayment may well seem in terms of the PD level to be making himself highly vulnerable; he is giving a gratuitous advantage to another over or against himself. But from the moral point of view kindness is valued for its own sake. Indeed, the more virtues there are which are valued for their own sake, the more stable the moral level becomes. The stability denied to moralities of the Morality$_A$ family by game-theory they win for themselves by the cultivation of the amiable virtues and the transformation of men's hearts.

There is a second way in which new virtues may develop at the moral level. While the members of a group may escape from PD situations in their relations with one another, these same individuals may form new emotions and new virtues when their group is in a PD situation *vis-à-vis* another group. These virtues and emotions are associated with concepts of solidarity, comradeship, fraternity, and loyalty, not to speak of patriotism.

Third, some of the things prized and valued at the moral level are quite different from those which may be traded off against one another at the PD level. Thus there are incommensurable goods or values like freedom, dignity, honour, and salvation, which many monolithic moralists (6.2), like the patriot, the knight of chivalry, and the saint, would on no account exchange for any amount of other goods, however large. It is such an attitude which the assembled Scottish nobles expressed in the Arbroath Declaration of Independence of 1320, when they maintained that 'not for glory, riches or honours do we fight, but for freedom alone, which no man loses but with his life.' Reverence for such values is not consonant with the coldly calculative world of bargaining and trade-offs. For men who prize goods and values of this kind the morality they follow is not a *pis aller*, and, in Burke's words about the state (*Reflections on the Revolution in France*, p. 93), 'ought not to be considered as nothing better than a partnership agreement in a trade of pepper and coffee, calico or tobacco, or some other such low concern, to be taken up for a little temporary interest, and to be dissolved by the fancy of the parties. It is to be looked on with other reverence; because it is not a partnership in things subservient only to the gross animal existence of a temporary and perishable nature. It is a partnership in all science; a partnership in all art; a partnership in every virtue, and in all perfection.'

16.2. My account of prophylactic morality makes it possible, I suggest, to resolve the autonomous/heteronomous antinomy. This antinomy only arises within moralities of the Morality$_A$ family which seek to restrict natural inclinations. That is why it is appropriate that its resolution has had to wait until the present stage of this enquiry.

The antithetical arguments in the autonomous/heteronomous antinomy may be stated thus. On the one hand, if a morality's judgements and imperatives are derived from specific human desires, they are tantamount to hypothetical moral judgements and imperatives, which merely prescribe means to already presupposed ends, on the value of which the morality is silent. This thesis, substantially Kant's, sees such moralities as defective and states that a rational morality ought to be autonomous. According to the opposing argument, since a morality is a human social phenomenon, it must have some connection with the actual desires of real human beings. Unless it did, nobody could ever be brought to accept it. It is only the connection with human desires which makes a morality truly ours. So-called categorical or autonomous moral judgements, on this view, are rationally-defective, because they lack the human connection and have been cut adrift from men's long-term desires and aims, their interests, and their conceptions of their well-being.

This antinomy can be resolved if we distinguish two standpoints from which prophylactic morality may be conceived. On the one hand, from the standpoint of individual rationality prophylactic morality may be conceived of as heteronomous; its grammatically categorical 'ought'-sentences may be represented as containing a concealed 'if' clause, namely, 'If you want to avoid PD situations . . .' On this view, duty is merely the necessity of avoiding PD situations. On the other hand, the underlying end of prophylactic morality, the end of avoiding PD situations, is not an end which a rational agent can deliberate about aiming at, for the co-operative ends which he desires can only be achieved if PD situations are transformed. We may, then, conceive the underlying end of prophylactic morality as being categorically prescribed. Once we have learnt, like Maggie Tulliver (14.2), to take our 'stand' outside ourselves, to take up a point of view other than and independent of individual rationality, we can kick away the ladder of self-interest and conceive even prophylactic morality as entirely autonomous. We can, then, resolve the antinomy by distinguishing these two points of view. From the point of view of individual rationality, Morality$_A$ and moralities of the same family are conceived of as prescribing means to evade or escape from PD situations and thus as being heteronomous. However, from the moral point of view the end of avoiding PD situations is itself categorically prescribed and hence these moralities are autonomous.

The distinction between two points of view also enables us to explain the diversity in the superstructure of moralities of the Morality$_A$ family. For once the moral point of view is adopted, justification of moral beliefs no longer has to be in terms of being conducive to evading PD situations. One may seek new ways of articulating and organizing the morality in question according as different ends or virtues are selected as central and all-important. Much past moral philosophy has consisted of trying to articulate and organize Morality$_A$ and its kindred without omitting anything regarded as intuitively acceptable and without including anything alien to the spirit of Morality$_A$. Thus there has developed a philosophically sophisticated part of Morality$_A$ and allied moralities which, working from the inside, has sought to adjust elements of the superstructure both to themselves and to the altruistic infrastructure. This part I shall call 'critical morality'.

16.3. I have tried in this chapter to depict in a speculative and not very argumentative manner the historical entity which I have called 'Morality$_A$'. While its superstructure is, like its infrastructure, altruistic in nature, yet part of its superstructure, as one might expect from a historical entity, is taken up by accretions, excrescences, ethical suburbs, as it were, whose logical connection, if any, with altruism may be obscure.

Historical accident, the incursions of primitive taboos, the conventional socio-economic wisdom, social prejudice, past and present theories and religions, all contribute ingredients of the traditional morality I have called 'Morality$_A$'. The elements of the superstructure do not cohere or harmonize with one another; they therefore set problems rather than provide answers to the perplexed moral agent. To deal with these problems the moral agent needs not a book of answers but a set of procedures. The required set of procedures for critical morality is to be found in the capacity for non-mechanical moral reasoning which (6.3) is part of what we teach when we 'teach morality'. Given the moral point of view, the moral agent has to discern rules and standards to apply to differing situations. The capacity for non-mechanical moral reasoning is evinced in 'distinguishing' situations to which similar epithets appear to apply under some initial description and in assimilating situations to which different epithets appear to apply under some initial description. Critical morality, then, operating from the moral (altruistic) point of view, does not start from scratch; traditional morality, the dominant morality of his society and his initial individual morality provide the critical moral agent with material for moral reflection, material which he has been taught to scrutinize. The tools which he may use are furnished by logic and by those of my structural principles which have a ground-level employment.

There are three semi-logical values which are essential in order that critical morality should operate. First, there is coherence or consistency. As has been remarked before (1.1, 11.5), coherence or consistency plays a different role in morals from that which it plays in the theoretical sphere. The totality of facts logically must be consistent, but the totality of values does not have to be, for if values or ideals are incompatible with one another, this is not a problem for the world, even for a 'world of value'; it is a problem for the moral agent, but one of which he is not expected to provide a definitive resolution. Consistency represents an ideal of practical reason rather than a mandatory requirement. In morals consistency may be the mark not of the sober thinker but of the fanatic. The attempt to ensure that diverse ideals are given due scope and are not crowded out gives rise to a higher-order ideal of balance.

To see 'life steadily' and see it 'whole' is a mark of having attained such balance. The second semi-logical value is that of weight. The principles of realism (11.5) bid one take account of available knowledge. This knowledge can be made available if we explore the situations to be assessed with a view to seeing as many aspects as may turn out to be morally relevant, one way or the other. The third semi-logical value is that represented by the tenth structural principle, that of unattainable ideal rationality. There can be no final judgement about any real situation, since because of the inexhaustibility of description one can never know that one has taken into consideration all morally relevant aspects. The complete moralist is one who realizes that his task is never finished.

However, the most important tool of critical morality is imagination. Its task is facilitated by the uncertainty of human affairs (11.7) and the way in which role-reversal occurs in real life. But life is short and men cannot wait for life to teach them its lessons. This is where the historian, the artist, the novelist, the dramatist, and the poet may come to the aid of the moralist. For the imagination can give concrete embodiment to situations whose bare description may arouse no response. More importantly, it leads one to reflect on situations which have no direct or obvious relation to oneself. Imagination is thus the means by which we may achieve a kind of objectivity, affording us an antidote to the inevitable self-centredness which characterizes every moral agent. It is the merit of PD situations that they introduce or show the possibility of a new point of view outside the self from which human actions may be appraised. In a religious morality a God provides a focus outside the self for men to judge themselves and others. It is not what the God bids which is important, it is the vantage-point which he offers. This is why many people find it possible to reach moral judgements by dialogue with their God.

The use of the imagination is bound up with the sympathetic emotions. One cannot imagine what it is like to be somebody else unless one is capable of sharing his or her emotions or at any rate of feeling a vicarious reflection of them. But the capacity to experience the sympathetic emotions is not equally distributed among men and therefore, as we saw in 14.4, they cannot be used as a fixed point enabling us to give definitive answers to questions of rationality or as a sifting device to eliminate moralities based on non-sympathetic emotions. While this is so, yet there is an important asymmetry in our emotional experience which gives leverage both to the imagination and to the sympathetic emotions which it utilizes. The asymmetry is this. Love and hatred are emotions which are associated respectively with doing good to people and harming them, where (paternalism apart) by 'good' and 'harm' is generally understood what the recipients regard as good or harm. Now it is not normal for people to want to be hated or to like being hated. Of course, sometimes tyrants want to be hated because this is a means to some other end, for example, continuing dominance. This presumably is behind the *oderint dum metuant* attitude. But this is not identical with wanting to be hated for its own sake. We do not wish to be harmed, unless we see the harm in question as being a means to our eventual good. Being loved is different. Being done good to (being benefited) and its emotional surrogate, being loved, are things which we want and like for their own sake. The logic of the emotions thus provides a point of leverage for an altruistic morality to act upon. In this sphere there is no distinction between an appeal to the emotions and the imagination and an appeal to reason; sense and sensibility are one. It is clear, then, that imagination is a disciplined affair, for we are not giving a *carte blanche* to the 'individual conscience' to run riot. It is constrained in the first place by the traditional morality and the contemporary social morality, both of which preserve the results of our ancestors' imaginative experiments, and secondly, by the individual's practised imagination, which can act like an external force in imposing a curb on his fancies and wishes. There is a natural tendency for people to universalize their own wishes and to pose as universal legislators. Our imagination, like King David's (14.4), can restrain this natural tendency and put to the test our attempts at universal legislation. The imagination thus provides 'rational means for constraining the universally legislative character of the individual conscience' (13.4).

16.4. The movement of this book has been from logic of morals to metaphysic of morals, from analysis to dialectic, from moralities to morality, from propositions to people, from argument to speculation. In Part I I set out somwhat austerely to give an account of what a morality is without begging any questions as to what a morality ought to be. The logic of morals was to apply to all moralities without distinction. In Part II I set out to show that objectivity is not the kind of characteristic which can usefully be predicated of any morality, a conclusion which appeared to lead to a sort of moral scepticism. In Part III I have tried to use rationality as a substitute for objectivity and have sought by extending that concept to find some cutting edge to distinguish what may and may not legitimately be said on matters of moral theory. Application of structural principles enables us only to prefer one style of morality to another. In seeking to do more than this and to justify altruistic morality I have had to deploy factual as well as structural constraints. It has been by doing this that I have been able to justify the moral point of view, the point of view of the altruist.

Despite the austerity of Part I and the scepticism of Part II we have reached a position not so very far from that of common sense and its morality. The common-sense view of the nature of morality and its message has never needed to be bolstered up by the belief that 'the true' morality was rooted in the nature of things, for a morality abstracted from all relation to mankind can neither exercise leverage upon us nor excite interest. The roots of any morality which has altruism at its core are in the human heart and the human situation, and this is a view eminently acceptable to common sense. In the concluding words of Berkeley's Philonous, 'You see . . . the water of yonder fountain, how it is forced upwards, in a round column, to a certain height; at which it breaks and falls back into the basin from whence it rose: its ascent, as well as descent, proceeding from the same uniform law or principle of *gravitation.* Just so, the same principles which at first view lead to scepticism, pursued to a certain point, bring men back to common sense.'

Bibliography

Including only works mentioned in the text and showing the editions referred to or quoted

Acton, H. B. 'Tradition and Other Forms of Order'. In *Proceedings of the Aristotelian Society*, liii, 1952-3, 1-28.

Aeschines. 'Against Ctesiphon'. In *Works*, tr. C. D. Adams, London, 1919.

Anderson, A. R. 'A Reduction of Deontic Logic to Alethic Modal Logic'. In *Mind*, lxvii, 1958, 100-3.

— *The Formal Analysis of Normative Concepts*. Technical Report, No. 2, US Office of Naval Research Contract No. SAR/Nonr-609 (16), 1956.

Anscombe, G. E. M. *Intention*. Oxford, 1957.

— 'On Brute Facts'. In *Analysis*, xviii, 1957-8, 69-72.

Aristotle. *The Nicomachean Ethics*.

Arnold, M. *Culture and Anarchy*. Cambridge, 1960.

Austin, J. L. *How to do things with Words*. Oxford, 1962.

— 'A Plea for Excuses'. In *Proceedings of the Aristotelian Society*, lvii, 1956-7, 1-30.

Bacon, F. *Bacon's Advancement of Learning and The New Atlantis*. London, 1906.

— *Essays*. London, 1906.

Banfield, E. C. *The Moral Basis of a Backward Society*. New York, 1967.

Barclay, W. *The Gospel of Matthew*. Edinburgh, 1956.

Bell, Q. *Virginia Woolf*. London, 1976.

Benson, J. 'Wants, Desires and Deliberation'. In *Moral Weakness*, ed. G. Mortimore, London, 1971.

Bentham, J. *A Fragment on Government and An Introduction to the Principles of Morals and Legislation*. Ed. W. Harrison, Oxford, 1948.

— *Works*. Ed. Bowring, New York, 1962.

— *Of Laws in General*. Ed. H. L. A. Hart, London, 1970.

— *Collected Works*, Vol. V. Ed. J. H. Burns and H. L. A. Hart, London, 1977.

Blackburn, S. 'Moral Realism'. In *Morality and Moral Reasoning*, ed. J. Casey, London, 1971.

Bradley, F. H. *Collected Essays*. Oxford, 1935.

— *Ethical Studies*. London, 1962.

Braithwaite, R. B. *Theory of Games as a Tool for the Moral Philosopher*. Cambridge, 1955.

Brentano, F. *Psychology from an Empirical Standpoint*. Ed. O. Kraus, English edition edited by L. McAlister, London, 1973.

Burke, E. 'Reflections on the Revolution in France'. In *Reflections on the French Revolution and Other Essays*, London, 1910.

Burnet, G. *Lives of Hale, Bedell and Rochester*. London, Dove (1830?).

Butler, J. 'Dissertation on Virtue'. In *Butler's Fifteen Sermons Preached at the Rolls Chapel and A Dissertation on the Nature of Virtue*, ed. T. A. Roberts, London, 1970.

— *The Analogy of Religion, Natural and Revealed to the constitution and course of Nature*. London, 1907.

Catullus. *Catulli Carmina*. Oxford Classical Texts, 1904.

Cohen, L. J. *The Principles of World Citizenship*. Oxford, 1954.

Coleridge, S. T. *Notebooks*. Ed. K. Coburn, London, 1957.

Collingwood, R. G. *An Essay on Metaphysics*. Oxford, 1940.

Cooper, N. 'The Aims of Science', In *The Philosophical Quarterly*, xiv, 1964, 328-33.

— 'The Concept of Probability'. In *The British Journal for the Philosophy of Science*, xvi, 1965, 226-38.

— 'Inconsistency'. In *The Philosophical Quarterly*, xvi, 1966, 54-8.

— 'The Law of Excluded Middle'. In *Mind*, lxxxvii, 1978, 161-80.

Crossman, R. H. S. *Plato Today*. London, 1959.

Davidson, D. 'Truth and Meaning'. In *Synthèse*, xvii, 1967, 304-23.

Donne, J. *Complete Poetry and Selected Prose*. London, 1946.

Dostoevsky, F. *The Brothers Karamazov*. Tr. C. Garnett, London, 1912.

Dummett, M. A. E. *Frege, Philosophy of Language*. London, 1973.

— 'What is a Theory of Meaning? (II)' In *Truth and Meaning*, ed. G. Evans and J. McDowell, Oxford, 1976.

Durkheim, E. *Sociologie et Philosophie*. Paris, 1967.

Eliot, G. *The Spanish Gypsy*. Edinburgh, 1868.

— *The George Eliot Letters*. Ed. G. S. Haight, London, 1954-5.

Fletcher, Fr. J. *Situation Ethics: The New Morality*. London, 1966.

Foot, Mrs P. 'Moral Arguments'. In *Mind*, lxvii, 1958, reprinted in *Virtues and Vices*, Oxford, 1978, pp. 96-109.

— 'Morality and Art'. In *Proceedings of the British Academy* (1970) and reprinted in *Philosophy As It Is*, ed. M. F. Burnyeat and T. Honderich, Harmondsworth, 1978.

— 'Morality as a System of Hypothetical Imperatives'. In *The Philosophical Review*, lxxxi, 1972, reprinted in *Virtues and Vices*, pp. 157-73.

Frankena, W. K. 'The Concept of Morality'. In *The Definition of Morality*, ed. G. Wallace and A. D. M. Walker, London, 1970.

— 'Obligation and Motivation in Recent Moral Philosophy'. In *Perspectives on Morality: Essays of William K. Frankena*, ed. K. E. Goodpaster, Notre Dame and London, 1976.

Friedmann, W. *Legal Theory*. 3rd edition, London, 1953.

Fuller, L. *The Morality of Law*. New Haven, 1964.

Fürer-Haimendorf, C. von. *Morality and Merit*. London, 1967.

Galsworthy, J. *The Silver Spoon*. Harmondsworth, 1967.

Gauldie, S. *Architecture*. London, 1969.

Gaunt, W. *The Aesthetic Adventure*. Harmondsworth, 1957.

Godwin, T. *Enquiry Concerning Political Justice*. Ed. K. C. Carter, Oxford, 1971.
Goldman, A. *A Theory of Human Action*. New Jersey, 1970.
Griffiths, A. P. and Peters, R. S. 'The Autonomy of Prudence'. In *Mind*, lxxi, 1962, 161-80.
Hampshire, S. N. *Thought and Action*. London, 1959.
— *Public and Private Morality*. Cambridge, 1978.
Hare, R. M. *The Language of Morals*. Oxford, 1952.
— 'Universalizability', In *Proceedings of the Aristotelian Society*, lv, 1954-5, reprinted in *Essays on the Moral Concepts*, London, 1972.
— *Freedom and Reason*. Oxford, 1963.
Hart, H. L. A. *Definition and Theory in Jurisprudence*. Oxford, 1953.
— 'Legal and Moral Obligation', In *Essays in Moral Philosophy*, ed. A. I. Melden, Seattle, 1958.
— *The Concept of Law*. Oxford, 1961.
Hepburn, R. 'Vision and Choice in Morality'. In *Proceedings of the Aristotelian Society*, Supp. Vol. xxx, 1956, 14-31.
Hobbes, T. *Leviathan*. Ed. M. Oakeshott, Oxford, 1951.
Holmes, O. W. jun. *The Common Law*. London, 1882.
Holton, G. *Thematic Origins of Scientific Thought*. Cambridge, Mass., 1973.
Hume, D. *Enquiries*. Ed. L. A. Selby-Bigge, 2nd edition, Oxford, 1902.
— *A Treatise of Human Nature*. Ed. L. A. Selby-Bigge, Oxford, 1888.
Hutcheson, F. 'Illustrations on the Moral Sense' (1728). In *British Moralists*, ed. L. A. Selby-Bigge, Vol. I, Oxford, 1897.
James, H. *The Spoils of Poynton*. Harmondsworth, 1963.
— *The Wings of the Dove*. Harmondsworth, 1965.
Joseph, H. W. B. *Some Problems in Ethics*. Oxford, 1931.
Justinian. *The Institutes of Justinian*, ed. J. A. C. Thomas. Amsterdam and Oxford, 1975.
Kant, I. *Critique of Pure Reason*. Tr. N. Kemp Smith, London, 1929.
— 'Groundwork of the Metaphysic of Morals'. Translated as *The Moral Law*, by H. J. Paton, London, 1947.
— *Kant's Critique of Practical Reason and other works on the Theory of Ethics*. Tr. T. K. Abbott, London, 1873.
— *Critique of Judgement*. Tr. J. C. Meredith, Oxford, 1928.
Keynes, J. M. *A Treatise on Probability*. London, 1921.
— *Two Memoirs*. London, 1949.
Kierkegaard, S. *Fear and Trembling*. Tr. W. Lowrie. Princeton, 1941.
Ladd, J. *The Structure of a Moral Code*. Cambridge, Mass., 1957.
Lakatos, I. *Philosophical Papers*, 2 vols. Ed. J. Worrall and G. Currie, Cambridge, 1978.
Lewis, C. S. *Mere Christianity*. London, 1955.
Locke, J. *An Essay Concerning Human Understanding*. Ed. A. C. Fraser, Oxford, 1894.
Luce, R. D. and Raiffa, H. *Games and Decisions*. New York, 1957.
Lucretius. *Lucretius on the Nature of Things*. Tr. C. Bailey, Oxford, 1910.

Macaulay, T. B. *Works.* London, 1879.

Machiavelli, N. *The Prince.* Tr. W. K. Marriott, London, 1908.

MacIntyre, A. *Against the Self-Images of the Age.* London, 1971.

— *A Short History of Ethics.* London, 1967.

Mackie, J. L. *Ethics.* London, 1977.

Medlin, B. 'Ultimate Principles and Ethical Egoism'. In *Morality and Rational Self-Interest*, ed. D. P. Gauthier, Englewood Cliffs, 1970.

Mill, J. S. *Autobiography.* London, 1924.

— *Utilitarianism, Liberty and Representative Government.* Everyman edition, London, 1910.

Moore, G. E. *Principia Ethica.* Cambridge, 1903.

Murdoch, I. 'Vision and Choice in Morality', In *Proceedings of the Aristotelian Society*, Supp. Vol. xxx, 1956, 32-58.

— *The Bell.* Harmondsworth, 1962.

Nietzsche, F. *Werke*, Zweiter Band. München, 1965.

Nowell-Smith, P. H. *Ethics.* London, 1954.

Oakeshott, M. *Rationalism in Politics.* London, 1962.

Olson, M. *The Logic of Collective Action.* Cambridge, Mass., 1965.

Passmore, J. *Man's Responsibility for Nature.* London, 1974.

Pears, D. F. *Questions in the Philosophy of Mind.* London, 1975.

Pitt-Rivers, J. 'Honour and Social Status', In *Honour and Shame: The Values of Mediterranean Society*, ed. J. G. Peristiany, London, 1965.

Plato. *Euthyphro.*

— *The Republic.*

— *Philebus.*

Pope, A. *The Correspondence of Alexander Pope.* Ed. G. Sherburn, Oxford, 1956.

Price, R. *Review of the Principal Questions of Morals.* Ed. D. D. Raphael, Oxford, 1948.

Prichard, H. B. *Moral Obligation.* Oxford, 1949.

Prior, A. N. 'Escapism: The Logical Basis of Ethics'. In *Essays in Moral Philosophy*, ed. A. I. Melden, Seattle, 1958.

Proudhon, P.-J. 'Qu'est-ce que la propriété?' In *Œuvres complètes*, Vol. IV, Paris, 1926.

Radcliffe-Brown, A. R. 'Social Sanction'. In *Encyclopaedia of the Social Sciences*, Vol. xiii, New York, 1959.

Ramsey, F. P. *The Foundations of Mathematics.* London, 1931.

Rawls, J. *A Theory of Justice.* Oxford, 1972.

Reichenbach, H. *Elements of Symbolic Logic.* New York, 1948.

Richards, D. A. J. *A Theory of Reasons for Action.* Oxford, 1971.

Samuelson, P. A. 'Pure Theory of Public Expenditure and Taxation'. In *Public Economics*, ed. J. Margolis and H. Guitton, London, 1969.

Searle, J. R. *Speech Acts.* Cambridge, 1969.

Sen, A. 'Isolation, Assurance and the Social Rate of Discount'. In *Quarterly Journal of Economics*, lxxxi, 1967, 112-24.

— 'Choice, Ordering and Morality'. In *Practical Reason*, ed. S. Körner, Oxford, 1974.

Shelley, P. B. *The Complete Poetical Works of Percy Bysshe Shelley.* Oxford, 1907.

Sidgwick, H. *The Methods of Ethics.* 7th edition, London, 1907.

Singer, M. *Generalization in Ethics.* London, 1961.

Skinner, B. F. *Walden Two.* New York, 1948.

Smith, A. *The Theory of Moral Sentiments.* Ed. D. D. Raphael and A. L. Macfie, Oxford, 1976.

Stephen, Sir L. *The Science of Ethics.* London, 1882.

Stevenson, C. L. *Ethics and Language.* New Haven, 1944.

— *Facts and Values.* New Haven and London, 1963.

Strawson, P. F. 'Freedom and Resentment'. In *Studies in the Philosophy of Thought and Action*, ed. P. F. Strawson, London, 1968.

Thucydides. *The History of the Peloponnesian War,* ed. Sir Richard Livingstone. London, 1943.

Titmuss, R. M. *The Gift Relationship: From Human Blood to Social Policy.* London, 1970.

Tolstoy, L. *What Then Must We Do?* Tr. A. Maude, Oxford, 1935.

— *Anna Karenin.* Tr. C. Garnett, London, 1901.

Toulmin, S. E. *An Examination of the Place of Reason in Ethics.* Cambridge, 1950.

Ullmann-Margalit, E. *The Emergence of Norms.* Oxford, 1977.

Veblen, T. 'The Theory of the Leisure Class'. In *The Portable Veblen*, ed. M. Lerner, New York, 1948.

Warnock, G. J. *The Object of Morality.* London, 1971.

Westermarck, E. *The Origin and Development of the Moral Ideas*, 2 vols. London, 1912.

Wheatly, C. *A Rational Illustration of the Book of Common Prayer.* Cambridge, 1858.

Wittgenstein, L. *Philosophical Investigations.* Oxford, 1953.

Index